Meaningful Resistance

Meaningful Resistance explores the origins and dynamics of resistance to markets through an examination of two social movements that emerged to voice and channel opposition to market reforms. Protests against water privatization in Cochabamba, Bolivia, and rising corn prices in Mexico City, Mexico, offer a lens to analyze the mechanisms by which perceived, market-driven threats to material livelihood can prompt resistance. By exploring connections among marketization, local practices, and political protest, this book shows how the material and the ideational are inextricably linked in resistance to subsistence threats. When people perceive that markets have put subsistence at risk, material and symbolic worlds are both at stake; citizens take to the streets not only to defend their pocketbooks, but also their conceptions of community. This book advances contemporary scholarship by showing how attention to grievances in general, and subsistence resources in particular, can add explanatory leverage to analyses of contentious politics.

Erica S. Simmons is a Lyons Family Faculty Scholar and assistant professor of political science and international studies at the University of Wisconsin–Madison. Her dissertation, on which this book is based, was awarded the Latin American Studies Association/Oxfam America 2013 Martin Diskin Dissertation Award. Her research has been funded by the Fulbright Commission and the Mellon Foundation, among others.

Cambridge Studies in Contentious Politics

Editors

Mark Beissinger   *Princeton University*
Jack A. Goldstone   *George Mason University*
Michael Hanagan   *Vassar College*
Doug McAdam   *Stanford University and Center for Advanced Study in the Behavioral Sciences*
Sarah Soule   *Stanford University*
Suzanne Staggenborg   *University of Pittsburgh*
Sidney Tarrow   *Cornell University*
Charles Tilly (d. 2008)   *Columbia University*
Elisabeth J. Wood   *Yale University*
Deborah Yashar   *Princeton University*

(continued after Index)

Meaningful Resistance

*Market Reforms and the Roots of
Social Protest in Latin America*

ERICA S. SIMMONS
University of Wisconsin–Madison

CAMBRIDGE
UNIVERSITY PRESS

University Printing House, Cambridge CB2 8BS, United Kingdom

One Liberty Plaza, 20th Floor, New York, NY 10006, USA

477 Williamstown Road, Port Melbourne, VIC 3207, Australia

4843/24, 2nd Floor, Ansari Road, Daryaganj, Delhi - 110002, India

79 Anson Road, #06-04/06, Singapore 079906

Cambridge University Press is part of the University of Cambridge.

It furthers the University's mission by disseminating knowledge in the pursuit of
education, learning and research at the highest international levels of excellence.

www.cambridge.org
Information on this title: www.cambridge.org/9781107562059

First published 2016
Reprinted 2016

A catalogue record for this publication is available from the British Library

Library of Congress Cataloging in Publication data
Names: Simmons, Erica, author.
Title: Meaningful resistance : market reforms and the roots of social protest in
Latin America / Erica Simmons, University of Wisconsin–Madison.
Description: New York, NY : Cambridge University Press, 2016. |
Includes bibliographical references.
Identifiers: LCCN 2015042175| ISBN 9781107124851 (hardback) |
ISBN 9781107562059 (paperback)
Subjects: LCSH: Social movements – Latin America. | Protest movements – Latin America. |
Political participation – Latin America. | Latin America – Economic conditions. |
Latin America – Social conditions. | Latin America – Politics and government.
Classification: LCC HN110.5.A8 S5526 2016 | DDC 303.48/4098–dc23
LC record available at http://lccn.loc.gov/2015042175

ISBN 978-1-107-12485-1 Hardback
ISBN 978-1-107-56205-9 Paperback

For my parents

Contents

Acknowledgments

For this work, I owe a number of debts. Most importantly, I am grateful to many people in Bolivia and Mexico for their willingness to share their lives and thoughts with me. My time in the field was made possible by support from a Fulbright-Hays Dissertation Year Fellowship, the Tinker Foundation, the University of Chicago, and the University of Wisconsin–Madison. It was only through friends and colleagues in Bolivia and Mexico, however, that I was able to put the financial support to good use. In Bolivia, I am grateful first to Santiago Daroca Oller and his wife, Cecita Espinosa, who not only provided important research contacts, but also invited me into their home and their lives in La Paz. Diego Ayo also offered me a place to stay, fabulous company, and critical advice on the project during my trips to Bolivia and once I had returned home. In Cochabamba, Carlos Crespo Flores not only facilitated research contacts, but also invited me to participate in his local networks engaged in water-related matters. Ida Peñaranda welcomed me into her family and her work. Fernando Mayorga opened the doors of the Centro de Estudios Superiores Universitarios (CESU) to me, offering an office space and additional support. I would not have been able to do my research in Bolivia without them.

My debts in Mexico are no less extensive. Ana Luisa Liguori and her husband, Carlos Aguirre, provided a home away from home throughout my stay, offering friendship, professional advice, engaging conversation, and wonderful food every time I visited with them, whether in their home in Mexico City or during a trip to their spectacular weekend retreat. Andres Antonious, Libby Haight, and Rachel and Chris Huk all took me in at various stages of my fieldwork. I am grateful to each of them for sharing their homes and their friendship with me. Susan Gzesh at the University of Chicago played a critical role in the early stages of my Mexico research, providing the initial contacts that got my investigation off the ground. Víctor Suárez and the entire team at *Asociación Nacional de Empresas Comercializadoras de Productores del*

Campo [National Association of Commercial Businesses from the Countryside] (ANEC) opened their doors to me, facilitating interviews and offering access to the documents and records of the *Sin Maíz No Hay País* campaign. Ivan Polanco and Enrique Pérez deserve particular mention. One contact within the Mexican government helped to facilitate nearly all of my interviews with governmental officials. I will not name him here, but he knows who he is and that I owe him an enormous debt. Finally, I am grateful to Jonathan Fox for the time and attention he dedicated to this project. His interventions came at key moments and encouraged me to see things in new ways.

At the University of Chicago the members of my dissertation committee pushed me at just the right moments and in just the right places, providing valuable advice and support at every stage in the process. I am particularly indebted to my chair, Lisa Wedeen, who introduced me to a new way of thinking about politics; she is the sole reason that I chose the University of Chicago for my doctoral studies. Dan Slater quickly became an exceptional interlocutor and much of the direction of this project came from long conversations with Dan over lunch. I now count them both not only as mentors but as dear friends. John Comaroff and Elisabeth Clemens provided critical interventions at key moments, never failing to remind me that there is a world outside of political science from which I have much to learn. Finally, Jorge Domínguez can claim responsibility for my interest in political science. Jorge has had the unenviable task of serving as a guide and mentor since my time as an undergraduate, when he provided unwavering (if always critical) support. I am grateful that he has stuck with me for so long.

The University of Chicago also offered invaluable support through the group of scholars and friends who joined me as graduate students in the Department of Political Science. Daragh Grant, Christopher Haid, Juan Fernando Ibarra del Cueto, Diana Kim, Sarah Parkinson, and Nick Smith provided seemingly never-ending sources of academic and personal support at every stage in the PhD process. I am particularly grateful to Juan Fernando, who offered crucial insights when it was time to begin fieldwork in Mexico. Sarah Johnson, J. J. McFadden, and Jon Rogowski also deserve mention here. Each offered important support and encouragement during the process of research and writing.

A number of individuals outside of my committee and cohort offered feedback on this project at various stages. I received valuable comments and questions from the Comparative Politics Workshop at the University of Chicago (which endured not one but three presentations on this project over the course of four years), the David Rockefeller Center for Latin American Studies at Harvard University, participants in the Young Scholars in Social Movements conference at Notre Dame, the Kellogg Institute for International Studies at Notre Dame, Yale Law School, the University of Wisconsin–Madison Comparative Politics Colloquium, the Sociology of Economic Change and Development Seminar at the University of Wisconsin–Madison, and George

Washington University's Comparative Politics Workshop. Alan Kolatta, Emilio Kouri, Adrienne LeBas, Lindsay Mayka, Jeremy Menchik, Mariela Szwarcberg, Alberto Simpser, Susan Spronk, Sidney Tarrow, and Mayer Zald all read drafts of chapters or discussed key issues with me and provided important feedback at various stages.

My colleagues at the University of Wisconsin–Madison helped to transform the dissertation into a book. I could not have asked for a better group of friends and scholars. I am particularly lucky to have been surrounded by an exceptional cohort of junior scholars who offered unflagging personal and professional support. Rikhil Bhavnani, Noam Lupu, Margaret Peters, Eleanor Powell, Jonathan Renshon, Michelle Schwarze, Alex Tahk, and Jessica Weeks deserve special mention. I also had two invaluable senior mentors, Katherine Cramer and Scott Straus, who provided important advice and encouragement throughout the process. In addition, John Ahlquist, Rick Avramenko, Mark Copelovitch, Christina Ewig, Scott Gehlbach, Yoshiko Herrera, Dan Kapust, Helen Kinsella, Jimmy Casas Klausen, Florencia Mallon, Melanie Manion, Benjamin Marquez, Michael Schatzberg, Gay Seidman, and Nadav Shelef all provided helpful comments on drafts of chapters, proposals, or the entire manuscript. Other colleagues offered kind words, coffee breaks, and conversations that were critical to keep me going. José Luis Enríquez, Diana Oprinescu, Rachel Schwartz, and Brianne Walsh each provided important research assistance.

Thanks to the generous financial support from the University of Wisconsin–Madison Political Science Department, I had the good fortune to host a workshop on the book manuscript. Many of my UW colleagues attended and offered important feedback. I am particularly grateful to the five outside scholars who took the time to travel to Madison for the day and offered thoughtful comments on the manuscript. Their insights transformed this book. Timothy Pachirat, Kenneth Roberts, Fred Schaffer, Joe Soss, and Deborah Yashar helped to improve this work more than they can ever know. Their interventions were truly critical and each of them has left a stamp on this project. Joe Soss deserves an additional thank you for coming up with the project's final title.

I am also grateful to four anonymous reviewers for their careful reading of the manuscript and important comments that pushed me in just the right ways at the final stages of the project. My editor at Cambridge University Press, Robert Dreesen, has provided unflagging support and editorial assistant Brianda Reyes demonstrated extraordinary patience. I thank them both. In September 2014 *Theory and Society* published an expanded discussion of the meaning-laden approach to grievances that is summarized in Chapter 1. Some of the analysis and evidence in Chapters 2 and 3 appeared in an article published in *World Politics* in January 2016. Similarly, a condensed version of the evidence and analysis discussed in Chapters 4 and 5 appeared in *Comparative Politics* in April 2016.

My parents, Adele and John Simmons, offered unflagging support throughout the process of researching and writing this book. My brothers also deserve mention here, as both were willing to lend an ear when the going got tough. My sister-in-law joined our family just when some sisterly support was necessary, and my little niece came along in time to offer smiles during the final revisions. My mother- and father-in-law, Dan and Nancy Balz, put up with long writing sessions over winter holidays and supported me at every stage. A number of friends outside of academia must also feel as though they, too, have written a book. I am grateful to each of them. Finally, I could hope for no better partner through the entire process than John Balz. He has lived with this project since the beginning, enduring every challenge and success along with me.

Abbreviations

ADOC	*Alianza Democrática de Organizaciones Civiles* [Democratic Alliance of Civil Organizations]
ANC	*Acuerdo Nacional para el Campo* [National Agreement for the Countryside]
ANEC	*Asociación Nacional de Empresas Comercializadoras de Productores del Campo* [National Association of Commercial Businesses From the Countryside]
ATEM	*Asociación de Trabajadores del Estado de Michoacán* [Association of State Workers of Michoacan]
CAP	*Congreso Agrario Permanente* [Permanent Agrarian Congress]
CCC	*Central Campesino Cardenista* [Cardenist Farmers' Union]
CNC	*Confederación Nacional Campesina* [National Peasant Confederation]
CNTE	*Coordinadora Nacional de Trabajadores de la Educación* [National Coordinator of Education Workers]
COB	*Central Obrera Boliviana* [Bolivian Workers' Central]
COD	*Central Obrera Departamental* [Departmental Workers' Central]
CODAEP	*Comité para la Defensa del Agua y la Economía Popular* [Committee for the Defense of Water and the Popular Economy]
CONAIE	*Confederación de Nacionalidades Indígenas del Ecuador* [Confederation of Indigenous Nationalities of Ecuador]
CONASUPO	*Compañía Nacional de Subsistencias Populares* [National Company of Popular Subsistence]

CONOC	*Consejo Nacional de Organizaciones Campesinas* [National Council of Peasant Organizations]
CONORP	*Consejo Nacional de Organizaciones Rurales y Pesqueras* [National Council of Rural and Fishing Organizations]
COMIBOL	*Corporación Minera de Bolivia* [Mining Corporation of Bolivia]
Coordinadora	*Coordinadora de Defensa del Agua y de la Vida* [Coordinator for the Defense of Water and Life]
CROC	*Confederación Revolucionaria de Obreros y Campesinos* [Regional Confederation of Workers and Farmers]
CSUTCB	*Confederación Sindical Única de Trabajadores Campesinos de Bolivia* [Confederation of Rural Workers of Bolivia]
ECNAM	*El Campo No Aguanta Más* [The Countryside Can Bear No More]
EZLN	*Ejército Zapatista de Liberación Nacional* [The Zapatista Army of National Liberation]
Fabriles	*Federación Departamental de Trabajadores Fabriles de Cochabamba* [Departmental Federation of Factory Workers of Cochabamba]
FAP	*Frente Amplio Progresista* [Broad Progressive Front]
FEDAT	*Federación Sindical del Autotransporte* [Federation of Auto Transport]
FEDECOR	*Federación Departamental Cochabambina de Regantes* [Cochabamban Departmental Confederation of Irrigators]
FEJUVE	*Federación de Juntas Vecinales* [Federation of Urban Neighborhood Organizations]
FDTFC	*Federación de Trabajadores Fabriles de Cochabamba* [Federation of Factory Workers of Cochabamba]
FSM	*Frente Sindical Mexicano* [Mexican Union Front]
FSUTCC	*Federación Sindical Única de Trabajadores Campesinos de Cochabamba* [The Unified (or sole) Union Confederation of Peasant Workers of Cochabamba]
LPP	*Ley de Participación Popular* [Law of Popular Participation]
MNR	*Movimento Nacionalista Revolucionario* [Nationalist Revolutionary Movement]
NAFTA	North American Free Trade Agreement
NPE	*Nueva Política Económica* [New Economic Policy]

OTB	*Organizaciones Territoriales de Base* [Territorial Base Organizations]
PAN	*Partido Acción Nacional* [National Action Party]
PRD	*Partido de la Revolución Democrática* [Party of the Democratic Revolution]
PRI	*Partido Revolucionario Institucional* [Institutional Revolutionary Party]
PT	*Partido del Trabajo* [Workers' Party]
PUMA	*Pueblo en Marcha* [People/Town on the Move]
PVEM	*Partido Verde Ecologista de México* [Mexican Ecological Green Party]
SAGARPA	*Secretaría de Agricultura, Ganadería, Desarrollo Rural, Pesca, y Alimentación* [Ministry of Agriculture, Livestock, Rural Development, Fisheries, and Food]
SARH	*Secretaría de Agricultura y Recursos Hidráulicos* [Ministry of Agriculture and Water Resources]
SEDESOL	*Secretaría de Desarrollo Social* [Ministry of Development]
SEMAPA	*Servicio Municipal de Agua Potable y Alcantarillado de Cochabamba* [Cochabamba Municipal Drinking Water and Sewage Service]
SME	*Sindicado Mexicano de Electricistas* [Electrical Workers' Union]
UAEM	*Universidad Autónoma del Estado de México* [Autonomous University of the State of Mexico]
UNAM	*Universidad Nacional Autónoma de México* [National Autonomous University of Mexico]
UNORCA	*Unión Nacional de Organizaciones Regionales Campesinas Autónomas* [National Union of Regional, Autonomous Campesino Organizations]
UNT	*Unión Nacional de Trabajadores* [National Workers' Union]
YPFB	*Yacimientos Petrolíferos Fiscales Bolivianos* [National Oil and Gas Corporation of Bolivia]

1

Introduction

During the past thirty years, market-oriented economic reforms have swept much of the globe. Privatizations, free-trade agreements, the elimination of subsidies, and cuts in social safety nets have dominated national and international economic policy agendas. Some communities have met these reforms with relative quiescence; in others, the reforms have generated sustained resistance. This book explores the origins and dynamics of this resistance through a careful examination of two cases in which social movements emerged to voice and channel opposition to market reforms. Protests against water privatization in Cochabamba, Bolivia, and rising corn prices in Mexico City, Mexico, offer a lens for analyzing and understanding the mechanisms through which perceived market-driven threats to material livelihood can prompt resistance. The cases prompt an overarching question: Why and how does the marketization of certain goods become the basis for broad-based mobilization? Through these cases, this book explores how everyday life is intertwined with extraordinary events and how the ideas with which some grievances are imbued can generate social mobilization.

The most basic claim of the book is this: studying the grievances around which a political protest emerges adds explanatory leverage to our understandings of the dynamics of contentious politics. Dominant theories explicitly argue that grievances, although a necessary condition for social mobilization, are constant and therefore have little explanatory power. Other approaches simply assert that particular threats (such as erosion of rights, state repression, or declining economic opportunities) are more conducive to social movements than others, without exploring the potential mechanisms at work.[1] Although

[1] Some scholarship does focus directly on grievances. See, for example, Snow et al. (1998), McVeigh (2009), and Snow and Soule (2010). See Simmons (2014) for a full treatment of these authors' contributions. More recent contributions (e.g., Cederman et al. 2013; Buhaug et al. 2014) are treated in this chapter and the conclusion.

political opportunities, organizational resources, and framing processes played critical roles in the events in Bolivia and Mexico, they leave gaps in our understandings of the mechanisms at work.[2] I aim to "help pluralize understandings of the microfoundations of contentious politics" (Pearlman 2013, 388) by encouraging scholars to study the ways in which the content of a movement's claims shapes its emergence and composition.

Instead of paying attention to the perceived or relative severity of a grievance, as much of the early grievance literature did (e.g., Smelser 1963; Davies 1969; Gurr 1970), I encourage the study of the meanings with which grievances are imbued (see Simmons 2014).[3] This approach is both in line with recent efforts to focus our attention on the mechanisms at work during contentious episodes (e.g., McAdam et al. 2001) and with important insights into the role of meaning-making in contentious processes (e.g., Kurzman 2004a; Gould 2009). When we study social movements – and grievances in particular – through the lens of meaning, we recognize that claims are both materially and ideationally constituted. The ideas with which some claims are imbued are more conducive than others to motivating political resistance; by paying attention to meaning we improve our ability to explain and analyze the dynamics of contention.

This approach serves as the basic premise on which to build specific theoretical propositions. The core theoretical argument of this book focuses on a particular category of grievances – threats to subsistence goods – and how the meanings these threats take on help to explain not only the mechanisms at work in the Bolivian and Mexican cases, but also broader patterns of mobilization and resistance. Because of their central role in daily life and practice, subsistence goods can signify not only "imagined communities" (Anderson 1991) but also what I call "quotidian communities" – communities that are built through routine, face-to-face interactions where members know each other personally. As a result, market-driven threats to subsistence goods can be perceived not only as material threats but also as threats to community. These perceptions help to bridge salient cleavages and forge understandings of common grievances and goals that allow for broad-based, widespread mobilization. We cannot explain the dynamics at work in the Cochabamban and

[2] See McAdam et al. (1996, 2001); Tarrow (1998); McAdam (1999); Aminzade (2001); and Goodwin and Jasper (2004) for overviews of dominant approaches to social movements as well as critiques of those approaches. I use the term *frame* in the way it is generally deployed in social movement scholarship. See, for example, Snow and Benford, who describe a frame as an "interpretive schema that simplifies and condenses the 'world out there' by selectively punctuating and encoding objects, situations, events, experiences, and sequences of action" (1988, 137). Framing refers to "the process of defining what is going on in a situation in order to encourage protest" (Noakes and Johnston 2005, 2). Although these usages draw on Goffman (1974), they imply a far narrower conceptualization of the term.
[3] Following John Comaroff, I take *meaning* to be "the economy of signs and symbols in terms of which humans construct, inhabit, and experience their social lives (and thus act in and upon the world)" (cited in Wedeen 2009, 81–2).

Mexican movements without paying attention to the ways in which water and corn meant "community" to many of the people who participated and how those meanings contributed to political resistance.

Building on classic works on markets and mobilization (e.g., Polanyi 2001) and moral economies (e.g., Thompson 1971; Scott 1976), as well as on more contemporary analyses of contentious politics (e.g., McAdam et al. 2001; Goodwin and Jasper 2004) and political identification (e.g., Brubaker 2004), this analysis investigates connections among marketization, local practices and understandings, and political protest to show how the material and the ideational are inextricably linked in resistance to subsistence threats. Threats to subsistence highlight the ways in which the material and the cultural cannot be pried apart. When people perceive that markets have put relationships with subsistence goods at risk, material and symbolic worlds are both at stake; citizens take to the streets to defend not only their pocketbooks but also their perceptions of community. By theorizing the connections among subsistence, markets, and social mobilization, this book sheds light not only on processes of political resistance but also on how identifications are mobilized and groups made (see Wedeen 2008).

The argument developed here deepens our understandings of responses to marketization and offers conceptual frameworks with which to explore an increasingly familiar collection of empirical events. As markets regulate relationships with water and basic foodstuffs, and global integration intensifies price fluctuations and insecurities, more communities are likely to perceive that subsistence resources are at risk. By rejecting the notion that goods such as food and water can simply be treated as "commodities" that do similar political work across time and place, the argument offers tools with which to understand variation in responses to price shocks. Why might rising corn prices spark civil unrest in Mexico but have little impact in Japan? This book suggests that we must look beyond comparative consumption levels. To fully explain both the outliers and the events conforming to expected patterns, we must understand the meanings these staples take on in particular times and places, and how those meanings might work to produce group identifications. The Bolivian and Mexican cases are not contingent events, but rather examples of a type – a type that has appeared throughout history and one that will take on increasing importance in the years and decades to come. The cases can teach us much about what we might expect as the welfare state continues to retreat and markets regulate access to increasingly scarce resources.

The claims I make are both constitutive and causal, but they are not claims for which I attempt to establish necessary and/or sufficient conditions for a particular outcome. The dynamics I identify are neither necessary nor sufficient for social mobilization.[4] Nor do I make the kinds of causal claims that are based

---

[4] See Ragin (2000) and Chapter 4, in particular, for a discussion of causal complexity and necessary and sufficient causes.

on the logic of statistical inference. An interest in dynamic, unfolding processes is ill-suited to that type of variable-oriented analysis (Simmons and Smith 2015).

Instead, this research employs a logic of inquiry that draws on relational approaches (Emirbayer 1997; Tilly 2002) in which actors are embedded in dynamic, shifting social contexts. A relational approach emphasizes the importance of practices in constituting individual and social relations, and it challenges conceptions of individuals or social groups as discrete units. First, I make causal claims about the ways in which subsistence symbolized community and how those meanings helped to produce broad-based, widespread mobilization in the Bolivian and Mexican cases. Second, I argue that these dynamics and mechanisms are likely to appear in other times and places. What I observed is both specific to Cochabamba and Mexico City respectively *and* suggestive of a broader relationship. I am identifying a particular set of relationships that sometimes work together to help produce political resistance. They will not do so everywhere and always; nor can the particular conditions under which these mechanisms are most (or least) likely to work in these ways be identified. Too much causal complexity exists in mobilization processes for this kind of inferential logic to be effective. Furthermore, although scholars may find that these mechanisms appear to be at work most frequently outside of fully "developed" contexts, there is no theoretical reason that the argument is not broadly applicable. I argue that subsistence goods will symbolize community in cases beyond the ones explored here and that, through investigating other times and places, scholars will uncover other moments when the community-related symbolic work done by relationships with subsistence goods plays a role in generating political resistance.

THE CASES: PROTEST IN BOLIVIA AND MEXICO

In January 2000, thousands of Bolivians took to the streets to protest the privatization of the water supply in Cochabamba, Bolivia's third largest city. Bolivians had previously voiced their opposition to the economic policy shifts that had begun almost fifteen years earlier. The mobilization in Cochabamba, however, grew to an unprecedented scope and scale. The protests were precipitated by the Bolivian government's sale of the rights to the Cochabamba's water to a private firm in June 1999. The firm gained rights not only to Cochabamba's municipal water system but also to water collected through private and communal wells. By the time ownership was formally transferred five months later, a cross-class, cross-ethnic social movement demanding access to affordable water had taken hold in the region. In January when bills came due for water that had, in some cases, doubled in price, the water wars began – shutting down the city for days at a time.[5] Protests spread throughout the country, and, by April, the

_____

[5] Some accounts of these events describe them as the "water war" in the singular. Others use the plural. I adopt the plural, "water wars" as there were multiple protest events, each of which can

government was forced to re-nationalize Cochabamban water. Although protest politics quickly subsided in the region, the Cochabamban movement was arguably the beginning of a period of political unrest that lasted for more than five years, removed two presidents from office, and dramatically reshaped the landscape of Bolivian politics.

Seven years later and thousands of miles away, in January 2007, Mexicans filled the central square in Mexico City to express opposition to rising corn prices and corn imports. Farmers drove tractors from Aguascalientes and Puebla, union members came on buses from as far as the Yucatán in the east and Chihuahua in the north, and urban residents of Mexico City came out to join them. The price of tortillas had been rising dramatically across the country – in some regions, prices had quadrupled since the previous summer. A combination of increased international demand and the reduction of tariff barriers on corn imports caused the price increases that became known as the *tortillazo*; it was no coincidence that the January demonstrations coincided with the final stages of implementation of the North American Free Trade Agreement (NAFTA). Marching under the banner *Sin Maíz No Hay País* [without corn there is no country], consumers, producers, middle-class workers, and *campesinos* united to demand access to affordable, explicitly *Mexican*, corn. Recently inaugurated President Felipe Calderón moved quickly to cap prices, and the movement largely collapsed. Nevertheless, social movement organizations continue to work to demand NAFTA's renegotiation and the protection of Mexican corn seed varieties.

The water wars were one of the most influential events in recent Bolivian history. Often given partial credit for current trends in Bolivian popular politics, they have been identified as one of many factors culminating in the election of indigenous activist Evo Morales to the presidency in 2006 (see Petras and Veltmeyer 2005). In offering additional analysis of these particular events, this book contributes to understandings of the changing dynamics of Bolivian social mobilization as well as the origins of what is often touted as the recent revival or "rise of the left" in Bolivia. In spite of extensive attention both to the Bolivian water wars (e.g., Crespo Flores 2000; García Linera et al. 2004; Peredo et al. 2004; Domínguez 2007; Spronk 2007a, 2007b) and to social movements in Bolivia more generally (e.g., García Linera et al. 2004; Crabtree 2005), the existing literature does not fully illuminate the mechanisms at work in the Cochabamba mobilization, and why that mobilization took the forms it did.

---

be understood and described as its own "war." Interestingly, most participants in the water wars call the entire set of events *la guerra del agua* using the singular. However, when they discuss different episodes of protest, they use *la primera guerra del agua* (the first water war) to refer to the January protests events, *la segunda guerra del agua* (the second water war) to refer to the February protest events, and so on. The plural, therefore, although not a literal translation of how most participants name the events, remains true to how they describe them.

The *tortillazo* cannot be similarly credited with setting Mexico on a new political path. Yet the events of January 2007 continue to shape Mexican public policy and helped spark a sustained movement that focuses on Mexico's countryside in general, and corn in particular.[6] More broadly, corn in Mexico has received extensive attention (Fox 1993; Hewitt de Alcántara 1994; Nadal 2000; Otero 2008a, 2008b; Fitting 2011), and Mexican social movements have generated significant scholarship, particularly since the Zapatista uprising in 1994 (e.g., Foweraker and Craig 1990; Harvey 1998; Williams 2001; Otero and Bartra 2005; Stolle-McAllister 2005). However, little attention has been devoted to connections between civil unrest and consumer staples.

The Mexican protests do not look precisely like the events in Bolivia to which they are compared. Indeed, we would never expect contentious episodes to map perfectly onto one another. The events in Mexico were brief and felt like a routine political protest to many residents of Mexico City. The protests in Cochabamba lasted almost nine months and shut down the city and later the country for days at a time. I want to leverage these differences to better understand how threats to subsistence might work both similarly and differently across contexts. Whereas at the meso-level the Mexican and Bolivian protests appear to be different categories of events entirely, a micro-level analysis reveals important commonalities. A comparison of the Mexican and Bolivian cases allows us to shed light on understudied events, look at well-travelled empirical terrain with new lenses, and theorize the dynamics of political resistance across space and time.

THE QUESTIONS

A number of specific questions motivate this book. What accounts for the broad-based, widespread composition of the movement to resist water privatization in Cochabamba? What explains cross-sector, cross-political cooperation in the Mexican protests? Why do responses to two different claims in two different contexts look so similar with respect to the diversity of the participants and the frames employed? In light of strong histories of sector-specific or identity-based mobilizations in both countries, how do we explain the cross-class, cross-ethnic, and cross-urban-rural nature of the two movements? More generally, varied responses to recent spikes in the prices of basic food-stuffs have generated questions in both policy and academic circles (e.g., see Hendrix et al. 2009; Leblang and Bernard 2011; Hendrix and Haggard 2015).

[6] I am referring here to the *Sin Maíz No Hay País* campaign, a social movement that followed the *tortillazo* protests, using language deployed during the earlier protests. The campaign was officially launched in June 2007. The campaign coordinated marches on January 31, 2008, and January 31, 2009. It has also coordinated a "National Day of Corn" celebration every September, beginning in 2009. As of the completion of this book, the campaign continued to hold meetings and events.

What might the Bolivian and Mexican cases tell us about why we see protest in only some times and places in spite of comparable increases in economic hardship when the prices of foodstuffs go up? And what might they tell us about who participates in these protests and why? More broadly, what can these cases tell us about why some claims become the basis for broad-based mobilization while others do not? In tackling these questions, this book explores the conditions under which social mobilization emerges and the forms it takes.

THE ARGUMENT

This research starts with the proposition that meanings matter. Everything we do (or do not do) in the world tells us something about the environment in which we are operating and has an effect on how our social and political worlds are constructed. Our worlds are socially made, and the "things" we see in the world index and generate meanings beyond what we might take as their face value.[7] This book focuses specifically on the content of a movement's claims and how that content is both materially and ideationally constituted. But is there a way to think systematically about those claims? Can we categorize grievances in ways that can help us better understand processes of social mobilization across time and space? I propose that the intersection of subsistence resources and market reforms serves as one of these categories.

The central argument develops as follows: Because of the ways in which daily life and livelihood often revolve around subsistence goods, these goods can come to signify community. They can signify both the "imagined communities" (Anderson 1991) of, for example, nation, region, or ethnic group, and quotidian communities. Quotidian communities are built through routine, face-to-face interactions where members know each other personally.[8] In other words, they are not mediated the way an imagined community is (by, for example in Anderson's case, the print media); members interact directly with one another.

Imagined communities are constituted by individuals who may never meet one another face to face yet they develop connections and have affinities for each other even in the absence of direct, personal communication. Anderson's original formulation emerges through the study of national attachments. The nation is "imagined because the members of even the smallest nations will

---

[7] I am using the word "index" methodologically. I intend to invoke the concept of indexicality whereby a sign (image, action, utterance, etc.) is indicative of something not necessarily present in the sign itself.

[8] The quotidian community concept has some resemblance to Tönnies's concept of "Gemeinschaft" insofar as the term refers to ties based on relationships developed through direct, person-to-person contact (Tönnies 1988). See also Gudeman for a discussion of the how economic practices help to create what he calls "on-the-ground associations" in addition to imagined solidarities (2001 p.1). Thanks to Dan Slater, Helen Kinsella, and Jackson Foote for helping me label this category.

never know most of their fellow-members, meet them, or even hear of them, yet in the minds of each lives the image of their communion" (Anderson 1991, 6). The simultaneous imagining of collective communion central to the concept of an imagined community is not limited to the territorially bounded communities implied by concepts like nation. For example, to imagine ties with others through a shared culture does not require notions of territorial connection. In the pages that follow I use Anderson's term to explore how other kinds of imagined communities – some tied to bounded territories like region or nation and others that may require only assertions of a shared culture – might be produced and reproduced.[9]

Subsistence threats can tap into these imagined and quotidian identifications, heightening solidarity through bringing to the fore common relationships with the threatened resource. As a result, market-driven threats to subsistence goods can be perceived not only as material threats, but also as threats to communities as large as a nation, or as small as a neighborhood.

These perceptions create the conditions of possibility for broad-based, widespread mobilization in the face of market-driven subsistence threats. The possibilities emerge through the ways in which subsistence-related communal identifications both bridge preexisting cleavages and appeal to everyday communal ties. The indiscriminate nature of the threat among poor communities creates the possibility for organization across ethnic and regional divides, while the potential appeal to imagined communities of nation, region, or ethnic group can both bridge divides among the poor and motivate middle- and upper-class participation by tapping into preexisting identifications and historical legacies or repertoires. These solidarities may be episodic, solidifying only when a threat is apparent, but they may also be more durable – lasting well beyond a particular threat and creating new possibilities for mobilized action.

But more unmediated identifications may also be at stake. As established community routines and centers for social interaction are altered, the foundations of social structures or interactions may be perceived to be at risk. These quotidian communities may help to produce strong identifications as well as the networks and ties that often prove critical in mobilization processes. When citizens perceive both imagined and quotidian communities to be at risk, individuals at odds over salient local divisions (e.g., those rooted in class, sector, occupation, gender, ethnicity, or geographies – urban, peri-urban, and rural) can coalesce around the perception of a shared threat. These overlapping identifications can help to create the conditions of possibility for broad-based, widespread resistance.

---

[9] My comments here recognize that, in fact, by the time we get to the twenty-first century (long after the period during which national imaginings began to emerge) assertions of cultural sameness are often anchored to ideas of territorially bounded communities. Thus, assertions of cultural sameness are often tied to territorially located political communities, although they need not be. Thanks to Lisa Wedeen on this point.

When markets threaten affordable access to or established relationships with a good broadly understood to be a subsistence resource, contested and varied conceptions of the resource can come together through shared understandings of insecurity and vulnerability. To threaten access to water in Cochabamba was to create perceptions that ancestral *usos y costumbres* (roughly translated as "traditions and customs" or "customary uses") were at risk. This threat also tapped into a legacy of cultivation and regional scarcity, undermined irrigation and water collection practices – as well as the community organizations that had developed to maintain these practices – and challenged a pervasive belief that water belongs to "the people." In Mexico, tortillas (and corn more generally) are a cornerstone of both urban and rural diets; they are included in well-known myths, serve as a centerpiece of daily ritual and social interaction, and are a part of how many conceive of themselves as Mexican. In each of their respective contexts, to threaten water or corn was to threaten not only a material relationship with a material good, but also perceptions of community, both imagined and quotidian.

THEORIZING AND STUDYING GRIEVANCES

Throughout this book, *grievance* is used to refer to the central claims a social movement makes – the practices, policies, or phenomena that movement members claim they are working to change (or preserve). For example, do participants claim to fight to stop climate change? To advocate for gay marriage? To reduce the size of government? The term is also central to literature on violence and civil war where it is often deployed not only to refer to claims an actor makes but also to the structural conditions – for example, political or economic inequality – from which violence emerges. This book advances the argument that we should treat these grievances as categories that require analysis because they are not just objectively identifiable conditions but also social experiences. As a result, both the explicit claims a social movement makes and the structural conditions from which it emerges are imbued with ideas – they index and generate meanings beyond the fact of climate change, gay marriage, the size of government, or political or economic inequality. Understanding these ideas furthers our understanding of contentious politics and opens up new possibilities for the study of social mobilization and conflict.

Building on the contentious politics literature

When I began this project I did not intend to focus on grievances broadly or subsistence specifically. I was intrigued by water's potential role in Cochabamba, but I grounded my analysis in the political process model (e.g., see Piven and Cloward 1977; McAdam 1982), looking for moments of political opening, the resources available to local social movement entrepreneurs, and the mobilization frames these entrepreneurs deployed. I also looked to literature that emphasized mechanisms of contention and paid particular attention to interactivity (e.g., McAdam et al. 2001). The focus on social construction that was critical to the so-called cultural turn (Bonnell et al. 1999; Sewell 1999; Goodwin et al. 2001; Goodwin and Jasper 2004) was also foundational to my early analysis. But I found that attention to elements central to political process theory could not fully explain the dynamics at work in the Cochabamban and Mexican cases. Political opportunities, organizational resources, and mobilization frames each undoubtedly played a role at various stages in the water wars and the *tortillazo* protests, and these factors provide an important foundation to understanding the dynamics at work. Yet they could not tell me why these particular issues at these particular moments brought such broad, unexpected coalitions to the streets.

Literature that looked to mechanisms in contentious politics (e.g., McAdam et al. 2001) shifted my analytical focus from outcomes to processes, providing useful guidance on how to identify and compare dynamics across contentious episodes. But how the content of a movement's claims might systematically relate to the mechanisms at work in social mobilization was under-theorized, if addressed at all. Furthermore, it appeared as though attention to a movement's claims might shed light on why some mechanisms worked the ways they did, when they did. For example, brokerage mechanisms ("the linking of two or more previously unconnected social sites by a unit that mediates their relation with another and/or with yet other sites" [McAdam et al. 2001, 102]) were clearly pivotal in the Cochabamban water wars and Mexican *tortillazo* protests. Yet attention to this mechanism suggests a prior question – what are the conditions of possibility for effective brokerage mechanisms in the first place? Similarly, mechanisms of social appropriation ("appropriation of existing social space and collective identities in the service of [attributions of threat and opportunity]" [ibid., 102]) played a critical role in both protest movements analyzed here. And once again, a prior question emerges – are there some conditions under which some mechanisms of social appropriation will be more effective than others?

Social movement scholars who foreground culture and emotions offered a critical ontological shift (e.g., Goodwin et al. 2001, 2004; Wood 2003; Gould 2009; Pearlman 2013). Protesters' lived experiences and affective orientations, not simply political contexts or physical resources, help us to understand why people engage in social mobilization when they do. Concepts like "moral shocks" (Jasper 1997) both draw attention to a social movement's claims and situate those claims in emotional processes and cultural perceptions.[10] But concepts like moral shocks raise additional questions. Why were some grievances

---

[10] Jasper defines a moral shock as "an unexpected event or piece of information [which] raises such a sense of outrage in a person that she becomes inclined toward political action, with or without the network of personal contacts emphasized in mobilization and process theories" (1997, 106).

understood as moral shocks? Could we think systematically about when a grievance is morally shocking, when it is not, and why?[11] What is the role of emotion cultures in social mobilization, and why are particular categories of claims particularly likely to produce particular types of emotions? Why do some grievances (and not others) generate specific feeling states? (see Jasper 1997, 126). More specifically, if "emboldening emotions can drive defiance" (Pearlman 2013, 392), are there particular kinds of circumstances generally and grievances specifically that might be likely to generate these emboldened states?

Grievances are not absent in social movement theorizing. Older literatures, often ignored or dismissed by the political process model, did place grievances front and center (e.g., Davies 1962, 1969; Smelser 1963; Geschwender 1968; Gurr 1970). However, a focus on relative deprivation or strain, which pervades this literature, tells us little about what particular circumstances mean in particular times and places, and seems to assume it is somehow possible to index suffering.[12] Other literatures look to threats (e.g., see Tilly 1978), but much of this work remains general and relies not on context-dependent, meaning-making work, but rather on the loss aversion theories of cognitive psychology (e.g., Kahneman and Tversky 1979). Even the literature that moves beyond the general category of "threats" remains largely committed to examining the work of a particular grievance (or collection of grievances) in a particular time or place (e.g., see Goldstone and Tilly 2001; Van Dyke and Soule 2002; Almeida 2003; Einwohner and Maher 2009; Maher 2010). The questions of why those threats might be more powerful motivators than others and how they might work to produce mobilization remain unexplored (see Simmons 2014 for a full discussion).[13]

[11] In their critique of Jasper, Polletta and Amenta ask, "Are some *kinds of issues* more likely to generate moral shocks than others?" (2001, 307). The analysis presented here is a direct response to Polletta and Amenta's call. This book shows how and why market-driven subsistence threats might be categorically understood as moral shocks.

[12] Grievances have also crept into social movement analysis through attempts to explain how third-world communities respond to fiscal austerity measures (e.g., Walton and Ragin 1990; Walton and Seddon 1994). But these approaches fail to explain variations within countries or across time, and also crucially miss the potential ideational power of the reforms in question. Indeed, in his study of Argentine protest, Javier Auyero argues that we must look carefully at the "local mediations through which adjustment is implemented and out of which protest develops" (Auyero 2001, 35) and encourages us to analyze "the ensemble of mechanisms and processes at the root of collective claim making" (ibid., 35).

[13] Most recently, David A. Snow and Sara E. Soule make the case for considering "mobilizing grievances" (2010). These grievances, they argue, are "shared among some number of actors…[and] are felt to be sufficiently serious to warrant not only collective complaint but also some kind of corrective, collective action" (ibid., 24). The concept does carve out a particular category of grievances, highlighting a distinction between grievances that might be experienced individually and those that are likely to be shared. The next step is to develop tools with which to understand when a grievance will be understood collectively (and, thus, have the potential to become a mobilizing grievance) and when it will remain an individual experience.

Dominant approaches to the study of civil war and violence have largely agreed that grievances provide little explanatory leverage (e.g., Fearon and Laitin 2003; Collier and Hoeffler 2004). These large-N studies do much to uncover potentially powerful macro trends in political resistance. Yet their methodological approach precludes them from being attentive to the kinds of dynamics this book proposes to explore and causes them to overlook the potential explanatory power of grievances. Recent scholarship has sought to bring grievances back into the study of civil conflict (e.g., Wimmer et al. 2009; Cederman et al. 2013; Wimmer 2013; Buhaug et al. 2014) and, in doing so, has raised some of the limitations with previous literatures posed here. Cederman et al. (2013) and Buhaug et al. (2014) propose that different types of inequality matter for whether or not we will see a relationship between inequality and civil conflict. By disaggregating inequality into "horizontal" and "vertical" categories these scholars produce an analysis that comes closer to incorporating how inequality is experienced on the ground than their predecessors. Indeed, they emphasize that grievances with strong "emotional power" (Buhaug et al. 2014, 421) will be the ones around which rebels organize and that inequality must be experienced as a "perceived injustice" (ibid., 422) for it to generate conflict.

While this scholarship makes some important advances, the empirical analysis and, indeed, the theoretical underpinnings of a "group-level" approach continue to treat grievances, whether horizontal or vertical, as if they can be coded simply by looking at particular structural conditions (e.g., Wimmer et al.'s emphasis on political exclusion). This book shows that grievances that appear to be the same cannot always be coded as such. What those grievances mean in a local context will change their potential for generating resistance. A focus on groups does not address the challenge; it only relocates the level at which critical assumptions are made. Only interpretive work can help us understand how and why income inequality, poverty, or even nationalism can have different meanings in different times and places, thus playing different roles in the origins and dynamics of social movements or civil wars.

Grievances and groups

By thinking about claims as materially and ideationally constituted, we are able to enrich interest-based accounts of politics and better understand how groups come to the fore as salient categories in particular times and places. Following Truman (1981) and Bentley (1994), this book argues that we cannot understand interests as existing separately from – or prior to – the actions and understandings that are continually creating and recreating them; it is through the processes of group activities that interests are forged.[14] As a result, interests

---

[14] Some of the earliest literature on the subject of interests and groups explicitly claims that the concept cannot be reduced and that our analysis of them should focus on observable activities, not "attributes" (Truman 1981; Bentley 1994).

can only be understood when embedded in a particular context (Bentley 1994; see also Emirbayer 1997).

By focusing on the meanings with which grievances are imbued and how those meanings help to create categories of practice that are then "invested with groupness" (Brubaker 2004, 12), this book sheds light on the mechanisms through which categories of practice come to be understood as groups, how dormant categories might become active mobilizing tools, how solidarities may happen episodically, and how perceived threats can heighten feelings of group belonging.[15] Perceptions of belonging can come from both the daily process of meeting physical needs and the notion that others have similar needs and face similar obstacles in their efforts to meet them. This works not just on the material, but also the symbolic level to produce socially constituted perceptions of what interests are. These perceptions may, in turn, bring groups to the fore as salient categories of practice.

The Bolivian and Mexican cases shed light on these mechanisms by highlighting the ways in which particular kinds of threats can help transform categories into groups and increase levels of groupness for particular categories. In Bolivia and Mexico, a variety of relationships with water and corn, respectively, helped to create a number of local, sometimes overlapping groups that frequently came into conflict with one another while broader group identifications around nation (and region in Bolivia) operated to produce a seemingly cohesive movement. In particular, both cases speak to the ways in which ordinary daily practices can produce connections not only to family members and neighbors but also to the imagined community of nation, and how those connections produce active categories of practice during extraordinary events.

Grievances and meaning-making

The analysis is inherently grounded in context – to understand how groups come to the fore as salient categories of practice we begin with the meanings that grievances take on in particular times and places. But it is also potentially generalizable; by uncovering the ways in which apparently different grievances may index similar ideas across time and place, producing groupness in similar ways, we can categorize those grievances similarly and explore their potential relationship to social mobilization.

By focusing our analytic lens on how different grievances are laden with similar or different meanings in various contexts, we can think of grievances not in terms of the relative gain or loss of a material "thing" or as a set of political privileges. Instead, we conceive of a movement's claims as part of the "*socially and culturally available* array of symbols and meanings from which

[15] I follow Brubaker and Cooper (2000, 4) to define categories of practice as "categories of everyday social experience, developed and deployed by ordinary social actors, as distinguished from the experience-distant categories used by social analysts."

movements can draw" (Williams 2007, 96, emphasis in original). When we approach the analysis through this lens, it is quickly clear that context is key – the same things (actions, objects, ideas, etc.) cannot always be coded the same. What grievances mean in a local context will change their potential for generating resistance. This book builds on Snow et al.'s (1986) emphasis on grievance interpretation to encourage the study of the *meanings* with which grievances are imbued. By understanding grievances as embedded in cultural context, we can productively engage with the question of how the claims themselves shape social movement outcomes rather than simply focusing on whether or how those claims are articulated by movement entrepreneurs.

The significations of grievances in the Bolivian and Mexican cases were often in tension with one another and yet coexisted spatially and temporally. Corn may signify physical nourishment, home, and nation to the same person at the same moment, and each of these answers to the question "what is corn?" is right. Similarly, water may signify regional struggle, ethnic heritage, or community dignity. To answer the question "what is water?" with "community dignity" is no less correct than to answer it with "the combination of two hydrogen and one oxygen atoms in liquid form." What water *is* varies depending on the context. The same speaker might answer the question differently in different contexts, whereas for some speakers, the correct answer to "what is water" may never be "community dignity." Furthermore, this approach focuses our analytical lens not on abstract theorizations but rather on routine practices, and it seeks to reveal how these practices constitute identifications.

Importantly, context does not simply mean reference to a particular region or time period; it also refers to the actions that are undertaken in relationship to a particular statement, the felicitous conditions accompanying the utterance, the "grammar" of particular concepts, and the micro-circumstances of a statement in relation to other statements.[16] Water may be H_2O to some people in some times and places, and it may be community to others – in the same time and place. Broader macro contrasts in, for example, time or place still matter, but so do micro-circumstances.

The meanings that grievances take on are multiple and fluid. The mobilization process puts at risk old understandings and generates new ones; meanings will no doubt shift over the course of a mobilization. Social mobilizations can be times when rules are "transgressed and categories confused" (Coronil and Skurski 1991, 317), rendering meanings particularly vulnerable to change. While these shifts are an important subject of inquiry, this analysis is primarily concerned with the kinds of meanings at work before a social mobilization begins and the role those preexisting meanings can play in generating and shaping contention. As a result, the discussion of the cases focuses on the meanings with which water and corn were imbued before the threat that

---

[16] Thanks to Lisa Wedeen for helping clarify this point.

sparked a mobilized reaction and how those meanings were at work in the early stages of mobilization.

Whereas many social movements can and do deploy alternative conceptions that unsettle dominant cultural meanings (Alvarez et al. 1998, 7), they can also grow directly from those dominant meanings. Indeed, they may emerge precisely because widely shared practices of meaning-making are at risk. In Bolivia and Mexico, movements emerged precisely at the moment when two practices that pervaded social encounters were put into tension with each other, when the practices that constituted a globalized, marketized world put at risk practices that produced and reproduced both imagined and quotidian communities.

THEORIZING SUBSISTENCE

The events studied here suggest that perceived threats to community can provide a powerful focal point for political protest. The conjecture is not surprising; the potential for connections between perceived community threats and mobilization is clear in cases as varied as antinuclear protests in the United States, peasant revolutions in Latin America, and uprisings in post-Mubarak Egypt. But these empirical events remain under-theorized. What does community mean, and why might threats to it be conducive to social mobilization? How can we further parse the category to better understand why, when, and how group members perceive communities to be at stake?

Through analysis of the Bolivian and Mexican cases, one potentially generalizable category of threats to community emerges: threats to subsistence. One need only conjure images of bread and the French Revolution, grain riots in nineteenth-century England, or austerity protests in Latin America to recognize the role of subsistence threats in mobilization. The connection between subsistence and material well-being – that people might protest rising prices of subsistence goods because of the impact on their wallets alone – is an easy one to make. But that subsistence threats work to produce mobilization through the ways in which conceptions of community and subsistence are intimately intertwined is less intuitive. In particular, the importance of daily practices in the process of the production of groups draws our attention to the broader category of subsistence and how subsistence practices in different times and places may help to produce understandings of groupness in similar ways. The cases suggest that subsistence-related social movement claims encompass the potentially incompatible paradigms of redistribution and recognition, making claims based both on concerns surrounding deprivation and on social patterns of representation (Fraser and Honneth 2003).

To understand resistance to market-driven subsistence threats, we must understand not only how norms of reciprocity or perceptions of a "just price" mediate relationships with subsistence goods, but also how subsistence goods can be imbricated in what the Comaroffs (1990) call an "economy of signs and practices." The critical material role played by goods such as bread in England

(Thompson 1971) or rice in Indonesia (Scott 1976) in physical sustenance cannot be disentangled from how the goods have come to operate as symbols, working to produce and reproduce understandings of self and community. Arnold helpfully proposes that scholars reconceptualize moral economy "in terms of social goods" (2001, 85). I take his suggestion that an emphasis on specific social goods will offer insight into moments of political resistance and offer a systematic approach to the study of one category of social good – subsistence resources. Even though a number of scholars from a variety of disciplines have focused their attention on subsistence, marketization, and community, the question of how the three intersect to produce patterns of contention is underexplored.

Defining subsistence

What is a subsistence resource? The definition is critical in our efforts to theorize the relationships between subsistence and mobilization. I want to draw explicit attention to the importance of local understandings (where *local* may be as small as a neighborhood or as large as a nation). The definition of subsistence resource used in this book has two central components. First, the resource or good must be one that is understood by claimants to be necessary for survival and for which substitution is either impossible or highly undesirable. Although humans need not consume corn to survive, if corn has formed a central component of a regional diet in such a way that communities do not understand it to be substitutable (e.g., with rice or wheat), corn may come to be understood as a subsistence resource (see Chapter 4). The caloric or nutritional contribution of a good such as corn may be relatively easily found in other resources. What matters for this definition is that claimants do not believe that bread is a substitute for corn. Local meanings and perceptions play an important role in how and whether any community understands a good as "subsistence"; material resources cannot be treated independently from the ideas with which they are imbued. Even a resource as objectively important to survival as water becomes subjectively politicized, generating protest in some instances and quiescence in others.

I consider the relationship between the material and the ideational in subsistence goods as reciprocal. The meanings with which subsistence goods are imbued are the product of their particular material histories. As Wedeen has argued, "material interests might be fruitfully viewed not as objective criteria but as being discursively produced: in other words, what counts as material interest is mediated through our language about what 'interest' means and what the material is" (2008, 183). The ideational and the material continually work in ways that are "reciprocally determining, that is, mutually implicated in the changes that each undergoes through time" (ibid., 49). Corn's role in providing physical nourishment to Mexicans over centuries has played an integral role in how the grain has taken on meanings. Similarly, the Cochabamba

Valley's initial dependence on water for its growth and its current struggles with drought continue to shape what water means to many Cochabambans. Furthermore, these meanings and relationships are not static. Histories are remade and redeployed in different and sometimes contradictory ways. Both the ideational and the material aspects of a subsistence good may differ from neighborhood to neighborhood or community to community, between social or economic classes, or over time. The attachments are lived in different ways by different people and may even be lived differently by the same person at different moments. But these attachments may also bridge personal and political divides – taking on similar meanings and material values in different communities at different times and in doing so, providing common ground across geographic or social communities that may perceive they have little to share.

Second, claimants must either have an "artisanal" relationship with the good or they must understand other members of their perceived community to have such a relationship (see Bakker 2003). Where water is artisanal, people interact directly with its cultivation and distribution. The good does not simply arrive at an individual's home daily by opening a tap. Instead, it is "drawn from local streams, wells, or ponds, or delivered by water vendors in jerrycans or tanker trucks to the home" (ibid., 42). People need to exert daily effort specifically and consciously to procure enough water to meet their needs. In much of the Global North, however, water is an "abstract" industrial product and "large amounts of [it] … are taken for granted as a necessary requirement for daily life in modern, industrialized societies" (ibid., 42, 46); consumers need only open a tap and the good miraculously appears.

This kind of relationship allows us to understand some material goods as divorced from our social worlds. When we "enframe" (Heidegger 1977) goods this way, we regard them purely on material terms for the components that make them up and that can be taken apart and redeployed elsewhere for a different purpose. Rivers are regarded for the energy that can be extracted from them, rather than as entities with which we participate in the day-to-day rhythms of life; forests are regarded in terms of "orderable cellulose" (ibid.), rather than as enchanted domains shared across the generations; corn is revealed as nothing more than the nutritional value and calories it provides.[17] Yet when these goods are central to life and livelihood, they are often perceived as more than simply their component characteristics. We interact with these goods in relationships with other people (building an irrigation ditch, consuming or cooking a meal), and the goods are no longer simply material things that can be divorced from our social worlds. Instead, they serve as integral parts of our relationships with others and become imbricated in the most fundamental meaning-making processes in our lives; subsistence goods can transcend the pure materiality of their role to take on social meanings.

---

[17] More recently Georgio Agamben makes a similar distinction between bare life, or *zoe* (Gk. ζωή), and meaningful life, or *bios* (Gk. βίος) (Agamben 1995).

When a resource is understood as nonsubstitutable and relationships with it are artisanal, it may take on particular meanings that place it at the center not only of communal livelihood, but also of communal life.[18] Community routines and practices may develop around the good, relationships may form with the good as the focal point, and identifications may develop with the good whereby the good itself helps to symbolize group membership. Here the good's meanings are bound up not just with its quotidian material use, but with the ritualistic aspects of its deployment. The good may take on sacral meanings, becoming part of a community's religious life, playing central roles in religious ceremonies or rituals. For example, as Chapter 4 explores, corn takes on a central role in Mexican myths of creation. Both Mayan and Aztec mythology include at least one god of corn. Through these quotidian practices, the good becomes inextricably bound up with spiritual practices and institutions, helping to create not only quotidian communities but also mediated connections across space and time constituted not by conceptions of shared bounded territory but rather ideas of shared cultural connections.

Importantly, in order for daily routines around subsistence goods to come to signify group membership, individuals need not participate in the routines themselves. Instead, in the very act of imagining that others are participating in these routines and valuing them as somehow constitutive of groupness, the imagining can be doing some of the work. Think of an annual ritual around the corn harvest, or even the seasonal practices surrounding tending a *milpa* (a small plot of land containing corn and other staples). Urban Mexicans may not participate in the rituals, but they may come to think that the practice of tending a *milpa* or participating in an annual event around the corn harvest is foundational to the continuation of Mexican culture. It is the idea that *milpas* still exist or that harvest rituals still take place that is important. The thought that those practices might be threatened, even if an individual does not engage in them him- or herself, helps produce a perceived threat to community. Something that is perceived as somehow constituting and defining the group might be lost.

Markets and threats

As used here, threats to subsistence resources occur when access to the good is challenged in such a way as to endanger established patterns of use or consumption. It is worth noting that this book takes care to focus specifically on subsistence resources or goods and avoids including more general subsistence

[18] Jung makes a similar observation with respect to corn, and my language is based on hers. Jung writes that plummeting corn prices were "devastating" to Mexican peasants because "corn, and farming, is additionally at the center of the communal life, not just the livelihood, of Mexico's rural population" (2003 8). But the development of this insight is not her primary purpose and, as a result, goes understandably untheorized.

threats in the theoretical discussion. Although an across-the-board increase in taxes may, indeed, threaten an individual's or a community's ability to subsist, for the mechanisms described here to come into play we focus on the object of taxation. What is critical is that a specific resource is threatened; an increase or imposition of a value-added tax may generate protest in some instances, but it is unlikely to be through the mechanisms discussed here.[19] An increase in taxes specifically on rice in Japan, however, might tap into the community solidarities proposed here and produce resistance as a result. A specific subsistence resource is the target of the threat, and as a result, understandings of community may very well be perceived as threatened as well.

Any number of events or policies might put subsistence at risk. Floods, droughts, civil conflict, and government regulation are just a few types of threats that could jeopardize established routines and relationships with subsistence goods. The mechanisms outlined earlier might very well work to generate political mobilization during any of these types of threats. However, this research concerns itself with a particular kind of threat – one perceived to be caused by the imposition of markets. Evidence from the cases suggest that markets interact with narratives about insecurity and state expectations in ways that threats created by natural disasters, for example, might not.

I focus on market-driven subsistence threats for two reasons. First, market-oriented policy reforms can create clear targets for resistance movements. A movement might seek to alter a specific policy (e.g., the lifting of a subsidy), or a movement may protest the activities of a private firm that has taken over a previously nationalized industry. The mechanisms outlined earlier may work in different ways when natural disasters or civil conflicts are perceived to be responsible for the subsistence threat. Second, the symbolic importance of a subsistence good can motivate resistance rooted in claims that the good should not be subject to the vicissitudes of markets. When access to a good is subject to the profit-making motives of private companies or the unpredictability of international commodity markets, perceived relationships with the good may be rendered particularly insecure. This kind of anxiety may be particularly well suited to motivating the broad-based, widespread political mobilization analyzed in this book. By focusing specifically on the intersection of markets and subsistence, this book lays important theoretical groundwork for further scholarship on subsistence threats and contention more broadly.

---

[19] Taxes are, of course, also meaning laden and may take on community-related meanings. The ways in which taxes are understood across time and place – and the connections between those understandings and contentious politics – would be an interesting avenue for further research. See Isaac Martin (2008) for a good discussion of property taxes and protest in the United States. Martin's analysis is, in fact, potentially consistent with the arguments made here, as the meanings that property ownership takes on in the United States help explain the mobilizations he studies. Thanks are due to Elisabeth Clemens for drawing this to my attention.

Deepening moral economies

Social science research is replete with references to social mobilization around threats to subsistence resources (e.g., Thompson 1971; Scott 1976; McClintock 1984, 1998; Bouton 1993), yet the relationship between marketization, subsistence, and social movements remains under-theorized. E. P. Thompson (1971) shows how community-established expectations of the prices of necessities help us to better understand eighteenth-century food riots, and James Scott's (1976) concept of a "subsistence ethic" draws our attention to the importance of community in establishing technical and social expectations and arrangements for surviving times of dearth.[20] When these scholars focus our attention on "moral economies" they are explicitly claiming that there is more to the processes of production, consumption, and exchange than market-determined prices.

Much of this scholarship, however, remains focused on the material qualities of subsistence. If there is, as Scott suggests, something systematic about threats to subsistence and peasant rebellions, and subsistence threats are perceived as more "exploitative" than other potentially equivalent material claims (ibid., 31), we need to pay attention to not only the material, but also the ideational elements of those threats. General references to necessities and food beg disaggregation, as not all food is likely to be encompassed by a subsistence ethic.[21] Although rice plays a prominent role in Scott's story, its particularities and the potential meanings with which it is imbued remain unexplored – the "nearly universal limits" he discusses may not simply be a product of rice's nutritional value. In particular, Scott's focus on the nourishment subsistence goods provide overlooks the ways in which the material and the symbolic work to constitute each other when subsistence is at stake. Livelihood strategies are not simply a mechanism to cope with times of dearth (à la Scott), but also practices that invest life with meaning. This book both deepens the moral economy approach and exposes some of its limitations.

Contemporary subsistence protests suggest that a subsistence ethic continues to exist and that the concept of a moral economy should continue to inform our understandings of world events. Scholarship that draws on these recent events, however, remains grounded in traditional paradigms. For example, whereas Hendrix, Haggard, and Magaloni (2009) find that "international

---

[20] Like Scott, Deborah Yashar (2005) links changes in the economic order to social mobilization. Yet for Scott, resistance emerges specifically around issues of subsistence, whereas Yashar looks to threats to autonomy. I posit that it is possible that threats to autonomy can begin with challenges to subsistence rights, and, therefore, subsistence can very well be at the heart of autonomy movements.

[21] See also William Sewell (1980) and Cynthia McClintock (1984, 1998), who both highlight the importance of particular subsistence goods (bread and potatoes respectively) in social mobilization, but do not systematically distinguish between food prices generally and those of bread or potatoes specifically. See also Bouton's (1993) historical account of the 1774 "freeing" of the grain trade in France and the riots that followed.

food prices are a significant determinant of the incidence of protest and riots," they look to political context to explain variation. Drawing on data from Asia and Africa from 1961 to 2009, they ultimately conclude that attention to regime type best accounts for differences across time and place. More recently Hendrix and Haggard (2015) add an additional layer to the analysis by examining the role of urban bias in food policy. Like Scott and Thompson, Hendrix et al. (2009) and Hendrix and Haggard (2015) treat rising food prices as if they could be coded similarly without attention to the particular goods that might be at stake. Including meaning-making in our analysis could shed light on the dynamics of the varied local responses to food price spikes.

Subsistence as symbol

Even literature that draws our attention to the ways in which subsistence resources come to signify community (e.g., see Moore 2000; Perreault 2001, 2005; Wolford 2003;) leaves the connection between these significations and mobilized resistance largely unexplored. Livelihood practices – the things we do every day as we pursue survival – are an important source of meaning in human lives. These practices can become things we do not only for the purpose of material survival, but also because they work to constitute our sense of self and perceptions of group membership (see Gudeman 2001). When practices become a part of everyday routines and rituals – when they are involved in our daily lives and are central to social relationships – they take on meanings beyond serving merely as "stuff." In this way, goods can be "a medium of transformation, in a total economy of signs and practices, between a material economy of things and a moral economy of persons" (Comaroff and Comaroff 1990, 196). Goods that embody value and meaning can serve as intelligible symbols for groups – symbols that are recognized across geographies and decades.

Subsistence goods are a particularly likely type of matter for the investment of identity. Although "any material can arbitrarily be endowed with meaning" and myths "cannot possibly evolve from the 'nature' of things" (Barthes 2012, 218), there may still be objects that are particularly likely to be sources of suggestiveness. The material role subsistence goods play means they will likely be, for example, spoken and written about, photographed, drawn, and included in cinema or sport. All of these speech acts invest subsistence goods with meanings that inextricably bind the material and the symbolic. As a physical foundation of livelihood, subsistence resources both construct and order community in the present and serve as the perfect vehicle through which identities can be projected through space and time (Munn 1977; Comaroff and Comaroff 1990). This happens in rural areas around the cultivation of crops or the collection of water – where the production of these goods provides for the reproduction of community and serves both as a performance and a mark of identity (see Gudeman 2001, 46–7) – and in urban areas around daily routines that might be structured around a trip to the *tortillería* or a mid-morning taco snack.

These practices constitute and structure our social worlds through socially constructed schemas that operate without conscious awareness – what Bourdieu calls *habitus* (1977, 1990). These practices, which are taken for granted as common sense or "natural," are so much a part of our lives that we engage in them without questioning their social production. Habitus helps us navigate the world by acknowledging that many of its elements seem obvious, and, as a result, they fall away from our conscious analysis of why we do what we do (ibid.). In this way, "mythical speech" (Barthes 2012) becomes "naturalized" (ibid., 240–1), and we consume meaning-making practices without seeing a semiological system at work.

This process of naturalization sheds light on how the past is constantly reactivated in the present – a critical element to understanding how the meanings of subsistence goods are produced and reproduced. The past is active in the present, Bourdieu argues, through its "reactivation in similarly structured practices" (1990, 54). These practices are invested with meanings that then work to "transform history into nature" (Barthes 2012, 240). Subsistence goods may take on new forms over time or may work to evoke connections to community even if how those connections are produced change. Even as we acknowledge that there is no fixity in myth (ibid., 230), the habitus that helps us navigate our social worlds may continue to help produce a relationship between signifier and signified that we read as part of a factual rather than a semiological system.

A number of scholars have, if unintentionally, shown the habitus concept at work through their explorations of the ways in which subsistence goods work to symbolize community in a variety of regions and economic circumstances (e.g., Ferguson 1985; Comaroff and Comaroff 1990; Ohnuki-Tierney 1993; Kaplan 1996; Moore 2000; Perreault 2001, 2005).[22] The role that cattle in southern Africa (Ferguson 1985; Comaroff and Comaroff 1990), rice in Japan (Ohnuki-Tierney 1993), or baguettes in Paris (Kaplan 1996) play in providing household food security is precisely how they come to signify community – it is their material role that provides the critical foundation. In his study of the "bovine mystique" in Lesotho, James Ferguson finds that cattle "are not treated as simple 'economic' goods (i.e., commodities)" (1985, 682); instead they are

(margin handwritten note: references other cultures)

---

[22] Writing at the same time as Scott, Marshall Sahlins (1976) also urges scholars to think about the symbolic nature of physical necessities. Sahlins turns to Marx, who, in Sahlins's words, insists that although analysis of men must start with material needs, "the contents of human need are not exhausted by any such reference to physical necessity" (ibid., 148). As Sahlins points out, however, Marx "only presented the concept of the need to eat; he did not develop the concept of its historical properties" (ibid., 148–9). The need to eat cannot be pried apart from the historical moment in which the need exists. Marx's "system of needs," Sahlins points out, "must always be relative, not accountable as such by physical necessity, hence symbolic by definition" (ibid., 150).

"culturally constituted as a type of property which is not to be sold" (ibid., 653). The Comaroffs (1990) build on Ferguson's insight with their argument that Tswana cattle are at once economic and symbolic objects. In his study of Old Regime Paris, Steven Kaplan offers both an urban example and one based on the production and transformation of a grain. The baguette, Kaplan argues, serves as a "metonym for the nation and its civilization in France" (1996, 3). For the French, he posits, "the loaf contained something more than calories and nutrients" (ibid., 23), conveying "social identity" (ibid., 46), and serving "at the core of both the material and symbolic organization of everyday existence" (ibid., 23).

These goods and practices are imagined to be a part of a group's past at the same time as they can be projected into a group's future. These spatial and temporal dynamics are part of what make subsistence resources such likely candidates for the production and reproduction of community-related meanings. The production and consumption of particular foods "are, in a profound way, the material and symbolic practices through which we define ourselves and our group, and maintain the boundaries that separate us from others" (Perreault 2001, 403). As a result, struggles around development are particularly good for revealing the intersection of the material and the symbolic in livelihood practices. As development interventions often seek to alter subsistence patterns, usually with a promise of material benefits, reactions to them can expose the ways in which these patterns work to signify community.

Even if particular subsistence goods become replaceable as a critical source of food security, they may continue to serve as markers of group identification. The daily practices of production and consumption can retain their meanings even if the practices themselves are no longer critical for physical nourishment (see Perreault 2001, 402).[23] Thus, even as daily life may no longer revolve around the production, cooking, or consumption of corn, the importance of the grain to identifications throughout Mexico continues to be produced through habitus.

In his research on *chacras* (loosely translated as "small farms") in the Napo region of the Ecuadorian Amazon, Thomas Perreault (2001, 2005) finds that the farms produce connections to imagined ancestors, to other Quichua whom Perreault's research subjects will never meet, and to an imagined future where what it means to be Quichua is preserved, in part, through the *chacra*. One source recounts how the traditions around food and drink were learned "from our grandparents and for that reason we should not forget our customs and traditions. Because if we were to lose them, we would not identify ourselves as Quichua people" (Perreault 2001, 402). Kaplan finds that this is exactly the dynamic at work in Old Regime Paris where the consumption of bread was no longer a nutritional necessity. Nevertheless, for Parisians bread was not substitutable. Bakers were both the "guardians of tradition" and the "artisan

---

[23] This is not to imply that the practices become static. They change constantly.

of today" (1996, 7), producing and reproducing what it means to be Parisian in the present while maintaining connections to an imagined past. Using Pascal's language, Kaplan argues that Parisians were attached to bread not by the "cords of necessity" but also by the "cords of imagination" (ibid., 3).

Food generally, and subsistence resources in particular, may be only one of many ways through which feelings of groupness are produced and reproduced. Yet evidence from southern Africa, Ecuador, and France cited here (see also Bouton 1993; Ohnuki-Tierney 1993; Moore 2000; Wolford 2003) speak to what we might call the "external validity" of the initial steps in the development of my theoretical argument. It is not just in Cochabamba or Mexico that water or corn, because of their role in daily life and practice, help construct and define community. We see similar processes at work in places as different as southern Africa (Ferguson 1985; Comaroff and Comaroff 1990), urban Paris (Kaplan 1996), and the Amazon basin (Perreault 2001, 2005).[24]

Importantly, these meanings do not simply disappear with the arrival of markets based on cash transactions. Even as goods are assigned a monetary value – tortillas at ten pesos per kilo or water at seven bolivianos per cubic meter – they do not lose the "grammar of social relations" (Comaroff and Comaroff 1990, 211) with which they might be imbued. Markets may transform how goods are conceptually and discursively represented (Bakker 2002), but markets do not, by definition alone, divorce goods from their meanings. Even as markets begin to play a role in how subsistence goods are obtained, consumption remains a highly social act.[25] Whether we produce a good in our own fields or buy it at a supermarket, the act of obtaining and consuming it adds to who we understand ourselves to be and how we understand ourselves to fit into the world. In fact, in the cases analyzed here, markets may illuminate a good's symbolic role, highlighting meanings that may otherwise be taken for granted in daily practice.

Double movements and subsistence

Should we expect broad-based resistance to marketization? The answer, of course, is not clear. Writing in the 1940s, Karl Polanyi famously argued that with the commodification of the fundamental bases of production we should see the emergence of a "double movement" – a movement to protect citizens from the dangers of unregulated markets (2001).[26] For Polanyi, land and labor

[24] Although the cases explored here (both in my own research and that of others discussed in this text) are largely limited to "developing" countries (with the potential exception of France during the Old Regime), it is likely that the arguments apply more broadly.

[25] Jonathan Friedman observes that "consumption within the bounds of the world system is always a consumption of identity, canalized by a negotiation between self-determination and the array of possibilities offered by the capitalist market" (1990, 314).

[26] Other authors have explored the connections between Polanyi's claims and resistance to market reforms in contemporary Latin America. Silva's (2009) is the most recent and comprehensive of these works.

are "fictitious commodities." They help to constitute society itself and, therefore, cannot be reduced to things that can be bought and sold.[27] "Fictitious commodification" disembeds land and labor from the social fabric, destabilizing society and economy – inevitably generating social tension and its own logic of resistance. Broad-based resistance crossing class, sectoral, and geographic lines coalesces in an effort to protect society from the detrimental effects of markets – largely by calling on democratic states to step in to regulate private interests. Yet – with some notable exceptions – this kind of a double movement seemed strikingly absent in the early decades of neoliberal reforms, and Latin America in particular appeared relatively quiescent. The earliest phases of economic adjustment faced weak opposition, if any at all. Why would policies that lowered wages, pensions, and social safety nets for so many Latin Americans face such limited mobilized resistance?

Some research points to the disorganizing, weakening, and/or atomizing effects of market-oriented economic policies on social movement or civil society organizations (e.g., Oxhorn and Ducatenzeiler 1998; Agüero and Stark 1998; Kurtz 2004; Auyero 2007). As relations of production evolve to meet the needs of the global economy, capital, labor, and markets are becoming increasingly flexible. As many industries, driven by the demands of global production and distribution, break down into smaller and smaller units, it becomes difficult for labor – the historical center of twentieth-century Latin American social struggles – to organize a large and cohesive base. Furthermore, with free markets, citizens may have "conflicting and often disparate material grievances" (Kurtz 2004, 294), making large-scale social mobilization even less likely. The disintegration of organized labor may help to explain why the 1980s and 1990s did not usher in the kind of double movement Polanyi saw in the 1920s and 1930s. A key element in Polanyi's analysis – strong organized labor – was missing.

Yet popular protest is far from dead in Latin America, and, in fact, some scholars argue that market reforms have actually served to repoliticize citizens throughout the region (e.g., Edelman 1971; Yashar 2005; Silva 2009).[28] Protest movements have forced presidents from office (e.g., Hochstetler 2006), asserted claims rooted in ethnic identifications (e.g., Yashar 2005), and expressed outrage with austerity measures (e.g., Walton and Seddon 1994; Auyero 2001, 2003; Silva 2009).[29] In their analysis of protests over sharp increases in food

---

[27] Polanyi argues that "man's economy, as a rule, is submerged in his social relationships" (2001, 48). He goes on to posit that man "does not act so as to safeguard his individual interest in the possession of material goods; he acts so as to safeguard his social standing, his social claims, his social assets. He values material goods only in so far as they serve this end" (ibid., 48).

[28] Roberta Rice (2012) takes a more nuanced approach, arguing that globalization has encouraged particular types of social mobilization while discouraging others.

[29] See also Alvarez et al. (1998). Arce and Bellinger offer an explicit critique of Kurtz, calling his evidence on declining labor mobilizations "circumstantial" (2007, 118).

prices and food shortages in 1989 in Venezuela, Coronil and Skurski (1991) show how links between hunger and resistance are connected to expectations of the state and morality while creating opportunities for new, imagined connections among affected populations. While a double movement has remained strikingly absent in much of the Global North, similar dynamics appear to have emerged, if delayed, throughout Latin America (Almeida 2007; Silva 2009).

However, many of these mobilizations took place well after neoliberal regimes had been firmly entrenched.[30] Some of this delay may be due not only to the demobilization and fragmentation that Kurtz (2004) and others find but also to citizens' tacit consent. Andy Baker (2003, 2009) shifts our attention from the labor market to consumer-oriented interests and adds important nuance in the process. He finds widespread support for globalization and free trade because it makes higher-quality goods widely available at lower prices. This popular approval provides an alternative story for how governments kept mass protest at bay during the early stages of market reforms.

But the question remains: What changed as policies became more entrenched? Attention to consumer interests could be part of the story. In many countries the second stage of market reforms involved the privatization of national companies and municipal services. Unlike free trade these proved widely unpopular – they often raised prices on utilities and put a heavy burden on middle-income consumers (Baker 2009). Attention to consumers is helpful insofar as it reminds us of the importance of how populations experience market-based reforms. But it keeps us firmly grounded in material conditions, tying popular protest to rising prices and taking us back to the problems with early grievance-based approaches.

Careful attention to the dynamics of these later anti-market mobilizations helps to shed light on the processes at work. The movements studied here looked decidedly different from the double movement Polanyi described. While labor organizations played central roles, so too did neighborhood organizations. In Cochabamba and Mexico City, collective imaginings emerged not only around class, but also around region, nation, and ethnicity. The protesters' place in the structure of the capitalist system mattered, but so too did conceptions of indigenous heritage, national belonging, and communal reciprocity. Furthermore, state regulation was not always the answer. While protesters in Mexico may have been calling for the state to protect them from "savage capitalism" in the form of unregulated tortilla prices, Cochabamban protesters explicitly rejected state interference in local affairs. To understand these mobilizations we should

---

[30] Almeida (2007) identifies a "second wave" of contention. Arce (2010) makes a convincing theoretical argument that some of this variation can be explained by the quality of representation at the government level. However, Arce focuses on party system institutionalization, as an indicator of representativeness. Slater and Simmons (2013) show how even well-institutionalized systems may not be representative. More importantly, the argument made here does not contradict Arce's theoretical propositions. Instead, it helps us explain contemporaneous subnational variation, something that Arce's focus on national political institutions cannot unpack.

look not only at material conditions but what those material conditions meant in the contexts in which they were experienced.

A focus on conceptualizations of communities and subsistence offers useful insights into these dynamics, deepening our understanding of what a contemporary double movement might look like and exposing the limitations with arguments that are over-reliant on economic structures. Throughout Latin America, political resistance has arguably migrated from shared identifications in the workplace to shared identifications across themes of subsistence rights, citizenship, race and ethnicity, and gender (Eckstein and Wickham-Crowley 2003). As June Nash argues, "the locus of working-class struggle in the workplace that emerged with industrial capitalism in the nineteenth century now takes place elsewhere" (2005, 3). Although the workplace has not been rendered obsolete as a location of resistance, individuals and groups have discovered, created, and strengthened new forms of collective identifications that serve as effective centers of protest in the context of a globalized, neoliberal world. Communities are created and conceptualized in new places and new ways, as new categories of collectivity and subjectivity emerge.

When factory conditions change such that they no longer create connections through shared labor experiences, it is logical to imagine that one of the most powerful communities left is constructed through the daily routines and practices of subsistence. Groups can find security in neighborhood-level mechanisms designed to provide for daily needs or in pride in national heritage or culture. These mechanisms are rooted not only in the social relationships to economy that Polanyi describes, but also in the meanings ascribed to these practices. If we understand subsistence practices as part of the sacra of a community, and the destruction of sacra is not only a social event but also a threat to the group, then it is not difficult to imagine that a threat to subsistence may also constitute a threat to community. When we bring meaning into Polanyi's account, we can better understand the contours of the contemporary double movement.

Furthermore, when we break from essentialist accounts of responses to neoliberal reforms we can see how market liberalization might simultaneously demobilize and fragment popular sectors (e.g., Kurtz 2004), receive high levels of popular support (e.g., Baker 2009), and stimulate social protest in defense of popular interests (e.g., Arce and Bellinger 2007; Silva 2009). The Cochabamban and Mexican cases help to reconcile this long-standing debate by revealing the contextual, conditional, and highly contingent effects of markets. A focus on how the material and the symbolic are intertwined in subsistence threats shows us how.

METHODS OF RESEARCH

This book is a work of comparative interpretive analysis. Most generally, this approach takes the world to be socially made – understandings are historically constituted, variable, and always subject to risk. Interpretive social science involves the study of what people say and do, but it does not take those practices at face value. Instead, an interpretive scholar will try to understand the meaning of the actions or utterances at hand. By employing an explicitly comparative interpretive approach, this book can both embed cases in their particular context, paying attention to the role meaning plays in generating contention in a specific time and place, and offer an analysis that explicitly shows how the claims might be generalized.[31]

The approach requires a methodological commitment to interpretive ethnography (a task that challenges even the most ambitious and skilled ethnographers when attempting to compare multiple cases), interpretive historical analysis, and careful process tracing.[32] The case discussion focuses on two particular movements at two particular moments, enabling the use of interpretive ethnographic and historical analysis while also creating an opportunity to leverage the insights gained from tacking back and forth between two different moments when similar political processes were at work.[33] This book further leverages each case through attention to within-case variation in meaning-making processes, highlighting the ways in which divergent practices and ideas can converge in an apparently single mobilization. Through these approaches, this book bridges gaps between arguments that privilege the importance of meanings in social science analysis and those that seek to focus solely on explicitly generalizable claims.

Interpretive analysis

Social movement scholarship has a rich tradition of taking culture seriously. This book draws on an anthropological conceptualization of culture as "semiotic practices" (Sewell 1999; Wedeen 2002). This approach pays particular attention to "what language and symbols *do* – how they are inscribed into concrete actions and how they operate to produce observable political effects" (Wedeen 2002, 714, emphasis in original).[34] These meanings are constantly contested, both by chronologically linear processes of change and by the

---

[31] Interpretive analyses often make explicitly generalizable claims. The comparative case analysis conducted here allows me to further refine my insights and think explicitly about how they might travel.

[32] For a good discussion of the difference between interpretive and noninterpretive ethnography, see Wedeen (2009, 2010). In particular see fn. 15 (2009). Most generally, noninterpretive ethnographers take their informants' actions and utterances at face value without looking for the meanings – contested and subject to risk – those actions or utterances might take on for the individuals or groups exposed to them.

[33] See Tarrow (2010) for a treatment of the benefits and pitfalls of paired comparisons.

[34] Much of the social movement literature attentive to culture focuses on what movements do *with* language and symbols, as opposed to the approach proposed here, which focuses on the work done not by movement activists, but rather by the language and symbols themselves.

multiple significations that may exist within social groups. When we look at how symbols operate in the world, understanding them as dynamic and conflicted, we can begin to ask questions about why and how meanings might work to generate moments of collective political protest.

Interpretive work helps us better understand how the people we study make sense of the world around them.[35] This approach is particularly well suited to the questions at hand for three reasons. First, through enmeshing myself in the worlds I sought to study, I hoped to better understand what particular actions, words, or other symbols might mean to the Cochabambans and Mexicans with whom I interacted. I was able to explore how practices that have never been "put to paper" (Parkinson 2013, 420) order daily lives and are rendered meaningful. Second, I was able to avoid individualist assumptions about the logics of collective action and instead treat actors as socially embedded (Wedeen 2002). This allowed me to explore questions about the ways in which communities were constituted and how the water concession contract or rising corn prices might be perceived as a threat to them.

Third, the combination of interpretive ethnography and historical analysis allowed me to explore meaning-making processes at both the micro- and the meso-levels. The two approaches helped me to understand how participants in the water wars and *tortillazo* protests made sense of the world around them and how those meanings interacted with meaning-making processes of Cochabambans and Mexicans from other neighborhoods, classes, or professions. I was able to explore the work that language and symbols did in various Cochabamban and Mexican contexts, constantly moving back and forth between what I observed during fieldwork and the accounts of daily life in Cochabamba and Mexico City produced before and during the water wars and the *tortillazo* protests. This ability to go back and forth among neighborhoods – and across time – brought to the fore the ways in which the particularities of water and corn's meanings varied but often remained consistent with a broader narrative of community autonomy or sovereignty, and dignity. It was this narrative that served to bring Cochabambans and Mexicans together during the protest events. Ultimately, the approach allows me to shed light on the ways in which everyday practices are part of the fabric of extraordinary events.

The interpretive approach also allows me to make a broader contribution to methods of inquiry. Scholars who study politics through regression analysis using a large number of cases need to be able to code each case, identify the relevant variables to help explain a particular outcome, and then quantify those variables. A scholar who is interested in the relationship between corn prices and social mobilization might count the number of protests in a number of countries and then see whether changes in corn prices help to explain

[35] See Walsh (2009) for an excellent example of how participant observation can shed light on how people make sense of their worlds.

those protests. However, he or she would be missing the different meanings corn takes on in different times and places. If scholars coded corn based on the meanings with which it is imbued, they might get different results. For example, if the first analysis studying only corn prices and protest had weak or insignificant results, a second study of corn prices in places where corn has come to mean "nation" to many consumers might yield stronger results.[36] By taking meaning-making seriously, quantitative scholars may be able to both explain outliers and strengthen the predictive value of the variables in question. Interpretive work reveals variables to which scholars employing other approaches should pay attention.

Case comparisons

Interpretive analysis serves as a critical foundation for this book. Yet the research is methodologically layered. Case comparisons offer yet another level of insight. Case comparisons in the social sciences often build on the methods of similarity and difference proposed by John Stuart Mill more than 150 years ago (e.g., see Przeworski and Teune 1970; Gerring 2007; Slater and Ziblatt 2013). These methods present a particular challenge for scholars of contentious politics; recent studies increasingly recognize the importance of contingency and equifinality (e.g., Ragin 2000; McAdam et al. 2001).[37]

The methods also present a challenge for scholars committed to interpretive analysis (see Simmons and Smith 2015). Precisely because interpretive work is committed to context, it does not translate easily into case comparisons. The approach's focus on dynamics and processes instead of outcomes, and its commitment to exploiting ambiguity and incoherence as politically revealing, further complicates the use of interpretive analysis in a comparative case research design. However, case comparisons pursued through interpretive analysis can yield valuable insights as they refine our understandings of primary cases, enhance our theoretical models, and help us explore the generalizabilty of our claims. But they must be employed in a way that appreciates the importance of bounded, specific analysis and does not run roughshod over ambiguities.

Analytically Parallel Cases
Analytically parallel cases (Locke and Thelen 1995, 344) are a particularly appropriate approach with which to explore the puzzle driving this research

---

[36] Attention to meaning-making might similarly help game theoreticians refine their analyses. Preferences are central to game theory. Scholars are continually making assumptions about the preferences of the actors in their models. If those models include the meanings with which certain outcomes are imbued, and not simply the material payoffs, scholars may become even better at predicting political behavior.

[37] However, it remains standard best practice among scholars of contentious politics to use a most similar-with-different-outcomes design. For an early example, see Skocpol (1979). For a more contemporary example, see Goodwin (2001).

because they offer a solid foundation for inferential analysis without sacrificing in-depth knowledge of a case. The emphasis on "contextualized comparison" (ibid., 1995) in this approach allows us to focus not just on objectively identifiable material conditions as the basis for comparison but also on how processes and mechanisms might influence these identifications in the first place. We choose cases where we see similar dynamics or processes at work, allowing ourselves the flexibility to identify complex causal processes as they unfold. From this in-depth knowledge we can develop portable insights. These insights are not contingent on problematic assumptions about what the theoretically relevant variation that needs to be controlled is or whether the same empirical phenomena work in the same ways across contexts (Simmons and Smith 2015).[38] Instead, the cases for comparison are selected based on the presence of apparently similar mechanisms, dynamics, and processes. This approach allows me to shed light on dynamics that are easily overlooked when we aim to select representative samples or ensure that we have both negative and positive cases (Ragin 2004; Small 2009).

While meanings are indexed to particular situations, examining how they work in mobilization processes in different times and places can add to our theoretical models of the dynamics of contention. By studying the cases in parallel with one another, we can investigate how subsistence goods produce group affiliations, how these affiliations impact political resistance, and what the mechanisms are through which markets, subsistence, and political protest intersect.

The goal is to focus on identifying "family resemblances" (Wittgenstein 1958, par. 67) – resemblances in the ways in which the ordinary activities tied to subsistence practices shape identifications, influence group attachments, and impact political resistance; resemblances in the ways in which perceptions of markets, subsistence, and the state combine to heighten insecurities and forge common, if potentially episodic, identifications. Much in politics is contingent, and this is nowhere more true than in the unfolding of contentious episodes (McAdam et al. 2001; Kurzman 2004b). Nevertheless, investigation of the processes and dynamics at work as citizens take to the streets can tell us much about contention in particular and the political in general.

Case Selection

In Bolivia, the puzzle at the core of this research presents itself starkly. Between 1985 and 1999, economic growth rates increased and hyperinflation disappeared. Yet the gap between the country's rich and poor grew. Real wages shrank and poverty increased. While the water wars were not the first time Bolivians

---

[38] McAdam, Tarrow, and Tilly (2001) effectively show how pairing decidedly different cases with similar contentious outcomes can better establish scope conditions for particular arguments and explore how a variety of mechanisms may be at work in shaping political processes.

took to the streets during the neoliberal era, the events in Cochabamba stood in stark contrast to their predecessors. Protesters did not represent a particular group of Bolivians (e.g., miners, coca growers, or indigenous communities) but rather were drawn broadly from Cochabamban society. The coalitions that formed in Cochabamba cut across long-standing cleavages and sociopolitical divisions, bringing former adversaries side by side during protest meetings, events, and negotiations.

By focusing on the Cochabamba case as the only protest event in the analysis, however, I am unable to explore how the mechanisms at work might appear in other times and places, and how they might work similarly when different goods are at stake. As many food staples are substitutable, whereas water is not, it is possible that only water takes on the meanings that contribute to the advent and shape of political resistance. When I limit my analysis to water, I cannot explore potentially broader patterns in the relationship between subsistence goods and social mobilization. By examining a case of protest around a different, technically substitutable good, in this case corn, I hope to show that two materially different goods can actually take on similar meanings and ultimately have similar causal effects when threatened by markets. By comparing the mechanisms I observe in Cochabamba to processes at work in ordinary relationships to corn in Mexico, as well as how those processes play a role in contentious episodes, I can advance our understandings of the relationships between subsistence, markets, and resistance more broadly.

The 2007 Mexican *tortillazo* protests do not perfectly resemble their Cochabamban counterpart. The Mexican movement was national in scope and brief in duration. After only a month mobilizations had largely collapsed. Furthermore, the *tortillazo* protests pale in comparison to many other Mexican movements. Yet the largest of these movements tended to draw support from particular sectors or regions – they often addressed *campesino*, labor, or indigenous claims without inclusive overlaps.[39] What makes the *tortillazo* an ideal case for comparison are the scale of the price increases, their widespread impact, the centrality of corn in Mexican conceptions of culture, and the diversity of the opposition coalition.[40] The *tortillazo* seemed to be an excellent case for exploring patterns in how markets, subsistence, and mobilization might be intertwined. By exploring the dynamics at work in both cases, this book

[39] The *Ejército Zapatista de Liberación Nacional* [The Zapatista Army of National Liberation] (EZLN) uprising is one exception. The movement galvanized urban and rural, rich and poor in Mexico. Although the timing of the claims – the EZLN made its first dramatic move on the eve of NAFTA's implementation – links the movement directly to marketization, the grievances around which the movement formed were rooted in a much longer history of indigenous exclusion and land claims. The narrative of the movement was decidedly an indigenous one – urban Mexicans who supported and joined the EZLN largely perceived themselves to be making claims on behalf of others (see Harvey 1998 for a comprehensive account of the movement).

[40] The different trajectories of the movements prompt additional, important questions, which I have explored elsewhere (see Simmons 2011).

pushes us to theorize the "network of similarities" (Wittgenstein 1958, par. 66) between subsistence-related and market-driven resistance.

Subnational Analysis

The research design employed here offers one additional benefit from a methodological perspective. The focus on relatively short periods of time (one to nine months) in geographically limited places creates the opportunity for both careful process tracing of these particular moments and intranational comparisons.[41] In arguing that corn and water are imbued with community-related meanings in their respective Mexican and Cochabamban contexts, this book covers a longer time period. But when this book focuses on the contentious episodes themselves, it offers a more nuanced, textured approach than many current treatments of the same or similar episodes. For example, Eduardo Silva's (2009) six-country comparison offers a comprehensive, empirically rich analysis of resistance to neoliberal reforms in Latin America. Yet in treating each country as a case (e.g., Bolivia is a positive case of resistance to neoliberal reforms; Chile is a negative case), he cannot address the nuance produced by intracountry variation. Silva cannot tell us why we see resistance to water privatization in Cochabamba in 2000, but not in La Paz–El Alto when the same good was privatized there three years earlier (or, for that matter, why resistance to the La Paz–El Alto privatization finally did emerge in 2005). Instead, as protest is coded at the country level, the events are simply understood as cases with resistance or as cases in which such resistance failed to emerge. More nuanced processes and dynamics, as well as variation at the subnational level, are left underexplored.[42] The reform-by-reform, city-by-city analysis that is possible by a within-country comparative approach can highlight new dynamics, allow us to focus on processes and mechanisms, and contest claims that seem unassailable when made at the country level.

Data

This book is based on fieldwork in Bolivia and Mexico and extensive historical research. Field research included in-depth ethnographic work and semistructured and open-ended interviews. I conducted fieldwork in Bolivia during the summer and fall of 2008, as well as the winter of 2010. I spent most of my time in Cochabamba and La Paz–El Alto but traveled to Santa Cruz for additional interviews and comparative analysis. I conducted fieldwork in Mexico during the winter, spring, and summer of 2009. The analysis is based largely on research conducted in Mexico City.

---

[41] This book does discuss the national nature of the Mexican protests; however, most of the analysis is of how events unfolded in Mexico City in particular.

[42] Silva does note changes over time in both cases but cannot account for the timing of the emergence of protests (or quiescence) in either case.

I identified interviewees through newspaper reports and other publications as well as "snowball" sampling, whereby an interview with one individual would yield connections to one or more others. In addition, I spent time in Bolivia speaking about water with local residents and observing local practices involving water governance, management, and collection. In Mexico City, I spoke with local residents about corn and observed practices of consumption, cultivation, and celebration. I was also able to participate in meetings and activities of the *Sin Maíz No Hay País* campaign. In both field sites, I participated in daily life by taking part in social gatherings, political events and protests, and office activities. I observed formal meetings and workshop sessions, read newspapers, went to plays, concerts, and movies, and watched local television. These experiences gave me the tools to make sense of particular actions or words in the contexts in which they took place or were deployed.

Historical research involved analysis of written materials including regional and national newspapers, primary source documents (including movement declarations, petitions, and pamphlets), and scholarly works.[43] For both Bolivia and Mexico, I relied heavily on video clips of the movements' activities or other relevant events as well as photographs taken by private observers or photojournalists. My observations of lived experiences in 2008 and 2010 in Bolivia and in 2009 in Mexico helped me to interpret these earlier texts, to understand the work that particular words or phrases may have been doing in movement slogans, and how particular symbols worked to generate unity on the streets.

That I was not in Cochabamba before and during the events of the water wars or in Mexico during the events of the *tortillazo* protests posed particular challenges. In Cochabamba in particular, the protests unsettled water's meanings in the region, producing new languages, conceptions, and relationships with each phase of the mobilization. For these reasons, I relied heavily on documents produced, utterances made, and images deployed during or before the protest events themselves. Newspaper accounts, film footage (including a number of documentaries produced in Mexico and Bolivia prior to the protests), scholarly works, and other written texts proved particularly useful. Analysis of the movements themselves relied heavily on media coverage and film footage produced at the time. While in some cases I used these sources to understand who was at a particular meeting or when it happened, most often I used the texts in an interpretive fashion. I analyzed the words or images deployed and

[43] For the Bolivian case, I systematically analyzed coverage (or noncoverage) of water between January 1998 and June 2000 in *Los Tiempos* (Cochabamba), *Opinión* (Cochabamba), *Presencia* (La Paz), and *El Diario* (La Paz). I conducted a more targeted analysis of water coverage from 1970 to 1998, looking specifically for articles on drought, irrigation, agriculture, and the Misicuni/Corani water projects. In Mexico, I looked to *El Sol de México, Milenio, El Universal, La Jornada*, and *Reforma* for newspaper coverage of corn and tortillas beginning in July 2006 and extending through the time of fieldwork. I conducted a more targeted search prior to those dates, looking for coverage of NAFTA specifically, and marketization more generally.

tried to understand what those words or images were doing in the contexts in which they were used. What was important was to know what a placard said, who held it, and what they were doing when they did – I could then interpret what it meant in that particular context.

In addition, in Cochabamba many of the practices around water access changed little in the eight years after the water wars. As a result, I was able to supplement this source material with interviews and participant observation. For example, I was able to attend meetings of water governance councils where they discussed the same kinds of routine challenges and daily operations as they might have eight or ten years prior. Little changed in how water in Cochabamba was managed or distributed from the pre-water wars days to the time of my fieldwork. While I was not in Mexico during the *tortillazo* I was able to draw on earlier experiences living, working, and researching in the country. I lived in Mexico in 1994, 1998, and 2001. These experiences shored up claims about corn's meanings prior to the *tortillazo*.[44]

OUTLINE OF THIS BOOK

The remainder of this book proceeds as follows. Chapters 2 and 3 turn to the Cochabamba case. Chapter 2 explores meaning-making processes related to water in Cochabamba, and in doing so, lays important groundwork for the analysis of the protest events that follows. The chapter focuses on explaining how water is constitutive of – and works to index – both imagined and quotidian communities in the Cochabamban context. Chapter 3 details how attention to these meanings helps us understand both the origins and the composition of the protests against water privatization that swept the region in 1999 and 2000. Chapters 4 and 5 focus on corn in Mexico and on the 2007 *tortillazo* protests. Like Chapter 2, Chapter 4 lays important groundwork for the analysis of the protest events. The chapter shows how corn symbolizes both

[44] I employed three strategies to address additional inferential challenges. I looked to the work performed by discourses, both those that emerged during the movement itself and those of actors as they recalled the events, to make the movements intelligible. In fact, whether a source has "mis-remembered" is largely unimportant to the interpretive component of the analysis conducted here. How sources remember their experiences sheds light on what those experiences meant and the work they do in the sources' understandings of the world. This is far more important than the "fact" of what may or may not have happened on a given day. Second, when attempting to piece together a sequence of events or actions I strove to determine the credibility of sources through thinking about any incentives to lie intentionally. For government officials and movement leaders (as opposed to participants), this was of particular interest. Their responses often actually ran counter to what I might have expected had the actors intended to misrepresent or knowingly alter accounts of events. In such cases, I found answers particularly credible. Third, when I did rely on newspapers and interviews to reconstruct a sequence of events, I ensured that similar accounts appeared in more than one source. Most importantly, whether the statements of interviewees are "true," is often less important than what they signal about dynamics of the protest movements and the subjects' relationship with water or corn.

imagined and quotidian communities in the Mexican context, detailing contemporary relationships with the grain (with particular attention to tortillas) and showing how those relationships help constitute understandings of what it means to be Mexican. Chapter 5 analyzes the protest events in January 2007. The core of the chapter is organized around a discussion of how domesticity, class, security, and nation intersected to help motivate broad-based resistance. This book concludes in Chapter 6 with a discussion of the potential implications of the research.

2

Water in Cochabamba

No había nada más importante que el agua para los cochabambinos.
(There was nothing more important to Cochabambans than water.)
— Rene Barrientos, president of the Civic Committee of Cochabamba

On a chilly Cochabamba morning, a man stands over a small, open dirt canal with a shovel in his hand. He says a few words to give thanks to the *Pachamama* (Mother Earth) and uses his shovel to open the canal, allowing water to flow into his adjacent field. He draws it down small rows between the crops, guiding it with the shovel. When his time is up, he walks back to the canal and patches the hole, returning the water to its original course. The man then joins other irrigators with neighboring plots for *chicha* (a fermented corn drink) while another takes his turn diverting water from the canal into his field. "Water," the irrigator tells me, "is sacred. It is the blood of the *Pachamama*. The canals are her veins." Neither the actions of the irrigators that day nor the comments on water's sacred status are unique in rural Cochabamba. In the moment described here, the irrigator engaged in a ritual – from the opening prayer to the closing of the hole in the canal – that, later in the day, he would watch his neighbors (as they watched him now) complete. He also recognized that other irrigators in the Cochabamba region and throughout the Andean highlands recited a similar prayer and used similar techniques to water their fields. Similarly, he described imagining his mother, father, grandfather, great-great-grandfather, and imagined precolonial ancestors engaging in the same ritual tens, hundreds, or thousands of years ago. He even spoke of picturing his own children going through the same steps in the years to come.

The practice serves as a connection to others in the present, past, and future. It helps define and constitute a variety of communities with water at their core. The anecdote shows how water can serve as the foundation for both quotidian communities (in this example, one forming around the face-to-face interactions taking place as irrigators water their fields on the same day) and for the imagined communities that emerge when they think of themselves as connected (in this example, through the practice of irrigation itself) to other irrigators in the past, present, and future, whom they may never meet.

Water's role as a symbol is not limited to Cochabamba's irrigator communities, nor is its meaning coherent or fixed among irrigators themselves. Generally speaking, however, water helps produce and reproduce conceptions of regional rights and communal identity for many Cochabambans, regardless of their occupation or place of residence within the valley. Water has a particular place in everyday Cochabamban practice; it is understood as "essential to communities and cultures" (Perreault 2006, 165).[1]

The purpose of this chapter is to explore these meanings and establish a foundation for the following chapter, where I show how these meanings worked to produce resistance to the Aguas del Tunari contract. Not surprisingly, the meanings water has taken on in the Cochabamban context are multiple, varied, and sometimes apparently contradictory. The particularities of these meanings differ according to time, place, and person. Yet most scholarship focuses specifically on rural Cochabamba, and irrigators in particular (e.g., see Peredo et al. 2004) or on Andean water practices more generally (e.g., Grillo Fernández 1994; Salazar 1997; Boelens et al. 2010a). Here I focus our lens on Cochabamba more generally, bringing together analysis of practices in urban, peri-urban, and rural areas while exploring how these practices can resemble, contradict, and come into tension with one another throughout the valley (see Maps 2.1 and 2.2). I argue that because of the particular roles water plays in daily life throughout the Cochabamba Valley, it produces both imagined and quotidian communities. A history of and contemporary experiences with scarcity combine with irrigation practices and understandings of an agricultural past to imbue water with meanings tied to local and regional identities. Whether through serving as the center for routine personal interactions or guiding region-wide political discourse, water has become coterminous with community for many Cochabambans. The Aguas del Tunari contract was perceived as a threat to quotidian communities and imagined communities, including those formed through the everyday challenges surrounding access to water and those produced through regional notions of autonomy and independence and conceptions of Andean heritage.

IRRIGATION IN THE COCHABAMBA VALLEY

Irrigation practices have profoundly shaped daily life in the Cochabamba Valley for more than 500 years (see Map 2.3). Indeed, many Cochabambans

---

[1] Water also has a powerful national significance rooted in the loss of access to the sea to Chile during the War of the Pacific at the turn of the century. These discourses did appear during the water wars but do not appear to have featured prominently.

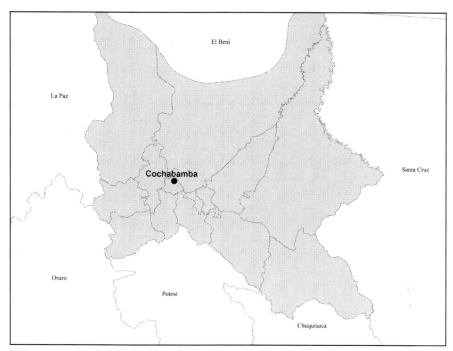

MAP 2.1. Cochabamba Province.

continue to understand them as a critical component of their regional heritage. The history of irrigation in the area dates back to before the Spanish conquest, when control over water was integral to control over territory. Irrigation practices remain central to daily life in much of the valley; in 1999, approximately 17 percent of land in Cochabamba was irrigated (Crespo Flores 2003, 130). Even for those Cochabambans who do not practice irrigation, it has become an idealized element of regional identity – a central piece of what it means to be Cochabamban. Defense of the *usos y costumbres* that govern Cochabamban irrigation became a central rallying cry during the water wars.

Irrigation systems arguably provided the material foundation for the development of what some scholars, albeit problematically, refer to as "Andean civilization" (Gelles 2010, 137). Whereas the idea that there is an "Andean civilization" to which we can refer produces and reproduces a problematic coherence in scholarly understandings of semiotic practices in the Andes, irrigation became central to daily life in many communities located in the Andean highlands. Anthropologist Paul Gelles observes that irrigation water "has long been one of the most culturally and ritually elaborated resources in Andean society and civilization; it has been used as a means of establishing identity for centuries" (ibid., 124).

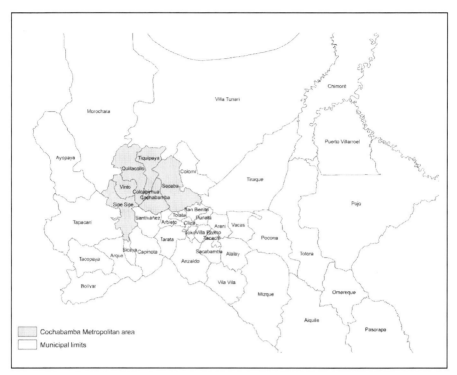

MAP 2.2. The Cochabamba metropolitan area.

Andean cultivators were initially attracted to the three contiguous valleys that make up the Cochabamba region (Valle de Sacaba, Valle Alto, and Valle Central) by their "extraordinary fertility" (Larson 1998, 3).[2] But colonization transformed regional society as Spaniards penetrated the Cochabamba Valley, bringing a market economy with them. Peasant sectors developed adaptive strategies of subsistence that "combined Andean forms of communal labor and reciprocal exchange with small-scale commodity production and marketing" (ibid., 7).

The transition to a republic (1810–1825) altered little when it came to the general political economy of colonialism. Water, however, now belonged to the state instead of the crown. Practically, the haciendas remained in control of water resources, and the changes that they underwent fundamentally shaped how relationships with water in Cochabamba would continue to develop.[3]

[2] The "Cochabamba Valley" refers to the three valleys that are generally understood to comprise the region.

[3] On a hacienda, Cochabamban peasants worked for landlords in exchange for access to subsistence plots, cash wages, or produce. There were also a few *reducciones*, small planned communities to which Andean people were relocated, in Cochabamba (Gotkowitz 2007, 10).

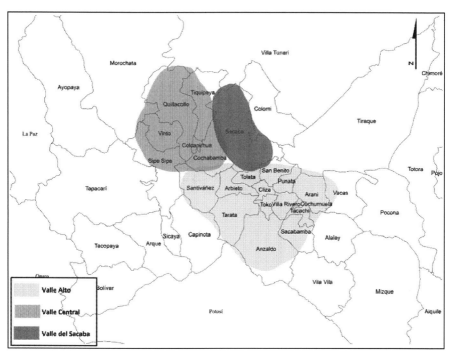

MAP 2.3. The Cochabamba valleys.

Gradually, the communal landholdings that the Spanish had allowed to exist alongside the haciendas were, according to historian Brooke Larson, "legislated out of existence" (1998, 310). By 1894, 60 percent of Cochabamba's communal lands had been converted into small, individually owned farms (Jackson 1994; Larson 1998).[4]

This development is crucial to understanding contemporary relationships with water in the region – the continued dominance of small landholdings maintains intimate, personal relationships with water and requires communal coordination for effective irrigation. Single families or small collections of families still cultivate small plots of land; without large, industrial irrigation systems, these families must use alternative methods to ensure that crops receive the water necessary for a good harvest. These methods all require intimate knowledge of water sources and patterns, as well as communal cooperation and vigilance of water use and management.

While local practitioners developed highly local systems for managing water, government officials also developed national-level policies. Almost 100 years after these systems were put in place, leaders of the water wars

---

[4] To my knowledge the creation of these individually owned farms generated little, if any, resistance.

invoked them while making their claims. The 1906 Water Law (*Ley General de Aguas*) established water as a public good but also stated that water that passed through a particular plot of land "belonged" to the landowner as long as his or her use did not affect others (Bustamante 2002). The law was vague and rarely applied; local practices went largely unchallenged and continued to shape water use and governance. The law, however, remained the central piece of national legislation governing water until the passage of Law 2029, which paved the way for the Aguas del Tunari concession in 1999.

The 1930s brought the first period of intense pressure on Cochabamba's water resources. The region came to know long droughts, which shaped relationships with water in both urban and rural Cochabamba. When the Great Depression hit Bolivia, declining tin prices sent many tin miners back to their original homes; a large proportion was from Cochabamba (Gotkowitz 2007). The population influx sent demand for water soaring, and the region increasingly turned to Cochabamba's extended network of underground aquifers to meet its needs. The aquifers, however, were unable to keep up with demand. Replenished by alluvial fans, aquifers could not refill themselves as quickly as Cochabambans used them. Water tables began to drop, making drilling increasingly expensive and controversial. Later conflicts in the early 1990s over aquifer access and drilling would serve as a precursor to the water wars.

Even as water became an increasingly important regional challenge, national politics took center stage. In 1952, the Bolivian National Revolution removed the traditional oligarchy from power, replacing it with popularly elected Víctor Paz Estenssoro and the *Movimiento Nacionalista Revolucionario* [Nationalist Revolutionary Movement] (MNR). Yet even as the MNR represented a fundamental change in Bolivian politics, the Revolution appears to have changed little in local relationships with water in Cochabamba. Highly anticipated agrarian reform was slow to come to Cochabamba, and unrest continued in the valley until the central government legislated widespread changes in August 1953 (Malloy 1970).[5] But the reform arguably altered little. There was a partial redistribution of land and water resources, but much of Cochabamba was already composed of small-scale plots, and most remaining haciendas went untouched, their access to water resources unaltered.

 The 1953 agricultural reform perpetuated conceptions of water as a resource belonging to the state, granting every peasant a water right (or *mita*) along with any land they owned.[6] The new policy gave legal authority to practices of communal management that had evolved over centuries, adapting to

[5] The 1953 agrarian reform distributed land to estate laborers, provided for the restoration of communal territory, and abolished the *latifundio* and *pongueaje* (domestic service for landlords) (Gotkowitz 2007, 278).

[6] The term *mita* is also used to describe a "shift" of water. Users are granted a *mita* to a particular source, allowing them to use the source for a particular "shift" or period of time. The term also describes the practice of forcing tribute in the form of labor during colonial and precolonial times.

conditions of haciendas, *reducciones,* and small landholdings. Principles of communal use and reciprocity had not disappeared during colonial rule or under the Republic.[7] Instead, they had adapted to (and helped shape) the social and economic conditions of the colony and the Republic. Many irrigation systems continued to be managed by small, local governance structures that relied on communal participation to clear channels and regulate consumption. Small landholdings remained the foundation of Cochabamba's agricultural economy, and local governance structures based on reciprocity continued to supersede the authority of municipal laws. Outside of the region's haciendas, user assemblies continued to make decisions not only about water use and access, but also about community norms not directly related to water management (e.g., some developed expectations around adultery or theft). These assemblies also developed systems for conflict resolution and punishment in the event of a violation of established norms.[8] Local governance structures continued to serve as the foundation for water management in rural areas and have, albeit in different ways, taken on an almost mythic status for many rural and urban Cochabambans.[9]

USOS Y COSTUMBRES IN CONTEMPORARY COCHABAMBA

Communal irrigation remains a fundamental component of daily life in much of rural and peri-urban Cochabamba.[10] Although residents of the three valleys maintain distinct water governance practices, residents generally refer to these practices with the same concept: *usos y costumbres.* Perreault describes *usos y costumbres* as "symbolic of livelihood strategies specific to Quechua and Aymara speaking people in the Bolivian Andes" (2008, 834). In Cochabamba, *usos y costumbres* have become a category of practice that can refer to an entire complex of meanings relating to water management. For example, a Cochabamban irrigator referencing *usos y costumbres* might at one moment be referring to a specific rule regarding water management in his or her community, and at another might reference a more vague notion of "this is the way things have always been done." As they are practiced among irrigators in Punata, just outside of the city of Cochabamba, *usos y costumbres* are both based on intimate knowledge of the local environment and signify a broader, valley-wide set of practices.

---

[7] See Holben (2007) for an example of reciprocal systems still in effect in rural Cochabamba.

[8] These systems will be treated further in the following section.

[9] In 1957, Bolivia adopted a new constitution that asserted that water was state property (Stallings 2006). But regional, local, and even national laws paid the constitution little attention on this point. Local governance structures of water use and management were the established and accepted law of the land.

[10] The Cochabamba Valley is the most irrigated region in Bolivia (Programa Nacional de Riego 2000). Most farms in the valley are smaller than five hectares (Stallings 2006, 36).

What is important here is *not* whether *usos y costumbres* are a concept or "tradition" with any observable connection to past practices. For the purposes of this analysis, the concept could have emerged any time prior to discussions of water privatization in the region. What matters is the way *usos y costumbres* worked in the Cochabamban context in 1999 and 2000. Furthermore, although *usos y costumbres* help govern relationships with water in the present, the concept remains firmly rooted in the past. Anthropologist Symantha Holben found that in spite of significant subdivisions to irrigation allocations in her field site in the Cochabamban Valley of Sacaba, the local irrigators' association continued to refer to an irrigation "table" from 1903 as the basis for local water rights (2007, 116–20). One *regante* (irrigator) from Punata reflected, "We have our *usos y costumbres* here, and they have theirs in Tarata [a nearby community in the Valle Alto]. They are different, but the same thing" (author interview, August 2008, Punata, Bolivia).[11]

Water is the fundamental organizing principle for many rural and peri-urban communities; elaborate, complex, and highly structured systems of obligations, rights, responsibilities, and justice govern relationships with water sources. Some communities define their membership by the kind of irrigation (e.g., rivers, dams, springs) practiced and others by a particular geographic area. The communities can overlap and complex governance systems are in place to resolve conflicts. Most generally, *usos y costumbres* outline the how a community will exercise what are understood to be communal rights to local water sources. They fit within a general notion of moral economy but often also refer to rules and responsibilities that have been explicitly codified. Each community has defined rights, roles, and obligations that each member is asked to respect and fulfill; *mitas* serve as the fundamental organizing principle. The *mita* remains effective because of the communal labor and resources devoted to the maintenance and governance of the water sources and routes; it remains necessary because of Cochabamba's long dry season and increasing drought. Communities will sometimes declare a period of *aguas comunitarias* (community water), when *mitas* do not govern access and individual farms can "liberally" use local water sources (Peredo et al. 2004), but these occur only during the height of the rainy season (December–April), if at all. Even during times of *aguas comunitarias*, roles and responsibilities remain clear.

In the wake of the water wars, two Cochabamban irrigators teamed with local scholar and activist Carlos Crespo to research and describe the intricacies of the *usos y costumbres* of Cochabamba's valleys. The team synthesized a definition of *usos y costumbres* into the following paragraph:

The *usos y costumbres* are the natural rights that god has given to man. The water is the *Pachamama* and the *Wirakhocha*, which isn't a person or a spirit, but rather the land

---

[11] Some of the interviews were conducted in confidentiality and the names of the interviewees are withheld by mutual agreement.

that gives us life, and its blood is the water that permits the life of the human race. They are all rights that were given to us by the grandparents, that is to say the originals, who inherited them from the patrones and that our parents and grandparents have carried on, and until now we use. It was custom from the beginning from our desire [*gusto*] we have woken up to this and this had been called *usos y costumbres*, the water is walking according to *usos y costumbres*, it was a path that is always open, no one can change it. There is no owner, for us there is no mayor, nor anyone who tells us what to do, then no one can tell us do this, that or the other. It is a Law that is not written on paper. For *usos y costumbres*, our fight will be permanent, for this cause we have fought and we will always defend it. (Peredo et al. 2004, 70)

The concept of *usos y costumbres* is grounded in a connection to the past – many Cochabambans (irrigators and otherwise) claim that *usos y costumbres* reflect the actual practices of generations of Cochabambans. The traditions were "given to us by the grandparents, that is to say the originals." They are imagined as rooted in the past, a connector to previous generations that is reproduced only through the continuing of the practices in the present and the assurance that the practices will continue into the future. They are something that current generations must care for, almost as if caring for an inheritance or stewarding a resource. They were "customs from the beginning," rituals that are imagined to have been static over long periods of time. But they are also a signifier of independence: "there is no mayor, nor anyone who tells us what to do." Maintaining *usos y costumbres* has become symbolic of maintaining not only a connection to the past, but also the ability to self-govern in the present.

Clearly, *usos y costumbres* in Cochabamba have also come to signify far more than that to which they technically refer. They are, as Perreault observes, a "symbol of traditional, place-specific and often culturally distinctive resource use practices" (2008, 840). To say you are defending *usos y costumbres* related to water has come to mean the defense of a conception of a particular way of life. The particular systems and management practices to which *usos y costum-bres* refer remain important, but the concept has also come to signify a connection with Andean custom, cultural autonomy, and independence from state intervention in communal governance.

Regardless of whether the current irrigation practices of the residents of the Cochabamba Valley resemble the practices of the Andeans who inhabited the valley before the arrival of the Spaniards, not only irrigators, but also many urban residents of Cochabamba, understand those practices to be a way of preserving a connection to their "Andean ancestry."[12] They have become a "cultural signifier" (Perreault 2008) that often suggests a highly essentialized

---

[12] Jake Kosek notes a similar phenomenon in his analysis of Truchas, New Mexico. Kosek describes how, when the U.S. government tried to persuade residents to adopt a more "efficient" system than the irrigation ditches already in use, one resident called the ditches the "lifeblood" of Truchas. Yet the resident also admitted that he had never relied on the ditches himself. He told Kosek, "whether I use the water or not, the *acequias* are still a part of who I am" (2006, 112).

conception of "Andeanness" and indigeneity. The importance of *usos y cos-tumbres* "lies less in their historical authenticity than in their symbolic role as signifiers of indigenous or *campesino* cultural continuity and political auton-omy" (ibid., 840).

These signifiers become as important to those who use them as the basis for local water management as for those who do not. *Usos y costumbres* provide a way for irrigators to make their lives intelligible to others. Irrigators' lives can be reduced to these practices (by irrigators and others), giving irrigators crucial cultural standing in the fight to preserve their "Bolivian heritage." For some, the value of *usos y costumbres* lies in the preservation of an imagined notion of their communal connection to an Andean past. *Usos y costumbres* pro-vide an easy way to conceptually capture, essentialize, and preserve *lo andino*. Irrigators have not shied away from the political work that *usos y costumbres* can do for them. As Perreault argues, the concept "provides an idiom through which indigenous and *campesino* peoples in Bolivia link the material practices of everyday life with politicized discourses of identity formation and citizen-ship rights" (ibid., 840). *Usos y costumbres* become a political tool, a short-hand for rural life and Andean custom.

Not surprisingly, the concept has gained powerful political force within the wider Cochabamban community. In Cochabamba's more urban areas, *usos y costumbres* tend to lose their referent to the specifics of water distribution or management. *Usos y costumbres* can refer to ethnic heritage, ideals of local governance, or a connection to the past. Invoking *usos y costumbres* might identify the speaker as someone for whom Bolivia's indigenous heritage is important, as someone who cares about a particular environmental ethic, or perhaps as someone who supports local self-governance. *Usos y costumbres* have become a "thing" to which not only irrigators, but also other *campesinos*, as well as urban and peri-urban Cochabambans refer, working to create com-monalities in the valley and serving as a piece of Cochabamban culture worthy of reification and protection.

For many urban Cochabambans, who may never have watched *regantes* irrigate a field, the preservation of irrigation customs has become an indis-pensable, if imagined, link to the past and the region's "Andean" heritage. This imagined link works differently for many urban Cochabambans than it does for their peri-urban or rural *regante* counterparts, yet as evidence in the pages that follow will show, it still produces and reproduces regional attachments. For many urban Cochabambans, the concept of *usos y costumbres* helps con-stitute a sense of self as Cochabambans that must be protected and preserved.

In holding up *usos y costumbres* as critical to regional heritage, and there-fore deserving of protection, activists during the water wars brought a sense of Cochabamban-ness to the fore. The references evoked a shared sense of regional experience and belonging. In invoking *usos y costumbres*, Cochabambans – both urban and rural – heightened their attachment to the region and helped to construct themselves as Cochabambans. It was not just the material impact of privatization that was at stake in the Aguas del Tunari contract. Many Cochabambans perceived the very "things" that make a Cochabamban a Cochabamban to be at stake as well. One of those things is tied to conceptions of *usos y costumbres*. The disruption of *usos y costumbres* has, for many Cochabambans, come to mean the disruption of both a contemporary way of life and long-held cultural practice.

Irrigation and quotidian communities

For many Cochabamban irrigators, water not only produces and indexes imagined Andean and regional irrigator communities, but also quotidian communities. The *usos y costumbres* that serve as a foundation for water management practices have produced and reproduced strong forms of local governance and organization among Cochabamba's irrigators. Face-to-face relationships form and are reproduced with water at the center. Water produces and reinforces quotidian communities among Cochabamban irrigators in three ways: through the local governance organizations themselves, through the practice of simultaneous irrigation, and through broader regional governance networks.

Local governance organizations provide the time and place for routine, face-to-face interactions for most of Cochabamba's irrigators.[13] Throughout the Cochabamba Valley, irrigators develop and implement their own systems for how responsibilities and water rights are allocated, as well as their own systems of punishment when rules are broken or obligations go unfulfilled. There are meetings, members, and officers of these associations. Many associations have names, subcommittees, and umbrella networks. These organizations form around water – regulating and managing access to irrigation water are their principal purposes. Members often pay regular monetary dues, elect officials, and are asked to follow rules. In the event that rules are broken (e.g., failure to attend a community workday or theft of water), members face sanctions. In some associations, rules govern not only activities related to water, but also crimes like adultery, property theft, or murder; in many communities, water has come to serve as the foundation for local governance.

The rural Cochabamban municipality of Punata exemplifies the ways in which irrigation practices shape local governance structures throughout the valley. Although some specific practices differ from association to association, the approach to water governance in Punata appears to resemble the broad contours of many water governance structures throughout the valley.[14] In

---

[13] Although I was unable to visit most of Cochabamba's irrigator communities and focused my own fieldwork in a particular place (Punata), the work of other scholars (e.g., Peredo et al. 2004; Holben 2007) suggests that there are, indeed, similar organizations throughout the valley.

[14] My own visits to Tiquipaya and the Upper Sacaba Valley suggested that what I saw in Punata was, indeed, exemplary. Peredo et al. (2004) and Holben (2007) offer further evidence to support this claim.

Punata, all members of the local irrigator association (*Asociación de Regantes de Punata*) have a time of irrigation in accordance with rights established by the organization and work during the *largada* (the irrigation period) in proportion to their right to water. To ensure equity, members rotate the timing of who gets water when with respect to the time of day and the timing of the *largada*. Everyone works to make sure the water gets to each of the member *chacras* (small farms). In addition to monitoring water use, the responsibilities of membership in the Punata irrigator association include communal workdays to clear canals. If a member does not show up for a communal workday, he or she is often fined. Members claimed punishments were more severe for water theft. One *regante* recalled a story of a member caught stealing a gas tank from a neighbor. The association declined to call the local police and, after a meeting of association leadership, chose to force the thief to return the gas and implemented a fine of various construction materials necessary for irrigation. The example illustrates one of the ways the Punata irrigators' association does far more than regulate local relationships with water.

Quotidian communities form not only in the process of governance, but also in the process of irrigation itself. Not every irrigator expects to receive water every day, but there are often days when all of the canals are open, providing water to each field. In Punata, when an irrigator expects water on a particular day, he or she can spend hours in the fields, preparing for his or her "turn." When a number of irrigators expect water on the same day, it is likely that many will be in neighboring fields conducting preparations at the same time. Irrigators might share food or drink, talk about local goings-on about town, or report on the health of a family member. A day of communal irrigation becomes a decidedly social event, even as irrigators work to ensure that their turns go smoothly.[15]

Quotidian communities have also formed through the development of a region-wide union whereby representatives of irrigators' organizations from throughout the valley meet to address perceived shared challenges. Most local water organizations throughout the Cochabamba Valley operated largely independent from one another until 1992. Where communities shared access to a particular watershed or river, or where other specific needs arose relating to the management of an individual water source, water organizations coordinated resources and developed joint structures for oversight. But as President Gonzalo Sánchez de Lozada began to develop what would become the Law of Popular Participation [*Ley de Participación Popular*] (LPP) – passed in 1994 – communities began to organize regionally to have a voice in shaping the pending changes. As originally proposed, the LPP was to transfer small irrigation systems to the municipality, giving the local government autonomy over local water infrastructure and administration, including irrigation systems

---

[15] Holben (2007) found a similar pattern during her research in the Sacaba Valley in Cochabamba in 2001, suggesting that the events I saw in Punata were not unique to that particular community.

smaller than 100 ha (Kohl 2003). Valley-wide irrigator associations formed in the Central, Upper, and Sacaba Valleys.[16] They then came together to form an ad hoc committee charged with influencing any provisions in the LPP that affected water (Peredo et al. 2004). The final version of the law affected neither local rights to water nor water infrastructure (ibid., 58) and, according to its organizers, the ad hoc committee, having achieved its objective, disbanded.

Local irrigators' organizations did not let the gains they had made through strengthened local networks and combined resources go to waste. Municipal efforts to dig deep wells to provide water for city residents had served as a source of urban–rural conflict since the 1970s. Irrigators continually argued, often with scientific support (author interview with Marcelo Delgadillo, February 2010, Cochabamba), that the city's deep well not only depleted, but also contaminated rural water supplies. This was, they claimed, not just about clean water supplies, but an entire way of life – water's symbolic capital surfaced to shape political protest almost a decade before the water wars. "We will have to give up our lives," one *regante* told me, "if the city uses all of the water. Of course we fought the city when it tried to dig more wells" (author interview, August 2008, Cochabamba). In 1992, irrigators in Sipe Sipe and Vinto, municipalities just outside of Cochabamba City, organized to oppose the drilling of additional municipal wells. Confrontation occurred again in 1994–1995 when other local organizations joined irrigators to form a defense committee (Assies 2003).

With Sánchez de Lozada's 1996 attempt to change Bolivia's 1906 Water Law allowing for private sale or concession of the resource, Cochabamban irrigators once again decided to organize formally, creating a second ad hoc committee. By the fall of 1997, irrigator leaders determined that a more permanent organizational structure was necessary and on October 3, with approximately 3,000 of them present, Cochabamban irrigators formally constituted the *Federación Departamental Cochabambina de Regantes* [Cochabamban Departmental Confederation of Irrigators] (FEDECOR) (Peredo et al. 2004).[17] FEDECOR went on to be a key player in Cochabamba's water wars. As described in a book coauthored by two of the organization's founders, FEDECOR is "the matrix organization of all of the systems and organizations of *regantes* in the

---

[16] Local organizing in response to the LPP resembles the process Yashar (2005) identifies in her analysis of indigenous mobilizations in Bolivia in response to "neoliberal citizenship regimes." Although there was limited public protest around water in Cochabamba in response to the LPP, the law's potential intrusion into local governance norms did apparently motivate organizing that would be foundational to the water wars six years later.

[17] According to *regante* leaders at the time, they tried to invite the *Federación Sindical Única de Trabajadores Campesinos de Cochabamba* [The Unified (or sole) Union Confederation of Peasant Workers of Cochabamba] (FSUTCC) to be a part of FEDECOR's governance structure. However, the FSUTCC opposed the formation of an independent irrigators' association, seeking instead the formation of a secretariat under the *campesinos'* union. From that time forward, the interactions between the FSUTCC and FEDECOR "*no fueron buenas* [were not good]" (Peredo et al. 2004, 61).

Cochabamba Valley whose principal characteristic is the integrated management of the resource of water through *usos y costumbres*" (Peredo et al. 2004,
57). In spite of its strong start, however, by the end of the 1990s, FEDECOR
no longer wielded enough organizational power to fight effectively on behalf
of its members. According to Perreault, it had "lost much of its initial energy"
and was "largely incapable of mounting a proactive campaign in favor of irrigator water rights" (2008, 842). Two of FEDECOR's founders and other interviewees agreed (author interviews with Omar Fernández and Carmen Peredo,
August and September 2008, La Paz and Cochabamba).

Nevertheless, FEDECOR served to create and sustain a region-wide, face-to-
face community through which irrigators throughout the valley got to know
one another and became increasingly connected. These networks put water at
the center of yet another quotidian community, this time directly connecting
regantes from regions throughout the Cochabamba Valley. As many *regantes*
understood the Aguas del Tunari contract to be a direct threat to their ability
to practice their profession, they also understood the contract to put these
quotidian communities at risk. A threat to water was not just a threat to *usos
y costumbres* or imaginings of *lo andino*, but also a threat to the regional relationships produced and reproduced through the *regantes'* practices.

"THE ANDEAN COSMOVISION": URBAN AND RURAL IMAGININGS

The prominent role water plays in rural Cochabamban life does not stop at
the city's edge and is not tied purely to irrigation practices.[18] Furthermore,
usos y costumbres do not stand on their own as signifiers of *lo andino* in
Cochabamba. Instead, they are imbricated in a broader concept often referred
to by scholars and community residents as "the Andean cosmovision." The
concept informs many Cochabambans' understandings of what it means to
be Cochabamban. To what, exactly, Cochabambans intend to refer when they
invoke the Andean cosmovision as it relates to water is often ambiguous. The
article "the" is a misnomer – there is no singular conception of what "the"
Andean cosmovision entails. For some, it appears to refer to a collection of
specific practices relating to how water is discussed and treated. These practices often but not always overlap; some sources had narrow conceptions of
the practices that did or did not qualify as being part of the cosmovision,
whereas others had a more expansive understanding. Even when invoked
abstractly, the concept works not just to reflect, but also to *produce* quotidian
and imagined connections.

---

[18] Information in this section comes from fieldwork in the city of Cochabamba, the rural municipality of Punata, and the peri-urban area of Tiquipaya. Information collected during fieldwork
is confirmed and/or supplemented by works specifically cited in the section.

In the context of the water wars, the Andean cosmovision appears to have symbolized "a way of life" (although what that way of life involved was certainly contested) that served to invoke an indigenous heritage or culture, to locate the region in a long history, and/or elevate conceptions of an indigenous past. Many Cochabambans describe the Andean cosmovision as rooted in ancient practices; they seem to adhere to an idea that the practices connected with the cosmovision work to preserve the region's connections to an idealized notion of what it means to be "authentically indigenous." Although many of the practices involving a direct interaction with water only appear in the valley's more rural areas, urban residents, too, have adapted and perform many purportedly traditional Andean rituals, ones that many practitioners claim have been practiced for thousands of years in the region and are part of Cochabamba's Andean roots.[19] The cosmovision is simultaneously particular to Cochabamba (sources call it part of "who we are as Cochabambans"), something that connects the region to an imagined past – "it is part of what our ancestors did"), and something that reflects both an ideal of what the region is, and an ideal of how it should be ("we should respect water like our ancestors did in the past"). References to the cosmovision reveal a nostalgia for what the past is thought to have been and a hope for what is possible in the present.

Yet the ideal remains vague. The Andean cosmovision is something the region should preserve, but exactly what that something includes isn't always clear. The comments of one source are illustrative. When asked what the Andean cosmovision was, a middle-aged factory worker and resident of Cochabamba's urban Southern Zone replied, "it is important. It is part of being Cochabamban." His response resembled not only those of his poor Southern Zone neighbors, but also those of many middle- and upper-class urban interviewees. When asked what, exactly, the cosmovision entailed, the factory worker went on to say, "it is doing what we have always done in the valley. I don't know. The *Pachamama*, I guess. We have to respect the way we've always done things. We would lose part of who we are if they took it away" (author interview with factory worker, September 2008, Cochabamba). The comments are vague, with unclear references to a notion of the way things have always been done, where who is actually "doing" anything is unclear. He does not seem to be speaking about his own way of "doing things" with water, as he gets it through a faucet in his yard. Yet he reveals a certain amount of collective ownership by saying it is doing what "we" have always done. What he, exactly, is doing, is unclear. It does seem as though he is imagining others to be doing something. The something itself is never specified, save for the reference to the *Pachamama*. There is a powerful notion that something important would be lost – a sense of self and/ or connection to the past – if Cochabambans were not able to put the tenets of the cosmovision (whatever they may be) into practice.

---

[19] See Abercrombie (1998).

The conception of an Andean cosmovision or *lo andino* is often derided as a product of essentialized views of Andean communities (Abercrombie 1991; Starn 1994).[20] Yet conceptions of the Andean cosmovision and elements of practices often described as comprising *lo andino* work in contemporary Cochabamba in two ways that are relevant to the questions at hand. First, some of the beliefs and practices with which even highly essentialized versions of the cosmovision are composed do form a critical component of daily life and aptly describe relationships with water, largely in Cochabamba's rural areas. For example, many Cochabamban irrigators practice *k'oas* – intimate ceremonies involving the burning of anything from a dried llama fetus to a miniature manufactured car, depending on the *k'oa*'s purpose, to ask for the blessing of the *Pachamama* – when they open a waterway.[21] It is also common to hear rural Cochabambans refer to water as a sacred, living thing, often with gendered pronouns.

Second, the concept of the cosmovision has come to be understood by many Cochabambans from a variety of income levels, occupations, and neighborhoods as an independent "thing" that should be preserved because of the work it does to simulate a connection to Cochabamba's Andean past. Conversations in homes around dining tables, at coffee shops, during long afternoon cookouts, while shopping at the local market, and while watching regional parades in the city square all revealed a powerful attachment to the cosmovision as something that grounded Cochabambans in who they understood themselves to be. Even a local business owner who sounded slightly exasperated when he brought it up revealed the power of the concept with his comment: "yes, yes, the *cosmovisión andina*. It comes up all the time here with almost everything we do" (author interview, September 2008, Cochabamba). Many who do not claim to believe or practice elements of the cosmovision, or may not have seen it practiced or understand what it might entail beyond treating water as sacred, claim it is a critical component of who they are as Cochabambans and, as a result, it is essential to "preserve."[22]

The cosmovision and daily life

Even many who do practice or subscribe to *lo andino* reinforce the essentialization when speaking about their contemporary relationships with

[20] Essentialism refers to the tendency to refer to categories of people as if particular attributes adhered to them directly and are necessary to their membership in a given group.
[21] Performing a *k'oa* can help to calm the angered water. The offering for water usually includes wine, coca, incense, *llamp'u* – llama fat and a llama fetus. The items are collected and burned.
[22] As the quotation marks in the previous paragraph indicate, what is important here is not whether or not the practices actually do replicate practices of Andean ancestors. Indeed, the concept of the cosmovision may very well be the product of savvy political entrepreneurs. What matters here is not how the practices came to take on the meanings that they have, but rather simply that those meanings are doing a certain work in the contemporary Cochabamban context.

water.[23] A central element of this cosmovision is the varied ways water is anthropomorphized. Water is often treated as a *ser vivo*, a living, thinking, and sentient being. It is described as a "compulsive walker," a living being without a waist or a spine that can't lift its head; water is an "animal without bones" (Salazar 1997). With life comes a personality;[24] in any moment water might be calm or angry. Water is both male and female – taking on different genders depending on the type of water or its temperament.[25] In addition to being alive, water gives life. It fertilizes the land and fertilizes man (Grillo Fernández 1994). It is the semen that fertilizes the earth, the blood that runs through its veins (in which the *Wirakocha*, the god responsible for the earth's creation, resides), and the milk that flows from a mother's breast to keep a child alive. One irrigator instructed me as we looked out over canals in Punata, "See, there they are, the veins of the earth, making everything grow." Water is rendered both sacred and vitalizing through these gendered objectifications. As water lives in the members of the community – through sexual fluids or a mother's milk – it also becomes a member of that community. Water becomes a foundation not only for reproduction, but also for communal ties.[26]

It is not only in Cochabamba's rural communities that water serves as a central part of sacred life. Many residents of the city of Cochabamba perform *k'oas* to bless the digging of a new well, the installation of new pipes, or a change in governance at a water cooperative. During these ceremonies, participants ask for the blessing of the *Pachamama* and often speak directly with the water, asking for it to arrive perhaps with abundance or without salt or mud. Some residents of the Southern Zone of the city claimed that the *Wirakocha* lives in a local well or spring. Many described their own anger in response to moments when they thought the water had been disrespected, perhaps through unsanctioned use of a well. In the Southern Zone of the city in particular, many

[23] What I analyze here are the ways in which the Andean cosmovision is described by Cochabambans today. Although my discussion draws on pan-Andean water scholarship, the practices are all ones I observed or experienced directly in Cochabamba. In subsequent chapters, I show how they played a central role in the water wars, as movement leaders and participants understood the cosmovision, articulated and understood in multiple ways, to be at risk.

[24] Some irrigators in Punata, just outside of the city of Cochabamba, claim that river water is offended when it is dammed and not allowed to continue its natural downward flow. The water is patient when there is drought but can be desperate and crazy; members of the Punata irrigators' association described water as *borracho* (drunk) during heavy rains (see also Grillo Fernández 1994, 141). The water can be capricious. But many rural Cochabambans also claim it offers wisdom; water will converse with people, bringing knowledge from the center of the mountains to inform crop choices or irrigation decisions (ibid.).

[25] Rivers are male or female, depending on the geography and contours of the particular river in a particular place; rain is male or female, depending on the strength with which it falls; lakes are female, married to the mountains around them (Salazar 1997) and connecting mountains and water in a symbology of power.

[26] This kind of gendered specificity appears less frequently in urban Cochabamba and appears to be almost absent among Cochabamban professionals, with the unsurprising exception of social movement leaders who focus on water-related issues.

residents refer to water with alternating gendered pronouns, although the male pronoun is more frequent.

The cosmovision as concept

Even those Cochabambans who do not engage with water in ways stereotypical to notions of the Andean cosmovision often discuss the cosmovision as something that is critical to preserve. The cosmovision works not as a meaning-laden praxis, but as a "thing," the components of which many Cochabambans claim they can clearly identify. These conceptions of connections to the past create a collective imagining of shared history that then informs notions of the self and the collective in the present. Anthropologists Jean and John Comaroff capture the coming together of past and present with their definition of heritage. "Heritage," they argue, "is culture named and projected into the past, and, simultaneously the past congealed into culture. It is identity in tractable, alienable form, identity whose found objects and objectifications may be consumed by others and, therefore, be delivered to the market" (2009, 10). Although the Comaroffs are concerned specifically with the marketization of ethnicity, their comments also shed light on how heritage can work to mobilize identities for political protest. Conceptions of a shared connection with Andean heritage worked throughout the water wars to summon groups both into being and onto the streets.[27] Movement leaders and participants during the water wars repeatedly claimed that the Aguas del Tunari contract violated the Andean cosmovision. Many Cochabambans perceived the contract as an affront to past, present, and future – to a shared heritage that was authentically Cochabamban. This, I argue in the following chapter, is part of what made the threat so powerful.

PRESENTS AND FUTURES: SECURING AND DISTRIBUTING MUNICIPAL WATER IN COCHABAMBA

The Andean cosmovision works in multiple ways in urban Cochabamba, most of which are shaped by the challenges of accessing water through the municipal system. The limited coverage of the networks by the *Servicio Municipal de Agua Potable y Alcantarillado de Cochabamba* [Cochabamba Municipal Drinking Water and Sewage Service] (SEMAPA) combined with poor water quality helped shape urban Cochabambans' relationships with water and, as a result, the meanings with which water was imbued in many Cochabamban neighborhoods. Whereas *usos y costumbres* often invoke the past, the Misicuni Multipurpose Project, a massive proposed water project, has come to signify a utopian, decidedly modern future, and SEMAPA – and the ways Cochabambans

---

[27] See Bourdieu and Thompson (1991), Butler (1997), Brubaker (2004), and Wedeen (2008) for discussions of this performative aspect of identity mobilization.

have coped with its failures in particular – has helped both articulate and add meaning to water in the Cochabamban present. Much of the discussion that follows is about access to water. I contend that through understanding the challenges Cochabambans face as they access water in their daily lives and the imaginings through which ideals of abundant water are surrounded, we can understand yet another way water's meanings in the region are produced and reproduced. The continued struggle to provide Cochabamba's urban areas with a reliable source of water produces both quotidian and imagined communities, providing the impetus for local water cooperatives and a source of heightened regionalism.[28]

In the postglacial period, the valley of Cochabamba was a large lake. Indeed, the name "Cochabamba" is itself a combination of the Quechua words for "lake" (*kocha*) and "plain" (*pampa*). The name reflects what made the Cochabamba Valley such a popular place for early settlers – the combination of water and plains made for a particularly fertile region. Cochabamba's water helped turn the region into the breadbasket of the country, fueling Bolivia's growth by providing grains to the miners who drove the country's development through both the silver and tin mining booms.[29] Cochabambans speak of this role with great pride and nostalgia – the region's history of cultivation produces notions of regional self-worth and recollections of it are infused with national pride.

Increasing water scarcity has served both to threaten many Cochabambans' conceptions of the region as a verdant, agricultural valley and to put water at the center of regional concerns. In the early 1930s, population growth and extensive agricultural development combined to fuel the overexploitation of groundwater supplies. By mid-decade, the region's residents were already voicing concerns about chronic water shortages. By the 1970s, droughts made headlines regularly. Communities commissioned studies on water table depth and debates took place over well construction. Studies about water loss and quality, as well as corruption within the municipal water organization, made front-page news. And every year, as the dry season reached its final weeks, conversations revolved around water – how many days a week people were receiving it, how much sediment came in it, and whether they would make it until the rains without a massive shutdown. Critiques of SEMAPA peppered newspapers. "Cochabamba dies of thirst" appeared repeatedly as a headline (Crespo Flores 1999). In 1997, the president of the Cochabamban Civic Committee declared that water was a "sacred issue" (*Presencia* 1997), and

---

[28] Although the focus of this section may appear more practical than the preceding discussions of the Andean cosmovision or *usos y costumbres*, this section remains concerned with what water has come to symbolize in Cochabamba. Water may have taken on the meanings discussed as a result of a long history of drought, disappointment in the municipal water company, or the region's historical role as Bolivia's breadbasket, but semiotic practices are at the heart of the analysis.

[29] On the silver boom and agricultural production in Cochabamba, see Larson (1998).

environmental activist and Cochabamban Gabriel Herbas described water as a "regional myth" (quoted in Crespo Flores 2003, 151). Not only had water become a central regional identifier, but Cochabambans themselves explicitly understood it as such.

The causes of Cochabamba's water woes are likely multiple, but as the 1990s wore on, market reforms became an easy scapegoat. Privatization of the tin mines in the late 1980s sent unemployed miners from towns like Oruro and Potosí to Cochabamba, and demand on the region's aquifers and SEMAPA's services rose. Water was increasingly pumped from aquifers faster than the natural rate of recharge (Crespo Flores 2003, 136). Furthermore, these natural recharge rates themselves began to decrease, as urbanization at the base of the rivers flowing from the Tunari Mountains increased runoff, reducing the amount of water absorbed back into the land and stored in the aquifers (ibid., 136). Market reforms could be blamed on both fronts – the arrival of unem-ployed miners both increased demand on the aquifers and led to settlements that obstructed aquifer recharge rates.

Not surprisingly, as Cochabamba continued to turn to its aquifers to meet regional demand, water conflicts intensified. Attempts at increased drilling roused local opposition as private and communal users worried that if municipal or state authorities were to tap into aquifers, their own supply would be threatened. In the early 1970s, residents protested the drilling of *Yacimientos Petrolíferos Fiscales Bolivianos* [The National Oil and Gas Corporation of Bolivia] (YPFB) wells in the Vinto District of Cochabamba's Quillacollo Province, kicking off a conflict that would last on and off for nearly thirty years and was called the "war of the wells." They returned to the streets again in 1976 and 1977 when SEMAPA drilled ten semideep wells in the Cochabamban community of Vinto (Crespo Flores 2003). In 1992 and 1994, SEMAPA tried again to dig wells in Vinto, but local opposition delayed the project (Crespo Flores 1999). During the 1994 protests, Vinto's Water Resources Defense Committee blocked access to the road leading to the drill site (ibid.). Foreshadowing the discourse that would appear again in 1999, and highlighting the salience of regional divides, the committee developed the slogan "Water Is the Patrimony of the Locality" (Assies 2003, 20). These claims of patrimony would later chafe against the privatization efforts in 1999 and 2000. Ultimately, the national government declared a state of siege and drilled three wells; by 2003, two had already drained the aquifer's water supply and were shut down (Crespo Flores 2003, 222). In 1997, SEMAPA yet again proposed to drill wells in Vinto and again it was met with opposition. Residents blocked access to the area and forced SEMAPA, along with its military escort, to withdraw (Assies 2003; Crespo Flores 2003).

Imagining a future: the Misicuni myth

With aquifers as a controversial and limited answer to the region's water concerns, Cochabamba looked increasingly to the surrounding mountains

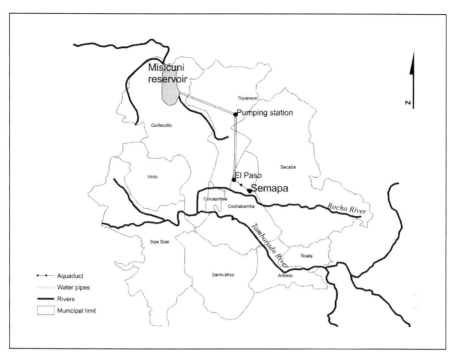

MAP 2.4. The proposed Misicuni Multipurpose Project.

for its water supply.[30] With the advent of large-dam technology in the 1950s, the Misicuni "dream" emerged. The proposal was to divert water from the Misicuni River to the Cochabamba Valley and create a local reservoir for water storage. The Misicuni Multipurpose Project (also known as the Misicuni Dam or just Misicuni) heightened regional identifications around the struggle to provide water to Cochabamba, becoming a source of conflict between national and regional priorities. It became an ideal around which Cochabambans could rally and an answer to the region's water woes that eliminated other possible solutions, including privatization, in the process.

The Misicuni project was perpetually in progress. At multiple moments, it appeared as though Cochabamba was on the verge of securing the project's construction, but an obstacle always arose that prevented adequate financing; the project required extensive tunneling through the mountains and would involve a significant investment of public funds.[31] As construction began for the second time in August 1998, a headline in the local paper *Opinión* read: "Work on the

---

[30] By the 1990s, the Tunari Mountains were supplying approximately 80 percent of the total water resources for human consumption and irrigation in the Cochabamba Valley (Crespo Flores 2003).
[31] One such moment was under General Banzer in 1971 when funds for Misicuni were diverted to development projects in Banzer's home state of Santa Cruz (Laurie and Marvin 1999, 1406).

tunnel has begun: the best proof that Misicuni is a reality" ("Empezó la obra del túnel: la mejor prueba de que Misicuni es una realidad" 1998).

Misicuni quickly came to mean far more than increased access to water for the region. According to Carlos Crespo, Misicuni became a "mythical discourse" (2003, 97). In spite of years of drought, many Bolivians continued to imagine Cochabamba as a "verdant agricultural valley" (Laurie and Marvin 1999, 1405). Many residents were nostalgic for the idyllic countryside that they imagined Cochabamba to have been, and they continued to proudly refer to their home as the "granary of Bolivia," or the "garden city." It was the "land of the eternal spring," a phrase that evokes not only an agreeable climate, but also perpetual growth, a verdant place in which flowers are growing and the grass is always green. Whereas much of Cochabamba is, indeed, green during the rainy season, June, July, August, and September are quite different. Looking out from the center of the city, hillsides are brown. In the rural areas, dust dominates the landscape. It is only where irrigation systems are well developed and maintained that anything appears to grow.

Many residents understood the region to be a "lost paradise," with Misicuni as the solution (Crespo Flores 2003, 152). Gonzalo Terceros, former mayor of Cochabamba, stated in 1996 that "with the Misicuni Project our agricultural lands will be replenished and we will re-find the former Cochabamba, where thriving agriculture was the feature of our Department" (quoted in Crespo Flores 2003, 152). The project would allow Cochabamba to "reassume the title of the Bolivian granary" and promised a "better quality of life" (ibid.). The image of a utopia, only possible through the construction of Misicuni, emerged. In 1994, a local magazine reported that Misicuni "continues to be a utopia" (*Datos y Analysis*, February 27, 1994), and the cover of a book on the project was adorned with a glowing water faucet, a colorful butterfly, and an image of the shape of the state of Cochabamba in green (Guardia 1994). Misicuni would bring with it color, life, and access to water via shiny new taps. Civil engineer Osvaldo Pareja called Misicuni "the beginning of Cochabamba's future" (quoted in Crespo Flores 2003, 152). It was a project for all Cochabambans, embodying "ideas of modernization and progress" (Laurie and Marvin 1999, 1406).

The project thus stands simultaneously for an idealized notion both of Cochabamba's past and of modernization. One resident commented that "Misicuni is an archetypal image; it's a hope; it's the idea that we can have water as we did before. It is a way to *recuperar* (regain/recover) the past" (author interview, September 2008, Cochabamba). Comments made by Amalia Ramírez, the president of the Women's Civic Committee of Cochabamba, at the inauguration of a new phase of work on the Misicuni tunnel in 1998 illustrate the point. Ramírez argued that the desertification of Cochabamba could only be reversed with the combination of the Misicuni project and the region's traditional irrigation practices ("Empezó la obra del túnel: la mejor prueba de que Misicuni es una realidad" 1998). Misicuni had quickly become the region's only alternative, and it allowed Cochabamba to both step into the future and preserve an idealized past. What is most perfect about past and present live alongside each other in the Misicuni myth.

Misicuni's mythical status even attained national attention. A headline on August 24, 1997, from the national newspaper *La Razón* reads: "*Misicuni: ¿un mito o una realidad?* [Misicuni: a myth or a reality?]" The article states that Misicuni is a theme of debate again in Cochabamba but acknowledges that it "never stopped being one" (Mallo 1997). "The first challenge for the region," the author argues, "is to demystify the Misicuni project" (ibid.), referencing how the debate around the Misicuni project referred not to the reality of what the project would or wouldn't do, but rather the understandings of the project as the region's economic and environmental savior. Understandings of what the project "was" had, in his estimation, become divorced from reality. As a result, to properly debate the merits of the project, it needed to be demystified.

Not surprisingly, the project became a political spectacle and a central component in regional political discourse. Visits to the Misicuni site served as a rite of passage for politicians – to oppose the project or offer anything less than a complete commitment to its construction was political suicide. Elected politicians, or those seeking office, appeared in the papers with their pictures at the tunnel site as they took part in the "pilgrimage" to Misicuni (Crespo Flores 2003, 154). The visits took on the flavor of a ritual, with each politician arriving at the project to pay his or her respects (ibid.). As it became a place to "show the pride and capacities of Cochabambans" (ibid., 154), no politician could avoid a trip to the tunnel. This political discourse reproduced and strengthened the Misicuni myth. Just prior to the water wars, geographers Nina Laurie and Simon Marvin wrote that Cochabambans "believe that Misicuni is the solution to their water problems because, for forty years, prior to each election every politician has promised to build this project in order to solve Cochabamba's water problem" (1999, 1409).[32] The tunnel meant independence and progress; it was a local source of pride and hope.[33] The Aguas del Tunari contract meant not only the privatization of SEMAPA, but also the end of the Misicuni dream.

The Misicuni myth had become so well established in the Cochabamban imaginary that alternatives appeared unacceptable. In the late 1990s, just as construction

[32] The unfulfilled promise of Misicuni did not appear to cause problems for politicians. Perhaps Misicuni was, indeed, so mythical that Cochabambans did not actually expect it to happen, so politicians did not need to be held to account when they failed to secure funding or advance construction plans.

[33] It is unsurprising that politicians not only made visits to the project site but also continued to fight for (or defend) the project's completion through the requisite political channels, albeit without success. In 1997, as the central government proceeded with plans for water privatization in Cochabamba, the mayor, Manfred Reyes Villa (who would still be mayor two years later when the Aguas del Tunari concession was signed), took out a court injunction arguing against the constitutionality of the privatization of a municipal resource like SEMAPA (Laurie and Marvin 1999, 1412). The Supreme Court ruled with the mayor and declared null the federal government's solicitation for proposals for a Cochabamba concession ("La Suprema falló a favor de la Alcaldía" 1997). A central concern appeared to be the uncertain future of Misicuni if SEMAPA were to fall into private hands.

for the first Misicuni tunnel got under way, the possibility for an entirely different approach to solving the region's water supply challenges emerged – the development of a neighboring reservoir, Corani, into a source of water for the valley. Constructed initially as part of a hydroelectric power project, the Corani project offered a potentially lower-cost solution to Cochabamba's water woes (Neal 2000). But by this point Misicuni had already become "emblematic of the region's identity and hopes for the future" (Laurie and Marvin 1999, 1409), and residents were skeptical that the Corani project could equal the promise of Misicuni ("Comité Cívico rechaza intento de imponer proyecto Corani" 1997). Misicuni's mythical status rendered the Corani project an unacceptable alternative. Whereas Corani might help solve the region's water challenges, Misicuni was expected to do much more. Corani could not bring with it the transformation with which imaginings of Misicuni were imbued. Corani was not the "cultural resource" (Laurie and Marvin 1999, 1409) Misicuni had come to be.

In addition to symbolizing past and future, the Misicuni project served to heighten divisions that existed just before the water wars. Misicuni both exacerbated and exemplified splits between the region and the central government. Cochabamban citizens and politicians had been engaged in an extended fight for regional and political decentralization; many residents understood the Misicuni project to be a central element in the region's struggle for increased autonomy (Crespo Flores 2003). Many Cochabambans came to understand Misicuni as something "owed" to the region by the politicians in La Paz. The project began to take on this meaning as central governmental officials continually diverted funds for its development away from the region; other projects were deemed more important at those times.

The market-oriented economic reforms of the 1980s and 1990s served to reinforce the earlier conception that somehow Misicuni was owed to Cochabamba. Many Cochabambans understood their water concerns as directly tied to the ways in which the central government's economic policies impacted the region. The particular impact of marketization on Cochabamba directly exacerbated the region's water shortages. As already mentioned, as miners lost their jobs, many settled in the Cochabamba Valley, putting a strain on the city's services, including its water infrastructure. Many Cochabambans claim that the arrival of migrants caused the region to unfairly bear much of the burden of Bolivia's market-oriented policies. As a result, the central government owed the region a debt – the "Misicuni debt," as many Cochabamban scholars, politicians, and professionals called it[34] – to help cope with the environmental strain caused by the arrival of thousands of unemployed migrants.

The Aguas del Tunari contract evoked strong attachments to region – to what Cochabambans "deserved." The extended struggle for water made these conceptions particularly powerful. Even though Cochabambans speak of

[34] I did not hear this phrase in Cochabamba's more rural areas nor in the poorer Southern Zone (where most of the migrants settled).

themselves as the breadbasket of Bolivia in the past tense – they clearly no longer envision the region as providing for the rest of the country – the language
they use suggests that because Cochabamba had used its water for so many
years to fuel the country, and the region had suffered disproportionately as a
result of the neoliberal reforms of the 1980s and 1990s, it now deserved better
where water was concerned.

These regional tensions are evident in comments made by the former director of SEMAPA:

Fifteen years ago Cochabamba was the second city; now it is in third place because of
the growth of Santa Cruz. Santa Cruz received extraordinary amounts of state funding. It is not disputed that Santa Cruz has huge economic potential because of oil, but
Cochabamba has not received any compensation for its suffering and taking on this
urban growth which has had a huge effect on Cochabamba's life. (quoted in Laurie and
Marvin 1999, 1411)

Misicuni became both a dream and a debt – something to which the region
aspired, but also something that the region was owed. Furthermore, access to
water was critical to Cochabamba's national standing. Santa Cruz was taking
Cochabamba's second-place spot because Cochabamba could not handle the
influx of immigrants straining the city's already beleaguered municipal water
infrastructure. Access to water was an issue of regional pride, serving to help
construct and bring to the fore regional identifications. The Aguas del Tunari
contract was an insult to Cochabamba perpetrated by officials in La Paz who
had no respect or understanding for what the region deserved. Furthermore, in
spite of reassurances by public officials, the Aguas del Tunari contract meant
an end to the Misicuni dream to many Cochabambans.

On the eve of the Aguas del Tunari concession, the Misicuni dream loomed
large in Cochabamba. Misicuni had so completely dominated the discourse
on what "progress" was that, as with Corani, any other attempt to solve the
region's water challenges would invariably fall short of capturing the public's
imagination. One of the first acts of protest against the concession was the
symbolic burial of Misicuni in Cochabamba's central plaza on July 26, 1999.
During protests the next winter, some participants sang the following verse in
Quechua, "For Misicuni we will fight, with the sellers of water we will come face
to face" (quoted in Crespo Flores and Fernández 2001).[35] The lines portray the
concession as a direct threat to Misicuni. Signs on placards during the protests
read, "*No al tarifazo, sí a Misicuni* [No to the rate hikes, yes to Misicuni]." The
contradictory hopes in the statement are clear – Cochabambans did not want to

---

[35] Quechua: "'*Misik'unirayku ch'allpanakusunchis*
Yaku rank'eroswan qonapakusunchis.'"
Spanish: "*Por Miscuni nos vamos a pelear*
Con los comerciantes del agua nos vamos a enfrentar."
As with all other translations, unless otherwise indicated, the translation from Spanish to
English is mine.

pay more for water through the current privatization scheme but did want an enormously expensive water development project that they had been expecting the state to deliver for decades. Even a state that had failed to provide was preferable to the unknowns of the market.

Producing a present: SEMAPA

Misicuni attained such an extraordinary position in the Cochabamban imaginary in part as a result of the failures of Cochabamba's municipal water organization, SEMAPA. In many of Cochabamba's poorer residential areas, SEMAPA's absence created the space for quotidian communities to form around water. In coalescing around water, communities made new claims for themselves, and water took on new meanings in the process. To threaten water was to threaten these communities; it was to challenge both the independence and the gains for which they had fought. The failings of the SEMAPA services tied many Cochabambans together, either intimately through quotidian communities or in a mediated fashion through a shared knowledge that Cochabambans throughout the region's urban and peri-urban areas faced similar daily challenges as they sought access to reliable, affordable water. The challenges to accessing water in Cochabamba became a regional identifier. They were (and continued to be) a shared experience that helped define the Cochabamban community. As a result, the Aguas del Tunari contract was perceived as a threat both to the quotidian communities that formed through the daily struggle to access water and to a regional notion of Cochabamban patrimony and independence.

Officially created in 1967 and given financial and administrative autonomy in 1972 (Crespo Flores 2003), SEMAPA slowly expanded to cover much of the larger metropolitan area of Cochabamba. By 1996, Quillacollo, Colcapirhua, Sacaba, Vinto, Tiquipaya, and the Cercado province (which overlaps directly with the Cochabamba municipal limits) were all included in the SEMAPA network. By 1999, SEMAPA covered approximately 292,000 people with 45,907 water connections (Crespo Flores 2003, 108). A total of 596,650 meters of pipe covered 50 percent of Cochabamba's urban area.[36]

But SEMAPA's networks failed to reach a majority of Cochabamba's residents, fundamentally shaping local relationships with water in the process.

---

[36] Prior to the concession, SEMAPA's tariffs functioned along two basic dimensions – metered and unmetered rates. Metered rates were calculated by a meter installed in a residence or commercial facility, and users were charged both for the amount they consumed and a minimum monthly fee. The consumption rate corresponded to the type of use. R1 users were on land without construction, R2 were on land with "*medias aguas*" or precarious construction, R3 were one-floor buildings, and R4 were larger residential buildings (Crespo Flores 2003, 122). Unmetered monthly rates were determined by the average consumption of a user's category. For example, if a residence was classified as R2 but did not have a meter, it was charged the average monthly rate for all of the residences in Cochabamba with the R2 categorization. In 1997, a new water connection cost US$85 and a meter US$50.

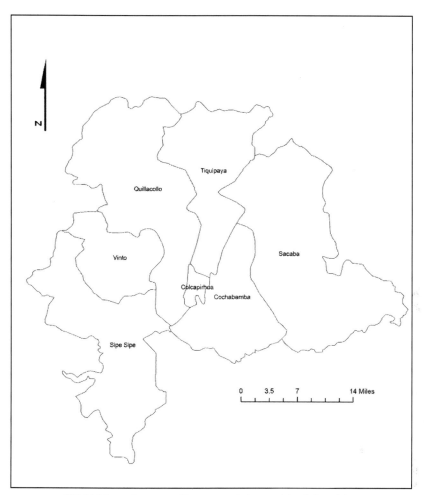

MAP 2.5. SEMAPA service area. City center is located in Colcapirhua.

In 1999, only 64 percent of the city's population had a SEMAPA connection in their homes (Laurie and Marvin 1999, 1406), most of them in the city's Northeast and Central Zones. Much of the south and the northwest were left unconnected. Furthermore, SEMAPA did not appear in a rush to reach them; at the time of the concession, SEMAPA had gone nine years without any network expansions. Those without coverage had to develop alternative means of accessing water. As discussed in the following pages, these alternatives became the core of local community relationships, shaping daily life through the efforts both to obtain water and to provide communal governance to manage it. The struggle to convince SEMAPA to extend its networks also served as an ongoing focus of community discussion and organizing efforts. Through these efforts, water not only produced and reproduced quotidian communities, it also came to signify dignity, autonomy, and reciprocity. As the evidence in the following pages shows, accessing water was not just about obtaining a particular material good; it was about fighting for justice, forging and sustaining community ties, and demanding recognition from municipal authorities.

But even for those Cochabambans with water connections, SEMAPA's miserable performance was a constant source of conversation; the water authority's failings created a sense of shared suffering (even if the degree and type varied greatly) among urban and peri-urban Cochabambans. "Our futures," one Cochabamban told me, "are all tied together in SEMAPA." Prior to the concession, SEMAPA was synonymous with poor quality and coverage. Users experienced problems with cloudy water and excess iron content, particularly during rainy months. Sediment came frequently out of Cochabamban taps. Furthermore, water provision through SEMAPA was insufficient to meet demand. In 1999, SEMAPA provided only 70 percent of the water demanded by the region's residents and businesses;[37] only 23 percent of the connected population received water for a full twenty-four hours a day, regardless of the season (Crespo Flores 2003, 119). In neighborhoods in Cochabamba's northwest, water came as infrequently as twice per week for periods of up to five hours. To make matters worse, the system was also inarguably inefficient, with water losses estimated at more than 30 percent (Laurie and Marvin 1999, 1405). For rich and poor alike, SEMAPA's failings produced perceptions of shared challenges.

SEMAPA's poor performance routinely made headlines in local newspapers, particularly during the final months of the dry season. The organization served as the butt of jokes and the object of derisive comparisons. The manager of a local hotel remarked, "we were always worried when the dry season arrived. How were we supposed to manage our business? We had to stay vigilant" (author interview, August 2008, Cochabamba). Although most residents of the south and northwest of the city did not have SEMAPA connections in their homes, some shared access to a communal tap. A resident of Villa Pagador, one of the neighborhoods in Cochabamba's south with access to a communal tap prior to the concession, did not mince words when asked how he felt about SEMAPA: "I had no use for them. We paid so much every month to get what? Muddy water once a week? They didn't seem to care. No one did. We were really on our own" (author interview, February 2010, Cochabamba).

The conversation I heard at a Cochabamban Sunday lunch more than eight years after the water wars could have easily taken place during almost any September since the early 1990s. "How was your water today?" one man asked of another sitting at the table. "Well, we had it in the morning, but nothing in the afternoon. Good thing we filled up the buckets." They spoke about SEMAPA's water service as if it were the weather – a mundane topic of daily

---

[37] Figure calculated from Laurie and Marvin (1999, 1405).

conversation during a lull in the meal. Whether rich or poor, Cochabambans have been left on their own to ensure daily access to water for their families and their businesses. This sense of shared struggle is something everyone can talk about – it creates a shared, regional vocabulary.

Constructing community in SEMAPA's absence

The north side of Cochabamba, where many of the city's wealthiest residents have made their homes, enjoys access to a local spring and a small river. Southern residents contend with deeper water tables and no flowing water. Furthermore, the urban water infrastructure is concentrated in the north, and the quality of service declines as you move farther south, until you reach zones without any connection to municipal water infrastructure. Those communities in southern Cochabamba that are connected to SEMAPA rarely receive water more than one or two days per week. Both Cochabamba's rich and poor must contend with SEMAPA's failures – some wealthy homes are also unconnected or receive unreliable service. It is undoubtedly easier to cope with SEMAPA's failures if you have financial means, yet Cochabambans of all income levels have developed their own mechanisms for accessing much-needed water resources. Many poorer communities rely on a combination of local water vendors and/or communally constructed and managed wells. Cochabamba's wealthy usually have an easier solution: private wells.

Private wells

Even though the challenges confronting those with private wells do not compare to those unable to afford private access, most Cochabambans do not take water for granted. During a lunch with a number of relatively well-off Cochabambans in their early thirties, one remarked, "water is something we all struggle with; we are all in it together. It is Cochabamba's curse." Her comment was not unique. These shared understandings help create a common, regional language around water; challenges are perceived as shared – a "curse" the region must endure – even if Cochabamba's rich and poor experience those challenges in very different ways.

Many of Cochabamba's wealthier residents living outside of the city center choose to dig their own wells, regardless of whether or not they have a SEMAPA connection in their homes. They can afford to dig far enough to access aquifers with more reliable and usually cleaner water than SEMAPA provides. One resident of Cochabamba's wealthier Northern Zone commented, "Have faith in SEMAPA? I don't think so. We knew we needed our own water so we built a well. We could usually rely on the well, but things would have been easier without it" (author interview, February 2010, Cochabamba). But even Cochabamba's privileged cannot entirely buy their way out of challenges that SEMAPA's poor service creates. Aquifers dry up and users must be careful to limit consumption to keep from putting excess strain on the resource.

Furthermore, privately owned wells cannot serve as an engine of growth for the region. This seemed to be a primary concern of many members of Cochabamba's business elite. Although wealthier residents do not engage in daily struggles to provide for their personal needs, many have ambitions for the region that they claim cannot be met without comprehensive, sustainable access to water. Their businesses can grow to be only so big, and they can attract only so many new partners to the region without adequate water infrastructure to support their needs. The comments of Mauricio Barrientos, president of the Civic Committee during the water wars and a prominent local businessman, reflect the comments of a number of interviewees: "SEMAPA alone was never going to be enough. We can't run our factories or develop our neighborhoods without water. We will be stuck – without development, without growth. Water is the key to Cochabamba's future" (author interview with Mauricio Barrientos, February 2010, Cochabamba). Barrientos's comments recall the utopian dream of Misicuni. They also suggest that the Misicuni dream may be far more salient to those whose immediate water needs are already met. Few Cochabambans in the Southern Zone spoke of regionally grounded aspirations for modernization or the return to past days of agricultural glory. Even though the specific understandings were different, water was a part of the Cochabamban imaginary, irrespective of personal access. The Aguas del Tunari contract threatened not only perceptions of individual access, but also of shared regional belonging.

Aguateros

For those Cochabambans without private wells or reliable SEMAPA connections, water vendors called *aguateros* provide an expensive and unpredictable alternative. *Aguateros* drive through the city's under- (or simply "un-") serviced areas in tankers filled with water. Residents come out to meet the truck with large water drums. The *aguatero* will continue to fill drums until the tank runs out. In 2003 the rate was approximately US$0.60/200 liters (Crespo Flores 2003, 116). The method is an unreliable, onerous, and expensive one for Cochabamba's residents. Someone must be home when the truck passes and hours are rarely predictable. Furthermore, the rate is twice the rate that residents can often get through communal management efforts (ibid., 116). The challenges of getting water through *aguateros* may not immediately recall the "artisanal" process that Bakker (2003) describes, but something similar is at work – getting water requires daily thought, planning, and effort. The story here continues to be about unpredictable and difficult access to water, but the analytical point is that the routines of contending with the challenges of relying on *aguateros* produced a shared vocabulary, summoning a group into being through the collective experience.[38]

The experiences of residents of Villa Pagador exemplify those of other Cochabambans who rely regularly on *aguateros*. Carlos Oropeza's comments

[38] See Wutich (2007) for an in-depth account of the challenges of relying on *aguateros* in the Cochabamban settlement of Villa Israel. Some residents claim that the community's name comes

echoed those of his neighbors: "When the *aguateros* come you have to watch out for them to get them to come to your house. Even then it can be hard. And the neighborhood can't really protest or make demands [*reclamar*] because they don't have another option. The *aguateros* can always sell to another neighborhood. We don't have any power" (author interview with Carlos Oropeza, February 2010, Cochabamba). For residents who rely on *aguateros*, water is never far from their minds. They organize their days around the potential visit of a truck and must ensure that they buy enough to last until the next visit, the date of which is always uncertain. For these residents, communities are formed, in part, because of a shared vulnerability. It is almost as if they share a common fate because they do not have the power to either ensure that the *aguateros* will visit on any given day or demand better service when the *aguateros* do pass through.

"Alternative" systems

When and where possible, many Cochabamban residents with limited or no access to SEMAPA's network have developed their own system of water cooperatives around communally constructed and managed wells or communal access to a singular SEMAPA connection.[39] These cooperatives are examples of the kinds of quotidian communities that emerge around water – they produce routine, face-to-face interactions among their members. Through them, water has helped to produce not only quotidian communities but also expressions of independence, reciprocity, dignity, and cooperation.

Carlos Crespo (2003) reports that in 1999, 15–20 percent of Cochabambans relied on these "alternative" forms of water distribution. Whereas each functions differently, many operate under the same general principles. Residents of a given community will contribute time and money to establish, maintain, and govern a communal system of water collection and distribution. The water comes from either a communally constructed well or a communally managed connection to SEMAPA, whereby the cooperative buys water in bulk from the municipal agency and then manages its distribution. In exchange, members will have the opportunity to access water at appointed times or for predetermined amounts. Most cooperatives have a system of punishment, usually fines, in

---

from the meaning of the name "Israel" as "one who fights." The literal translation is "struggles with God." Thanks to Nadav Shelef for bringing this to my attention.

[39] In writing about largely rural water systems, scholars Rutgerd Boelens, David Getches, and Armando Guevara-Gil argue that "in situations of scarcity and mutual dependence on a shared water resource, collective action is necessary and communities take up this task" (2010b, 11). Indeed, although they refer only to water, Boelens et al.'s observation, when understood more generally, is at the core of this book's argument – when thinly coherent communities rely heavily on a particular good for survival, the good will become important not just for its own sake but for the communities that form around it and the meaning the resource takes on as a result. The cooperatives also recall Ostrom (1990) and Ostrom et al. (1994) in reference to institutions that develop to manage common pool resources.

place for those who violate the communally agreed-upon rules for water collection and management.

Water cooperatives may be a part of the *junta vecinal* – the local neighborhood organization – or operate with independent legal status or no legal status at all. They can have as few as 40 and as many as 1,000 members. One resident offers his account of the development of water cooperatives in Cochabamba's south:

> In the Southern Zone, the people come from the countryside or from the mines. The mining centers were very well organized to demand things. They knew how to organize to ask for change. While in the countryside, they know how to solve their own problems through their own efforts. The combination of miners who knew how to organize to make demands and the country people who knew how to simply do it themselves was very powerful in the south. So they have built and learned how to manage their own systems. (Author interview, February 2010, Cochabamba)

The water cooperatives serve not only as a source of water, but also of pride for the communities that have developed them. The cooperatives are a reflection of their hard work, commitment, and entrepreneurship.

Cochabambans throughout the Southern Zone have actively formed communities to ensure regular, albeit limited, access to water. These communities, in turn, have come to play critical roles in building and sustaining local relationships and governance structures. As a result, water has become tied to ideals of communal governance and neighborly relations. Through these local cooperatives, water has come to signify independence and dignity, as well as ideals of reciprocity and collaboration. One resident commented, "Water dignifies people. Water brings us together. It gets us to work together. There aren't political divisions with water. It doesn't have a political color. It brings everyone together" (author interview, February 2010, Cochabamba).

The language of this interviewee is at once global and highly grounded in the context of those communities in Cochabamba without regular access to the municipal water network. Water is without political color – yet it brings everyone together in this particular context because its absence presents a challenge that the community can best meet by working together. The interviewee credits water for his community's organization. His remarks are not unique. In their efforts to organize around water, many communities established cooperatives that served not only to arbitrate water disputes or develop better water services, but also to resolve community problems or fight for community needs not directly related to water. Cooperatives worked to extend electricity, improve roads, and resolve disputes when residents were caught stealing or violating other community norms. Water cooperatives often served as local governance structures that met a wide variety of community needs and made residents increasingly independent from municipal services. This is not to say that the police weren't called if something was found missing, or that local leaders didn't advocate for new roads at the municipal government offices. But even those advocacy attempts were often rooted in the governance structures established by the water cooperatives.[40] In the words of one Cochabamba resident, "Water makes the community organize; it brings the community together" ["*El agua hace que la comunidad este organizada; aglutina la comunidad*"] (author interview, August 2008, Cochabamba).

Of course water does not always work this way. Communal governance structures are not the product of, nor do they continually produce, a constant state of collaboration and harmony. Meetings are contentious, and members do not always believe that others are doing their fair share, that the fees are appropriate, or that the water is being well managed. Furthermore, as already cited, water produces conflicts not only within neighborhoods but also across them. Urban residents lobbying for continued well drilling met sustained opposition from their peri-urban and rural counterparts. Water can be a source of conflict in Cochabamba as various groups fight for access to a scarce resource. Yet even as these tensions produced and revealed divisions within Cochabamba, they also helped produce the remarkable unity evidenced in the water wars. A threat from outside – a private company, the national government – highlighted the shared struggle and allowed common experiences to dominate discourse.

CONCLUSIONS

Writing in 1999, before the privatization of SEMAPA and the beginning of the water wars, Laurie and Marvin observed that in Cochabamba, "water has become intimately linked to issues of regional identity and privatization has heightened struggles against governmental influence in La Paz" (1999, 1404). Carlos Crespo's observations echo Laurie and Marvin's contention: "The chronic water shortage in the Cochabamba Valley has made water a very sensitive issue in the region, and water conflicts have been part of Cochabamba's history" (Crespo Flores 2003, 51). This chapter shows how those sensitivities are reflected in daily practices and the varied meanings water has taken on as a result.

Water in Cochabamba helps shape, constitute, and define communities, whether they are as small as an irrigation council or urban water cooperative or as large as the Cochabamban Valley itself. The water wars were not the first time these communities mobilized around water-related issues. Irrigators mobilized in the early 1990s when they perceived a threat from the LPP, *juntas vecinales* organized routinely to mount small protests and make demands that SEMAPA improve or extend services, and urban and rural groups mobilized throughout the 1980s and 1990s to express either support for or concern over potential new wells. Protest over water in Cochabamba was not new. What

---

[40] Evidence from the urban water management structures in Cochabamba echoes research on more rural Andean communities that finds that collective water management arrangements can be "the most essential fibers of … community social fabric" (Boelens et al. 2010b, 6).

was new was the apparent unity with which Cochabambans took to the streets. Water is a subsistence good that everyone – rich and poor – needs to consume to survive. Yet it is, in part, through its absence in Cochabamba that water takes on the subsistence-related meanings that are at the core of this book's theoretical argument. Micro-level understandings of the ways water and community were intertwined coalesced at the meso-level. Multiple understandings of water were not in conflict or competition but fit within an overarching master frame of opposition to the Aguas del Tunari contract. The contract simultaneously threatened regional autonomy; undermined ambitions for a regionally rooted, independent solution; was perceived to put network improvements and expansions at risk; and was understood by many Cochabambans as a challenge to local water practices and to their Andean heritage.

3

¡El Agua es Nuestra, Carajo! The origins of the Bolivian water wars

The 1999 privatization of water in Cochabamba brought Bolivians to the streets. And it was not just those who suffered from rate increases who joined the protests. Bolivian researchers Bustamante, Peredo, and Udaeta argue that "almost the entire population of the region participated [in the water wars], no matter what their social class" (2005, 72). It is clear that participation was not limited to any one class or identity group. During the water wars, "diverse popular sectors and their respective cultural tactics combine[d] as a plural political subject" (Albro 2005, 254). How and why was the formation of this "plural political subject" possible? What were the dynamics at work that enabled such a diverse coalition to come together in the streets?

To answer these questions, we must look to water, and what it meant in the Cochabamban context. For many Cochabambans, water symbolized community; these meanings help explain the dynamics at work in protests that rocked the region in early 2000. The privatization contract provoked a resistance rooted in specific community needs and relationships, which were expressed in familiar, long-standing discourses that cut across salient divisions. To many Cochabambans, water was not only a critical component in their continued livelihood, but also a good that took on national, regional, and ethnic significance. Many perceived the privatization contract as a threat to both local relationships and regional heritage. Individuals and groups came together around the "material and symbolic urgency of water" (Albro 2005, 255) to voice their objections through social mobilization.

Water helped resolve what had been, in Schelling's (1960) terms, a coordination problem. Water emerged as a focal point, something that brought together diverse groups with diverse interests to fight for a common goal. Why and how did water play this role? Was there something unique about the physical properties of the good itself – its biophysical characteristics or role in securing human survival? Although these aspects of water's materiality are important to understanding how and why it worked the way it did in Cochabamba, a focus on materiality alone would leave us wondering why threats to water provoke resistance in some times and places and not in others. The Aguas del Tunari contract not only threatened relationships with a critical material good, but also with imagined communities of nation, region, and ethnicity as well as with the quotidian communities – communities constituted by face-to-face interactions – created by everyday social interactions and relationships. To understand the water wars we must understand how water worked as a symbol in the Cochabamban context and how those symbols contributed to political resistance.

This chapter accomplishes three tasks. First, it offers the economic and political context for the Aguas del Tunari contract. Second, this chapter establishes the broad-based and widespread characteristics of participation in the social mobilizations. Finally, the analysis shows how attention to water's meanings in the Cochabamban context is critical if we are to understand the mechanisms at work in the emergence and composition of the early protest events. The analysis that follows allows me to make both particular claims about the events in Cochabamba and generalizable claims about how a market-driven threat to a subsistence resource can work to produce political resistance.

BOLIVIA'S NEOLIBERAL EXPERIMENT

Bolivia was arguably one of Latin America's earliest experiments with market-oriented economic reforms. Suffering from large foreign debt, negative GDP growth, and inflation that reached an annualized rate of 60,000 percent from May to August 1985 (Sachs 2001), Bolivia seemed the perfect test case for a package of economic adjustments later labeled the "Washington Consensus."

Reforms and reactions

Víctor Paz Estenssoro, Bolivia's president, initiated the New Economic Policy (NEP) in 1985, reducing trade barriers, slashing public expenditures, devaluing the currency, and privatizing national industries. More than 24,600 public employees lost their jobs between 1985 and 1986. Between 1986 and 1987, the workforce of the *Corporación Minera de Bolivia* [Mining Corporation of Bolivia] (COMIBOL) shrank from 30,000 to 7,000 (Silva 2009, 107). The policy met significant opposition, but Paz Estenssoro averted sustained resistance through the imposition of a state of siege (Klein 2003, 245). Government officials arrested union leaders and strikers, undermining already weak public sector unions. Although the *Central Obrera Boliviana* [Bolivian Workers' Central] (COB), Bolivia's umbrella union organization, continued to call strikes, it proved unable to mobilize large numbers of people, and government officials successfully contained whatever protests did take place. The lack of sustained opposition is particularly surprising in light of the high levels of mobilization that characterized Bolivia in the years prior to Paz Estenssoro's presidency (see Dunkerley 1984; Klein 1992, 2003).

Throughout the 1990s, Paz Estenssoro's successors deepened their commitment to Washington Consensus policies. Jaime Paz Zamora (1989–1993) further reduced public sector employment and passed legislation permitting the privatization of most remaining public sector firms (Grindle 2003). Gonzalo Sánchez de Lozada (1993–1997) breathed new life into Paz Estenssoro's reforms and pursued privatization policies with "enthusiastic abandon" (Shultz 2003, 34). At the center of Sánchez de Lozada's reform efforts, the *Plan de Todos* [Plan of/for Everyone] called for sweeping structural and economic changes, including constitutional reforms that paved the way for continued privatization. By the end of 1997, Sánchez de Lozada had privatized Bolivia's oil and phone companies, the national airlines, the national electric company, the national train system, and the water in La Paz–El Alto. In total, Sánchez de Lozada oversaw the privatization of fifty-six public companies, and Supreme Decree 24716 officially recognized concessions as the mode of transfer of water to the private sector (Crespo Flores 2003). Sánchez de Lozada also successfully overhauled the education system and reformed pensions to create privately managed funds and individual accounts (Grindle 2003).[1]

As the 1990s drew to a close, fourteen years of neoliberal economic reforms had arguably yielded impressive results. Growth averaged 4.8 percent from 1995 through 1998 (Inter-American Development Bank 2006), and inflation was no longer a primary concern. However, the benefits of the impressive growth rates were not evenly distributed. In 1998, the real urban minimum wage was 37 percent of what it had been in 1980 (Kurtz 2004). By the time Hugo Banzer (who became Bolivia's president in 1997) privatized Cochabamba's municipal water company in 1999, more than 70 percent of the national population remained below the poverty line (Nickson and Vargas 2002, 110).[2] The Gini Index hit 57.9 the same year. Furthermore, Bolivia's growth rate took a

---

[1] The Education Reform Act did trigger a response, largely among teachers, who took to the streets in large numbers in March 1995. They were not, however, able to mobilize significant opposition outside of their own ranks (although the peasants' union did block roads on occasion in solidarity with the teachers' union). Sánchez de Lozada also had to contend with opposition to the Zero Coca program. The program was not a market-oriented reform, but rather a response to U.S. pressure to reduce Bolivian coca production. The peasants' union (Confederation of Rural Workers of Bolivia [CSUTCB]), dominated largely by coca growers in the Chapare, led mobilizations against the government's coca eradication efforts. The movement culminated in August–September 1994 with the "March for Life, Coca, and National Sovereignty" that began in Villa Tunari and ended in La Paz. Neither movement galvanized the kind of broad-based resistance that would emerge in Cochabamba in 2000.

[2] See also World Bank (2006), which estimates that 62.7 percent of the national population (81.7 percent of the rural population and 50.6 percent of the urban population) lived in poverty in 1999. Although the figures do not agree, the point is clear – poverty was widespread.

dramatic turn, slowing to less than half a percent (Inter-American Development Bank 2006).

Privatization of the Cochabamban water system began in 1997 when the Bolivian government announced that it would offer SEMAPA, the Cochabamban municipal water company, to private bidders. The government entertained no serious bids until 1999 when it "made the conditions more 'flexible,' and at this point the only enterprise that showed interest was Aguas del Tunari" (Assies 2003, 21).[3] The final contract granted Aguas del Tunari a forty-year concession and what amounted to monopoly rights over the region's water. Law 2029, signed by President Banzer on October 29, 1999, served to legitimate the contract itself, granting private control to any wells that had been locally paid for, built, managed, or run.[4] On November 1, Aguas del Tunari assumed management of community-based water resources and residents were expected to pay accordingly. By January, Cochabambans from every class, age, and occupation were in the streets protesting the contract.[5]

The water wars were not the first time Bolivians took to the streets during the neoliberal era. An indigenous movement emerged in the Amazon in the early 1980s (prior to the adoption of the NEP), focusing on concerns of indigenous autonomy and territory (see Yashar 2005). The movement garnered significant national attention in 1990 with a March for Territory and Dignity, which helped to secure a number of indigenous territories via executive decree. Bolivian unions mounted powerful opposition to the NEP in 1985 and 1986, but were quickly demobilized by a state of siege. In 1994 coca growers mobilized to resist Sánchez de Lozada's Zero Coca plan, coordinating a "March for Life, Coca, and National Sovereignty" that began in Villa Tunari and ended in La Paz (see Yashar 2005). Teachers took to the streets in large numbers to protest education reform in 1995 (see Gill 2000). Road blockades occurred regularly throughout the country, and residents of La Paz and El Alto repeatedly demonstrated their ability to shut down both cities for twenty-four-hour "*paros*" (stoppages) to draw attention to any number of issues, from garbage collection to road construction.[6]

---

[3] Aguas del Tunari was a subsidiary of the U.S. Bechtel company. Bechtel's relationship with Aguas del Tunari was not uncovered until protests were well under way.

[4] The contract required the changing of Bolivian law (the passage of Law 2029) for it to be legal.

[5] Protests remained contained to Cochabamba until April when mobilizations began to occur throughout the country, most notably in La Paz. However, even though water remained at the center of the Cochabamba movement, the protests that took place in other regions adopted other demands rooted in those protesters' own grievances. There was little coherence to the mobilizations outside of Cochabamba; I would argue that they were not part of the "movement" even if national mobilizations were clearly feeding off the events in Cochabamba.

[6] Silva (2009) groups these movements into three "waves" of anti-neoliberal contention. The first occurred in response to the NEP's initial adoption and was quickly shut down. The second occurred under Sánchez de Lozada and included limited resistance on behalf of the COB and the CSUTCB to the Capitalization Law and the Popular Participation Law, as well as the more extensive resistance to education reform and to the Zero Coca program. The third began with the water wars discussed here.

Social movement
Is sustained

With the mobilizations in Cochabamba, however, the patterns of resistance changed. Blockades were not singular events but rather part of a sustained series of actions coupled with massive street mobilizations. Furthermore, protesters did not represent a particular group of Bolivians (e.g., miners, coca growers, or indigenous communities) but rather were drawn broadly from Cochabamban society. The coalitions that formed in Cochabamba cut across long-standing cleavages and sociopolitical divisions, bringing former adversaries side by side during protest meetings, events, and negotiations. See Figure 3.1 for a brief outline of the sequence of events in the Cochabamba water wars.

The Cochabamban water wars

Cochabambans began to organize against the Aguas del Tunari contract well before the concession was signed or the company arrived in the region. A number of existing local organizations, including the *Federación Departmental Cochabambina de Regantes* [Departmental Federation of Peasant Irrigators] (FEDECOR), the College of Engineers, and a coalition of nongovernmental organzations (NGOs) and environmental groups were quick to voice their objections. The *Comité de Defensa del Agua y la Economía Popular* [Committee for the Defense of Water and the Popular Economy] (CODAEP) grew out of the opposition of local professional groups and attempted to raise public awareness about the pending changes (author interviews with Gabriel Herbas Camacho, co-founder of CODAEP, September 2008, La Paz; and Omar Fernández, former president of FEDECOR, September 2008, La Paz; Cecena 2002). The committee held a public forum in July and went door to door throughout the summer and fall to explain potential problems with the privatization plan and encourage opposition (author interviews with Herbas Camacho, September 2008, La Paz; and Fernández, September 2008, La Paz). The first protests began in the fall when FEDECOR joined with CODAEP, peasant organizations, and water user groups in the urban periphery to construct roadblocks throughout the peri-urban areas (Maldonado Rojas 2004; Bustamante et al. 2005, 79). The mobilizations caused significant local disruption and the municipal government immediately revisited the Aguas del Tunari contract. However, the negotiations resulted in few policy changes. Significant rate hikes and the monopoly over communal resources remained unaddressed (ibid., 79).

On November 1, Aguas del Tunari officially replaced SEMAPA and on November 12, FEDECOR joined forces with the *Federación Departamental de Trabajadores Fabriles de Cochabamba* [Departmental Federation of Factory Workers of Cochabamba] (Fabriles), rural and urban teachers, neighborhood organizations, university students, regional workers' associations, and CODAEP to create the Coordinator for the Defense of Water and Life [*Coordinadora de Defensa del Agua y de la Vida*] (Coordinadora). CODAEP's incorporation into the alliance broadened the constituency to include members of the NGO community, civil engineers, and other local professional organizations.

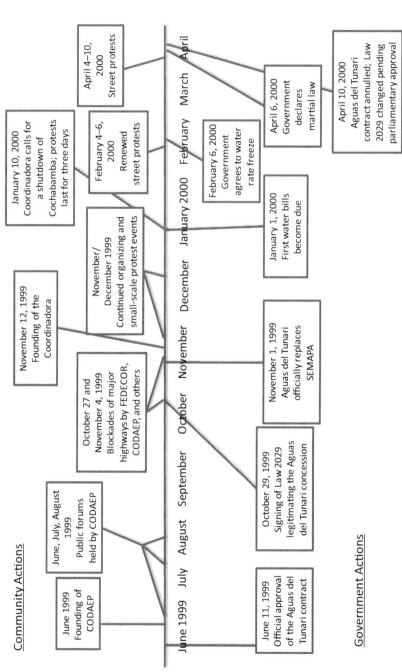

Community Actions

June 1999
Founding of CODAEP

June, July, August 1999
Public forums held by CODAEP

October 27 and November 4, 1999
Blockades of major highways by FEDECOR, CODAEP, and others

November 12, 1999
Founding of the Coordinadora

November/ December 1999
Continued organizing and small-scale protest events

January 10, 2000
Coordinadora calls for a shutdown of Cochabamba; protests last for three days

February 4–6, 2000
Renewed street protests

April 4–10, 2000
Street protests

June 1999 July August September October November December January 2000 February March April

Government Actions

June 11, 1999
Official approval of the Aguas del Tunari contract

October 29, 1999
Signing of Law 2029 legitimating the Aguas del Tunari concession

November 1, 1999
Aguas del Tunari officially replaces SEMAPA

January 1, 2000
First water bills become due

February 6, 2000
Government agrees to water rate freeze

April 6, 2000
Government declares martial law

April 10, 2000
Aguas del Tunari contract annulled; Law 2029 changed pending parliamentary approval

FIGURE 3.1. Sequence of events in Cochabamba.

Cochabambans saw their first rate hikes in early January. In some cases, hikes were as high as 200 percent (García et al. 2003; Peredo 2003; Shultz 2003), although the average increase appears to have hovered closer to 60 percent.[7] For those Cochabambans paying the lowest possible rate for their water (categorized as R2 users), the average cost of water went from 7 to 11 percent of the minimum monthly wage (355 Bs or US$60.01/month).[8] For the approximately 55 percent of Cochabambans living below the poverty line (293 Bs/month or US$41) (Instituto Nacional de Estadísticas 2006), the minimum monthly payment (assuming they were connected to the municipal water system, which many were not) would have exceeded 35 percent of income, not including additional meter fees.

At a January 10 Coordinadora meeting, the leadership decided to call for a shutdown of the city; on the morning of January 11, the water wars began. Between the 11th and the 13th, irrigators' associations effectively blocked strategic roads and neighborhood associations on the periphery set up barricades. The center of the city was closed off to vehicle traffic and storeowners closed their shops for the day. Protests shut down the regional airport as well as the two major highways into and out of the city (Shultz 2003). National governmental officials called in hundreds of police officers to control the march to the central plaza and attempt to reopen the roads. At the end of three days, government officials entered into negotiations with the Coordinadora. The water wars were far from over, but the coalition that would drive them had been defined.

Attention to water's meanings in the Cochabamban context fill in critical gaps in our understandings of how and why the movement came together in the way that it did. Water's meanings shed light on the extraordinary breadth of the coalitions that emerged, the conditions of possibility that allowed the Aguas del Tunari contract to be transformed into a political opportunity, and the extended resonance of the frames deployed.

It is difficult to understand developments in movement organizational capacity – including the broad-based nature of the initial alliance, CODAEP, and the subsequent emergence of the Coordinadora – without taking into account the ways in which different micro-level processes of meaning making could coexist within and resonate with broader frames of regional and national patrimony or ethnic heritage and local autonomy. Strong preexisting networks and ties were critical to the movement, and brokerage mechanisms were clearly at work. Cochabamba was home to a number of mobilizing structures – unions and neighborhood organizations in particular – that proved critical to the emergence of resistance in the region. Yet associational resources available to

---

[7] See http://democracyctr.org/bolivia/investigations/bolivia-investigations-the-water-revolt/bechtel-vs-bolivia/ for sample water bills. These figures reflect the increase in rates for R2 households – homes with indoor toilets but no showers.

[8] Figures are normalized for 2002.

local organizers varied little in the late 1990s, and in spite of a variety of grievances, large-scale, widespread protest did not emerge until the privatization of
water. Furthermore, similar organizational networks existed in other regions
of the country that also endured significant material hardship throughout the
neoliberal era, yet broad-based protest did not emerge in the rest of the country
until after Cochabambans had been in the streets for more than three months.
When we understand the ways in which water worked as a symbol throughout
Cochabamba we shed light on why so many networks were available to be
mobilized and why and how those brokerage mechanisms were effective.

Similarly, a focus on changes in political context cannot explain all of the
dynamics at work in Cochabamba. Local changes in the political opportunities
available to social movement organizers in the spring of 1999 – prior to any
significant mobilization – do not appear to be unique to the water movement,
and national changes in political opportunities such as, perhaps, the slow erosion of Bolivia's major political parties (see Slater and Simmons 2013) or the
election of a conservative former military dictator to the presidency were not
unique to Cochabamba. Attention to this dynamic cannot explain the mechanisms at work in bringing a diverse group of Cochabambans to the streets in
the movement's early months.

Collective action frames play a central role in the pages that follow.[9] The
threat to water resonated with Bolivian, Cochabamban, and indigenous nationalist master frames, allowing the issue to appeal even to those not severely
affected by the rise in water rates. One of the tasks of this book is to help us
understand why these frames were available to this particular movement at
this particular moment.

EARLY OPPOSITION: THE FORMATION OF CODAEP

Early opposition to the Aguas del Tunari contract foreshadowed the diverse nature
of the movement that was to come. With the formal approval of the contract on
June 11, 1999, a small group of professionals, including environmentalists, engineers, teachers, lawyers, and economists, met to discuss how best to organize
opposition (author interviews with Delgadillo, February 2010, Cochabamba;
and Herbas Camacho, September 2008, La Paz; Herbas Camacho 2004). They
created the Committee for the Defense of Water and the Popular Economy[10]

---

[9] I use the term "frame" in the way it is generally deployed in social movement scholarship. See,
for example, Snow and Benford (1988, 137), who describe a frame as an "interpretive schema
that simplifies and condenses the 'world out there' by selectively punctuating and encoding
objects, situations, events, experiences, and sequences of action." Framing refers to "the process
of defining what is going on in a situation in order to encourage protest" (Noakes and Johnston
2005, 2). While these usages draw on Goffman (1974), they imply a far narrower conceptualization of the term.

[10] Also called the Committee for Defense of Water and the Family Economy.

and began to work to inform Cochabambans of the impending changes to their water supply. Beginning in mid-June, committee members met twice weekly in the Plaza Principal to distribute flyers and speak with residents (author interviews with Gonzalo Maldonado Rojas, January 2010, Cochabamba; and Herbas Camacho, September 2008, La Paz; Herbas Camacho 2004). According to early leader Marcelo Delgadillo, the movement was "all impulse driven at this point, there was little strategy ... but it was clear that there was far more going on than an environmental threat. This was about survival; a resource of life was under threat" (author interview with Delgadillo, February 2010, Cochabamba).

It is impossible to explain the emergence of CODAEP without engaging the role water had played in Cochabamba's recent and extended history, and what it meant to Cochabamba's professional sector in particular. A diverse group of individuals, associations, and interests joined CODAEP (and later the Coordinadora); for them, water was one of Albro's (2005) "points of mutual recognition." But it is hard to explain their participation if we understand water only in material terms. Even though CODAEP's founders anticipated that rates would rise, most members would not have to make life-altering material trade-offs in order to pay their bills; members were largely comfortable middle-class Cochabamban professionals. The "point of recognition" came through the central role water had played in the region and the conception that privatization meant far more than potential rate hikes; the contract was a betrayal of a long regional effort to secure and distribute a sustainable water supply.

For nearly fifty years, Cochabamban engineers, architects, economists, environmentalists, and lawyers had been researching and advocating for various solutions to the region's limited access to water. The debates about the benefits of Misicuni or Corani – two extensive construction projects proposed to help alleviate water shortages discussed in Chapter 2 – had raged within meetings of the Engineers' Society and inside the mayor's office for almost two decades. Communities commissioned studies on water table depth and debates took place over well construction. Studies about water loss and quality as well as corruption within SEMAPA made front-page news. And every year, as the dry season reached its final weeks, conversations revolved around water – how many days a week people were receiving it, how much sediment came in it, and whether residents would make it until the rains without a massive shutdown.[11] An epistemic community of Cochabamban professionals formed with common water-related policy goals and experiences at the center.

Every CODAEP founder interviewed for this research offered lengthy treatments of how water had been a constant reference in both personal and professional life. Drought meant that water projects came across the desks of engineers and architects. It also made water a central concern for

---

[11] See Chapter 2 for an in-depth treatment of each of these factors.

environmentalists. Even business leaders were affected as limited water supplies put constraints on growth in manufacturing and other business developments. One architect commented that "we all shared an interest – water was
affecting each of us" and the foundation of CODAEP was simply a logical
outgrowth of that overlap (author interview, February 2010, Cochabamba).
The communities that formed around water were both imagined and quotidian – water was the subject of face-to-face professional discussions and something that lawyers or engineers, for example, could imagine that other lawyers
or engineers whom they might not know or ever meet were also talking about.
The idea that "water was affecting each of us" expressed earlier comes from
face-to-face interactions but refers to a community beyond people the speaker
knows directly. For many of these early activists, opposition to the Aguas del
Tunari contract provided common ground. They did not need to discuss the
merits of Misicuni or Corani or propose solutions to SEMAPA's failures –
debates that could have fueled disagreements in the past. Instead, they could
unite around common claims that privatization would exacerbate the region's
water struggles.

Participants understood not only that water was important to them, but
also that it was grounded in a shared set of experiences that worked to make
it important to the broader community. Water was understood to affect not
"me," but "us," and participants spoke as though they expected everyone else
to understand the threat in similar, communal terms. Environmental activist
and CODAEP founder Gabriel Herbas Camacho recalled, "We knew this was
important to every Cochabamban. We each fought in different ways, but it was
our shared fight" (author interview with Herbas Camacho, September 2008,
La Paz). Even if the particularities of how water affected environmentalists,
engineers, or architects were different, a sense of a communal "us" emerged.

These understandings quickly translated into collaboration. Water became
an issue around which groups that had worked together little in the past –
environmentalists, teachers, engineers, economists, and architects, to name
just a few – could easily unite, even if the particular meanings drawing participants into the coalition were different. For Herbas, the central issues
revolved around the environmental community's long history of commitment
to water-related issues. The valley's search for water had raised environmental concerns and groups had formed to evaluate the potential environmental
impact of the Misicuni and Corani projects, as well as to advocate for sustainable water policies (author interview with Herbas Camacho, February 2008,
La Paz). For engineer Antonio Siles, the issue at stake was the technical quality of the project itself: "it was simply a bad project," he stated. "After all
these years, we deserved a better project" (author interview, January 2010,
Cochabamba). For many of Cochabamba's professionals, water was part of
their regional identity with respect to both a historically grounded pride in
cultivation and recent efforts to overcome shortages.

CODAEP's actions slowly drew attention from additional, already established Cochabamban organizations. Midsummer, the leadership of *Pueblo en Marcha* [People/Town on the Move] (PUMA), a small organization of political activists, joined CODAEP's biweekly meetings in the plaza (author interviews with Delgadillo, January 2010, Cochabamba; and Víctor Gutiérrez, January 2010, Cochabamba). PUMA had already been organizing politically against neoliberal reform; the fight against Aguas del Tunari was a natural fit, and PUMA leadership argued there was potential for widespread participation. PUMA activist Víctor Gutiérrez recalls, "I knew it could be big – *campesinos*, *regantes*, families in the city – everyone cared about water. Maybe for different reasons, but it was important to everyone" (author interview with Gutiérrez, January 2010, Cochabamba). Movement leaders noted the potential for unity around water as a grievance from the start, and they began to frame their message, discourse, and outreach accordingly. Attention to the different ways in which water symbolized community to different people, and to how individuals understood those communities to be threatened by the Aguas del Tunari contract, explains why these frames were not only possible, but also successful. Separate mobilization identifications could coalesce at the meso level without threatening participants' individual conceptions of what was at stake. Water provided an opportunity for unity, but to understand why and how the opportunity was understood as such we must pay attention to water's role in the Cochabamban imaginary.

BRIDGING THE URBAN–RURAL DIVIDE

Even with the combined efforts of CODAEP and PUMA, resistance remained marginal and largely urban through the end of September 1999. However, with the passage of the legal prerequisite for the Aguas del Tunari contract – Law 2029 – in October, the dynamics began to shift. On October 27, one day prior to the official passage of Law 2029, FEDECOR joined CODAEP in Vinto, a Cochabamba suburb, to block the highway connecting Cochabamba to Oruro and La Paz – a central national artery – and demand the repeal of the law.[12]

The cooperation between urban Cochabambans, many of whom had migrated to the region in the wake of the privatization of the mines in the mid-1980s, and rural groups was particularly noteworthy. Urban–rural differences – both in policy concerns and in organizational structures – ran deep. Political scientist Spronk writes, "despite their common indigenous heritage, miners tended to view peasants as 'backwards' politically" (2007b, 12). These understandings appear to be rooted in conflicts that arose during the 1970s when political leaders used "anti-worker policies" as a wedge issue to divide the two groups. Policies toward

[12] See Chapter 2 for a discussion of FEDECOR's origins and activities.

unions, and miners in particular, had little impact on *campesinos'* daily life; *campesinos* were largely supportive of political leaders' efforts to curtail the miners' power and received benefits in exchange for political support (see Cusicanqui 1990, 105). The war of the wells had brought the two sectors into conflict only a few years earlier; cooperation was largely unprecedented, particularly on the scope and scale seen during the water wars.

Yet at the same time as the blockade bridged regional divisions, it also literalized a divide between Cochabamba and the nation's functional capital.[13] The blockade was a physical manifestation of the ideational divide between the valley's inhabitants and the officials in La Paz who had made, and would continue to make, policies with little understanding of local meaning and practice.[14] Urban and rural understandings of and relationships with water were both recognized and contained in the regional identifications that brought Cochabambans together to resist the Aguas del Tunari contract.

The *regantes'* participation in opposition to the Aguas del Tunari contract and Law 2029 seems logical – both policy changes struck at the core of the *regantes'* daily life on personal and professional levels. For *regantes*, both policies threatened imagined and quotidian communities in fundamental and tangible ways. Water is the core of *regantes'* professional lives. To threaten their well-established practices for constructing, regulating, and monitoring rural irrigation systems was to threaten the strong professional ties that formed not only through daily work, but also through the organization of FEDECOR itself. The utility of an organization that had served to channel collective grievances, unite disparate groups throughout the valleys of the department (province), and cultivate empowerment and independence was threatened.

But it was not simply about the community structures that FEDECOR maintained and what those structures meant to Cochabamban *regantes*. Meanings associated with an imagined community were also at stake. The *usos y costumbres* vary from region to region, and the practices associated with the Andean cosmovision are not uniform. Throughout the water wars, protestors repeatedly held up an abstract notion of the Andean cosmovision as both sacred and at risk. In a short film on the water wars, the narrator declares that Law 2029 prohibited *campesinos* from using water as they had since "time immemorial ... the law *pretendía* [aspired to or attempted to] eliminate peasant tradition" (Rioja Vasquez 2002). The violation is described as something in which not only peasants, but also Cochabambans and even Bolivians more broadly, had a stake. Here, even in the face of the urban–rural divides that dominated Cochabamban political discourse, the rural serves as a synecdoche for both the

---

[13] The legal capital of Bolivia remains Sucre, yet most matters of national government take place in La Paz. The only major exception is the country's Supreme Court, which continues to be housed in Sucre.

[14] See Simmons (2011) for a discussion of the ways in which divisions between La Paz and Cochabamba influenced the trajectory of the movement.

regional and the national. To undermine conceptions of a rural way of life was to threaten Cochabamba and Bolivia.

Even those who do not hail from Quechua or Aymara families[15] speak of the importance of the *Pachamama*, or Mother Earth, and practice *k'oas* to give thanks before opening or closing a river. *Regantes* claim to have understood the Aguas del Tunari contract and Law 2029 to violate these long-held beliefs and customs and hence to be an affront to a widely practiced way of life. The community at stake included not only the people with whom they worked directly (their quotidian community) but also individuals on the other side of the valley, the other side of the country, or even those who had lived centuries before. "This is the way we have always done things, the way our ancestors did things. They cannot ask us to change them," one *regante* told me (author interview with Cochabamban *regante*, September 2008, Cochabamba).[16] The failure to protect *usos y costumbres* violated perceptions of imagined communities that spanned history and geography. The *regantes* fought for what they called an Andean way of life.

FEDECOR President Omar Fernández recalls the organization's initial involvement in opposition to Aguas del Tunari and Law 2029: "From the start we were worried about how we would be affected. And then we learned more. We saw that *usos y costumbres* were not being respected, that they weren't even a part of the contract. So we knew we had to act" (author interview with Fernández, September 2008, La Paz). The material and the ideational are intertwined in Fernández's statement. Fernández refers to the need for explicit incorporation of preexisting water governance structures as outlined by local *regantes'* associations and the broader idea that practices considered part of tradition should be respected.

Throughout the summer, the *regante* leadership organized seminars and workshops, developing alternative proposals and informing constituencies throughout the Cochabamba Valley (author interviews with Carmen Peredo, August 2008, Cochabamba; and Fernández, September 2008, La Paz; Peredo et al. 2004). Echoing the language leaders used to describe the emergence of CODAEP, Fernández recalled that the October and November blockades seemed like "logical results" of the summer's seminars (author interview with Fernández, September 2008, La Paz). They wanted to see "how far [they] could go" (ibid.). *Regante* leadership was overwhelmed by the turnout.[17] One participant reflected, "[T]hey [the central government] were taking away our rituals,

---

[15] Identification as Quechua is far more prevalent in Cochabamba than identification as Aymara, although immigration that began with the closures of the mines and continued through 2013 is slowly changing this distribution.

[16] Some of the interviews were conducted in confidentiality and the names of the interviewees are withheld by mutual agreement.

[17] *Regantes* from Valle Alto did not participate to the same extent as those from the other Cochabamban valleys. Omar Fernández cites poor organization among Valle Alto's *regantes* as the explanation for the low turnout. His observation points to the importance of the factors

our way of relating to the water, of managing it. It was our lives we were defending" (author interview with blockade participant, February 2010, Cochabamba).
This participant's observation references far more than defending physical life –
it was, instead, a way of life. Water evoked, at once, attachments to imagined
and to quotidian communities representing perceived ties to a past, a way of life
in the present, a neighborhood, a region, and an ethnic group.

Leaders from both CODAEP and FEDECOR considered the October 27
blockade successful as it garnered significant attention from the national government and raised awareness among the general population. But the negotiated outcome was unsatisfactory to movement participants and leaders alike;
government representatives agreed to vague language surrounding the revision
of both Law 2029 and the Aguas del Tunari contract (author interview with
Delgadillo, January 2010, Cochabamba).

GROWING URBAN PARTICIPATION: THE CIVIC
COMMITTEE AND *JUNTAS VECINALES*

The coalition continued to grow, now largely through increased urban participation. Most notably, the Cochabamban Civic Committee officially joined the
ranks of the opposition. *Juntas vecinales* [urban neighborhood organizations
that are together called FEJUVE], acting largely through neighborhood-by-
neighborhood leadership, also increased their involvement and ultimately
proved a powerful tool for bringing Cochabambans, neighborhood by neighborhood, to the streets.[18] *Juntas vecinales* were one of the ways community
structures were already in place to inform, organize, and channel movement
activities.[19]

---

included in a resource mobilization argument – without strong organizational structures already
in place, the movement could not have succeeded – but why those resources were marshaled
effectively for this grievance and not others remains the central question.

[18] *Juntas vecinales* gained political power and prominence as a result of the 1994 Law of Popular
Participation. They are often called *organizaciones territoriales de base* (territorial base
organizations, OTBs) in rural areas. In an effort to decentralize resources and responsibilities,
the Law of Popular Participation transferred 20 percent of Bolivia's budget to 311 municipalities and "mandated grassroots participation in local planning and budgetary oversight"
(Kohl 2003, 153). The law officially recognized already existing OTBs – and encouraged the
development of more – giving them the responsibility for community development plans and
implementation. Although the law is not without its problems or detractors, grassroots community organizations grew and strengthened with local residents in both urban and rural
areas taking increasing initiative for community development.

[19] While *juntas vecinales* played a key role in the mobilization, they are only one piece of the
puzzle. First, the organizations were not unique to Cochabamba – they grew and strengthened
throughout Bolivia. For example, FEJUVE El Alto had been mounting various small-scale protests against everything from high electricity prices to poor garbage collection since at least as
early as 1996. Second, these organizations had been accumulating strength since the implementation of the law in 1994. Why the Cochabamban water reform would provoke such a powerful

On November 1, Aguas del Tunari officially replaced SEMAPA; on November 4, Cochabamban *regantes* led a second blockade, this time on a larger scale and with increased participation from both urban and rural groups. The *regantes* were joined now not only by CODAEP, but also the Cochabamban Civic Committee and local *juntas vecinales* (Peredo et al. 2004). Omar Fernández called this urban–rural alliance "a peculiar characteristic" (Peredo et al. 2004, 126) of the November blockades, clearly alluding to the unique nature of the collaboration and recalling the divisions that had surfaced so clearly only a year earlier during conflicts over proposed wells in peri-urban areas. The coalition successfully blocked both the highway linking Cochabamba to Santa Cruz and Sucre (the second major artery that passes through Cochabamba) and the Cochabamba–Oruro–La Paz connection.

The participation of both the Civic Committee and the *juntas vecinales* demonstrated the broad, urban resistance to Aguas del Tunari's arrival. Civic committees emerged throughout Bolivia in the 1950s and 1960s to articulate and represent regional interests. Although not officially tied to the government, they achieved local recognition as legitimate representatives of civic interests, and policy makers often included them in government plans and negotiations. The Aguas del Tunari contract was no different. Edgar Montaño, president of the Cochabamban Civic Committee until August 1999, participated in the contract negotiations (author interview with Mauricio Barrientos, former president of the Cochabamban Civic Committee, February 2010, Cochabamba; García et al. 2003; "Reyes Villa, Montaño, y otros aprobaron tarifazo" 2000). Montaño and Mauricio Barrientos, his successor as Civic Committee president, initially favored both the concept and the contract (author interview with Barrientos, February 2010, Cochabamba; "Reyes Villa, Montaño, y otros aprobaron tarifazo" 2000). It was not until the extent of the rate hikes became clear that Civic Committee leadership began to call for widespread resistance; participation of the Civic Committee in early protests was a reflection of popular demand, not the result of top-down instigation or leadership. Even years later, Barrientos declared his commitment to water privatization as the only way to "modernize" Cochabamba (author interview with Barrientos, February 2010, Cochabamba). Yet as his constituents were pushing for opposition, Barrientos brought the Civic Committee officially into the movement's fold.

response within both urban *juntas vecinales* and rural OTBs cannot be explained simply by pointing to the financial and organizational resources these groups began to develop and deploy in 1994. The organizational resources of these grassroots organizations were available to be mobilized to oppose market reforms in any region of the country and had existed for five years prior to the water wars. Here the point is not that rising levels of social organization should rapidly translate into social protest. Instead, it is that Cochabamba (like El Alto) was highly organized *and* experiencing a variety of grievances. Yet it was a threat to water that sparked broad-based, sustained mobilization.

Cochabamba's *juntas vecinales* participated under similar circumstances. FEJUVE President José Orellana was in favor of the contract and did not encourage or support the participation of his member organizations (author interview with Orellana, FEJUVE President, February 2010, Cochabamba; and Oscar Olivera, Fabriles Executive Secretary in 1999, September 2008, Cochabamba); individual *juntas*, without region-level direction, decided to work together with the *regantes* to mount the blockades. The Barrio Petrolero *junta vecinal* (located in the southern part of Cochabamba City where most residents live well below the poverty line) was one of the first to become actively involved in resistance. Raúl Águilar, its president, explains the involvement of his neighbors with "had-to" (*tenía que*) language: "We had to organize. And to organize other OTBs as well. We went door to door explaining the problems to come" (author interview with Raúl Águilar, president of the Barrio Petrolero *junta vecinal*, January 2010, Cochabamba). Águilar's language of necessity works to make a moment of political contingency seem like a moral imperative. He suggests that no other course of action was imaginable, yet resistance was far from inevitable. The language describes the origins of Águilar's participation, yet it also took on a life of its own as the protests grew. By continuing to argue that they "had to" organize, the ability of participants to imagine another course of action became increasingly difficult. The affective orientation appears not to be one of fear or futility, but hope (see Pearlman 2013). Águilar's language was not unique. A film on the water wars uses similar discourse as the narrator says that "what they did in the water war was what they had to do" (Rioja Vasquez 2002). The outcome was, of course, unknown, and participants had no reason to think that the protests would end in the annulment of the contract. Yet their words suggest that, even in the face of uncertainty, doing something was the only imaginable option.

Águilar's reflections also reveal understandings of the role of the state in water provision. He argues, "it was the obligation of the state to provide affordable water. They didn't, so we made our own wells. Then [with the arrival of Aguas del Tunari] they were going to take away these wells. With them we would lose our dignity, our community" (author interview with Águilar, January 2010, Cochabamba).[20] The comments expose a tension in what is expected of the state while directly invoking water's community-related meanings. There is both a longing for the state to fulfill the basic needs of the community and a lack of trust when the state travels down a path that could result in the provision of those very needs. The state had never provided water to most communities in the Southern Zone, and part of the promise of the Aguas del Tunari contract was that the company would have sufficient capital to invest in new connections. Whether these connections actually would have happened

---

[20] Recall that the Aguas del Tunari contract included provisions for the company to manage privately constructed communal wells. The contract gave the company the right to regulate and charge for water provision from wells constructed by local water cooperatives.

is a subject of debate; even so, for those Cochabambans who did not have reliable water connections (or any connection at all, for that matter), an absent state appeared to be preferable to a private company. With an absent state Cochabambans knew what they needed to do to meet their personal water needs – they dug wells and formed cooperatives. If poor, access to water was at least predictable. Privatization rendered relationships with water insecure. One elderly woman who never had a municipal water connection told me, "We do it with our own hands now and we know what we get. With the private company? Who knows. They'll charge whatever they want" (author interview, February 2010, Cochabamba). Her comments were not unique. Residents routinely expressed a lack of trust in a private company and fears that prices would be unpredictable. *- economic factors*

Yet even in its absence, the state helped shape these Cochabamban communities. By leaving neighborhoods to fend for themselves in their pursuit of water, the state created opportunities for community activism and connection. Notions of community became directly tied to water management and the practice of maintenance and management produced and reproduced community ties. These communities then found themselves at the center of the perceived threat and quickly emerged as loci for resistance. As outlined in the previous chapter, Cochabamban communities not hooked up to the municipal water infrastructure developed their own systems for accessing water, ranging from the simple to the sophisticated. With many of these systems came community organization, interaction, and perceptions of independence and self-sufficiency.[21] It was in the very absence of the state that community ties were forged.

Carlos Oropeza echoed the sentiments of other Southern Zone interviewees when he said, "thanks to water, we are organized ... we have dignity. Water gets us to work together ... The contract would have taken that away so we all participated" (author interview with Carlos Oropeza, February 2010, Cochabamba). The Aguas del Tunari contract threatened not only those who would pay increased rates, but also those whose hard-won structures of local governance and reciprocity would be put in jeopardy. Because of water's material role in survival, local communities had formed to help ensure reliable access. Through these communities, water took on the meanings that Oropeza cites – dignity, organization, and participation. In threatening established mechanisms for accessing and regulating water, the contract threatened these community structures and with them firmly held notions of community pride. It did not require leadership from the FEJUVE or Civic Committee presidents to tap into these anxieties; from the beginning, participation was truly a bottom-up phenomenon driven by the meanings water had taken on.

The failings of the SEMAPA services tie many Cochabambans together, either intimately through quotidian communities, or in a mediated fashion through a shared knowledge that Cochabambans throughout the region's

---

[21] Some of these systems recall Ostrom's (1990, 1994) work on common pool resources.

urban and peri-urban areas face similar daily challenges as they seek access to reliable, affordable water. The challenges to accessing water in Cochabamba have become a regional identifier. They are a shared experience that helps to define the Cochabamban community. As a result, many Cochabambans perceived the Aguas del Tunari contract as a threat both to the quotidian communities that formed through the daily struggle to access water and to a regional notion of Cochabamban patrimony and independence.

THE FORMATION OF THE COORDINADORA

On November 5, 1999, just twenty-four hours after the blockade began, leaders of the various participating *juntas vecinales* and FEDECOR agreed to sit down with representatives of regional and national governments to negotiate an end to the protest.[22] The participating individuals reached various agreements, including the commitment to maintain the *regantes'* access to established water sources in accordance with the *usos y costumbres* of each valley (Peredo et al. 2004). Movement leadership called off the blockade, claiming to have achieved a significant victory. In spite of participation in the negotiations by high-level government officials (including the minister of housing and the Cochabamban superintendent of water), opposition leaders immediately called the validity of the agreement into question. CODAEP's legal experts quickly pointed out that the concession contract took legal precedence over the agreement signed at Vinto. Omar Fernández observed that "what we had accomplished in Vinto was a step, but it was necessary to modify or annul the Contract of Concession with Aguas del Tunari and Law 2029" (quoted in Peredo et al. 2004, 130; author interview with Delgadillo, January 2010, Cochabamba). Empowered by the impressive participation in mounting the blockades, FEDECOR, CODAEP, and various neighborhood groups continued to inform Cochabambans about the pending changes to Cochabamban water.

With a variety of civic groups now mobilized to protest the Aguas del Tunari contract and Law 2029, movement leaders worked to better coordinate strategies for how to proceed. The organization that grew out of this coordination effort – the Coordinator for the Defense of Water and Life [*Coordinadora de Defensa del Agua y de la Vida*] (Coordinadora) – served as the center of the movement through the final April protests. The Coordinadora brought together strong preexisting organizations to work together in common cause – something they had not done when faced with market reforms in the prior fifteen years. In response to a broad call from FEDECOR, leaders of the movement met on

---

[22] Importantly, CODAEP did not participate in the negotiations. Its participation might have averted the disappointing outcome for movement leaders insofar as a CODAEP legal expert may have been able to alert participants to the nonbinding nature of the final agreement (author interview with Marcelo Delgadillo, January 21, 2010, Cochabamba; author interviews with Víctor Gutiérrez, January 2010, Cochabamba).

November 12 to discuss their next steps. That evening, those in attendance founded the Coordinadora, bringing together FEDECOR and CODAEP with Fabriles, the *Central Obrera Departamental* [Departmental Workers' Union] (COD), the teachers' union, the transportation workers' union, the peasants' union, and others. The alliance spanned not only urban–rural divides, but also social and class boundaries. Local leaders who had never met before were now seated around the same table, determining how best to work together. Omar Fernández recalls, "it was in this meeting that I first met the leaders Oscar Olivera [Fabriles Executive Secretary] and Walter Antezana [COD Executive Secretary]. I didn't know what type of leaders they were, if I could trust them, etc., but this is how the activities of the Coordinadora began" (quoted in Peredo et al. 2004, 131). Without prior experience working together, or any foundation for mutual trust, Cochabambans from various walks of life came together to form the Coordinadora.[23] Urban–rural alliances bringing together peasants and professionals were evident in the October and November blockades, yet not until the formation of the Coordinadora did a truly broad-based movement begin.[24]

Water brought engineers, teachers, economists, factory workers, peasants, irrigators, university students, the unemployed, heads of households, and business owners together to fight for the same cause. Oscar Olivera's comments echo those of his peers: "Before, we tried to resist the pension reform, but it was only us – just the workers. But water is everywhere. It belongs to everyone and no one. ... It is part of our history, part of who we are, all of us in Cochabamba ... it was like giving a piece of our territory away. So of course we came together" (author interview with Olivera, September 2008, Cochabamba). Omar Fernández remarked that "water made unity, it is an element that reaches everyone, this is what made the Coordinadora" (author interview with Fernández, September 2008, La Paz). Water's historical and contemporary roles in the region combined, allowing water to be perceived as shared by groups as disparate as *regantes*, factory workers, and business owners.

Even as the Coordinadora began to mobilize for larger marches, neighborhood affiliates continued to organize on a local level. The movement was not

---

[23] A "horizontal" leadership structure, naming only rotating *portavoces* or "spokesmen" as Coordinadora members who tried to maintain a "collective authority," appears to have emerged in an equally smooth fashion (Herbas Camacho 2004).

[24] Social scientist Assies (2003) credits the shift to connections made between FEDECOR and the *Federación de Trabajadores Fabriles de Cochabamba* [Federation of Factory Workers of Cochabamba] (FDTFC) (the factory workers' union). My interviews, however, suggest that the Coordinadora's founding can be explained by the combination of widespread distrust of the Civic Committee (by signing the Aguas del Tunari contract, the committee lost the credibility to represent Cochabamban dissatisfaction with the privatization) and the broad appeal of water as a grievance (author interviews with Walter Antezana, Mauricio Delgadillo, Víctor Gutiérrez, Gabriel Herbas Camacho, Maldonado Rojas, and Oscar Olivera, 2008 and 2010, Cochabamba and La Paz). Notably, neither Civic Committee nor FEJUVE leadership attended the November 12 meeting – even while their membership participated in Coordinadora-convoked marches, the leadership of both organizations distanced themselves from the Coordinadora's activities.

simply a product of a central or prominent leadership structure; it emerged from the neighborhoods themselves. FEJUVEs across the region began to convoke independent marches. On December 13, Fejuve-Pueblo rallied close to 199 *juntas vecinales* from the Cercado province (which includes Cochabamba City) to march against what they understood to be the impending 35 percent rate increase ("Fejuve-Pueblo: Resistencia civil contra del tarifazo" 1999). With little traditional social movement leadership, Cochabambans were taking to the streets.

As soon as the scale of the impending rate increase became clear, the Civic Committee and the FEJUVE leadership joined the Coordinadora in opposition to the Aguas del Tunari contract. The Civic Committee and FEJUVE, however, focused on possibilities for renegotiation, not annulment, and stayed largely away from discussions of changes to Law 2029 (author interviews with Barrientos February 2010, Cochabamba; and Orellana, February 2010, Cochabamba). On December 20, the Civic Committee called an Assembly of the *Cochabambinidad* and approved plans for a citywide shutdown on January 11. The declared purpose was to oppose rate increases for services that had not improved ("Cochabamba en emergencia exige rebaja de tarifas de agua" 1999). A photograph that appeared in *Opinión* shows businessmen, authorities, and leaders in attendance at the meeting, and the article quotes the "representative of private business to the Civic Committee," Carlos Olmedo, as saying, "we have to adopt protest tactics to defend the interest of the Cochabambans" ("Cochabamba en emergencia exige rebaja de tarifas de agua" 1999).

The Coordinadora, however, did not want to wait until January 11 and organized its first demonstration for December 22. Approximately fifty organizations participated in a march to the center of Cochabamba, where they called for a renegotiation of the Aguas del Tunari contract and of Law 2029 ("Cochabambinos protestarán hoy contra subida de precios" 1999). The participation of the transport union was particularly notable. The local newspaper *Opinión* reported that the transportation union participation came after nineteen years of silence. Maclovio Zapata, the union's leader, said they had not joined past marches addressing other economic reforms "because there were misunderstandings with the other labor organizations, but now the problem affects all Cochabambans" (quoted in "Cochabamba unida, rechaza reajuste de tarifas de agua" 1999). The threat to water created a perception of shared destiny. In spite of shared grievances in the past, Cochabamban unions had been unable to unite to fight for shared goals. The education workers, the Fabriles, and the transportation union, for example, had fought for their individual issues, often antagonizing other unions in the process. Water was a common language that each union could speak. A threat to it led many to put divisions behind them in an effort to fight for "all Cochabambans."

In early January perceptions of unity manifested in calls for large-scale protest. The first water bills came due on January 1, and the Coordinadora called for a popular refusal to pay. COD Executive Secretary Antezana echoed the Civic Committee's earlier call when he urged Cochabambans not to pay their water bills, arguing that the rate increases were "an increase for nothing because we are not receiving more water or better service" ("Comenzará hoy resitencia civil por el 'tarifazo' de agua potable" 2000). On January 4, the Coordinadora, including representatives from CODAEP, COD, FDTFC, FEJUVE, and the Federation of Auto Transport [*Federación Sindical del Autotransporte*] (FEDAT), among others, called for protests against the rate increases ("Coordinadora definó acciones contra el 'tarifazo' del agua" 2000). At a January 10 meeting, the Coordinadora decided to call for a shutdown of the city to coincide with the Civic Committee's actions scheduled for the following day ("Comité Cívico no busca anual el contrato, sino modificarlo" 2000).

Ultimately, water simultaneously threatened perceived material interests and indexed some combination of nation, region, ethnicity, heritage, or local community. These varied symbols brought Cochabamba's disparate groups together, apparently united in a single cause. I do not seek to undervalue the importance of the material claim. In fact, many interviewees cited the rate increase as the "*detonante*" (detonator) for the large-scale protests in December.[25] Yet while the rate increases mattered – I do not expect that we would have seen large-scale mobilization without them – there is clearly something more at work. In the days to come, those who could afford the rate hikes, as well as those who were not connected to the municipal water system, could be found holding banners and flags in the streets and invoking a violation of *usos y costumbres* and "the" Andean cosmovision. As the president of Barrio Petrolero put it, the reform "affected everyone; it did not matter what salary or sector" (author interview, Águilar February 2010, Cochabamba). The rate hike hit Cochabambans in more than simply their *bolsillo* (pocket/wallet), providing opportunities to both the leaders who had battled for years to oppose neoliberalism and to those who had never imagined themselves at the center of a political campaign.

Yet even as the evidence supports the claim that we can only understand the dynamics of resistance to the Aguas del Tunari contract by paying attention to water's meanings, attention to these meanings raises additional questions. If water symbolized imagined and quotidian communities in Cochabamba, and the perceived threat to community is part of what produced widespread resistance, why hadn't decades of state-generated threats to water generated similar political protest? Cochabambans had long faced water-related challenges. Many of these challenges came at the hands of a state that proved unable to provide reliable water services. Why did they wait to mobilize around water issues until the services were privatized?

[25] Although rate changes varied dramatically, with some residents claiming as much as a 200 percent increase, users throughout the region appeared to have experienced systematic increases of more than 60 percent ("Nueva tarifa pone en apuros a Aguas del Tunari y gobierno" 2000; Shultz n.d.).

In fact, Cochabambans had been mobilizing around water for decades – they had mobilized in individual neighborhoods to demand improved SEMAPA services, they had mobilized to advocate for the Misicuni project, they had mobilized to form an irrigators' union when a new water law threatened irrigators' interests, and they had mobilized to both fight for and try to stop new wells in peri-urban areas. The water wars were unique because these groups, many of which had been organizing around sector-, class-, or neighborhood-specific claims, found a common cause without challenging the particularities of the understandings of water that emerged through context-dependent relationships. Common cause was, in part, easier to find because the state's role in creating water threats was at once more ambiguous and more regionally varied than the perceived threat posed by Aguas del Tunari. Water-related demands on the state had varied – different individuals and group members had different perceptions of priorities and interests when it came to making claims. Solutions to problems of scarcity, corruption, and poor service might look different depending on differences in water-related practices. Disparate understandings made unity difficult when it came to advocating for changes in state policy. Furthermore, state officials could often claim that progress was being made, new plans were in the works, and improvements were just around the corner. The implementation of a private concession was clear and easily identifiable and the potential implications were easier to identify as well. Opposition to Aguas del Tunari could emerge even in the face of multiple meaning-making practices and understandings of water. Individuals may not have agreed about exactly what it was that markets were rendering insecure or which practices they feared would be destabilized. Yet with the contract perceptions of specific insecurities or particular concerns about daily practices could be subsumed under broad articulations of insecurity or violation of a way of life. Interests and understandings, even if only for the months of the mobilization, overlapped in the face of the Aguas del Tunari contract.

THE FIRST WATER WAR

On January 11, the "blockade for dignity" began. For three days, irrigators' associations effectively blocked strategic roads, and neighborhood associations on the periphery set up barricades. The Civic Committee joined the Coordinadora in rallying thousands of Cochabambans to the streets. The center of the city was closed off to vehicle traffic and stores were closed for the day – photographs show the central plaza filled with people and signs ("Tarifazo: una semana de conflicto en Cochabamba" 2000). *Regantes*, fabriles, architects, engineers, environmentalists, students, transportation workers, COD members, teachers, students, neighborhood organizations, and local water committees all came out to participate. The Civic Committee officially withdrew after twenty-four hours, but under the Coordinadora's leadership the protests continued for three days, shutting down the regional airport as well as the two major highways into and out of the city (Shultz 2003). According to the local newspaper *Los Tiempos*, the "the blockade was total" ("Tarifazo: una semana de conflicto en Cochabamba" 2000). Furthermore, Cochabamba was not the only city affected – the blockades of major highways paralyzed transportation and commerce throughout the country (García et al. 2003). City officials called in hundreds of police officers to control the march to the central plaza and attempted to reopen the roads, but protestors stayed put. In direct defiance of Law 2029, Cochabambans burned hundreds of water bills in the plaza ("Queman centenares de facturas del tarifazo de Aguas del Tunari" 2000; Olivera 2004, 32) and called for the annulment of the Aguas del Tunari contract and a rejection of the law.

In seven months, the movement had grown from a small group of professionals to include department-wide unions, neighborhood associations, and even previously unorganized Cochabambans. As a leadership structure, the Coordinadora effectively served to bridge the gaps that could have made coordinated struggle impossible. The appeal to water made the Coordinadora "at once rural and urban, multi-class and multiethnic, straddling what have historically been often fractious divides" (Albro 2005, 251). From the early moments of the struggle, the Coordinadora brought together farmers, factory workers, white-collar workers, and members of the informal economy. The protest events saw "a new world of work [come] out into the streets: the unemployed, the self-employed, the young and the women" (Olivera 2004, 47). Anecdotes describe children creating roadblocks out of bicycles and sticks, elderly women lying across the streets, and bank employees offering aid to protestors (Shultz 2003; Olivera 2004). Even José Antonio Gil, the commander of the army unit stationed in Cochabamba, recalls, "my wife, my child, my *empleada* [household employee] – they were all in the streets" (author interview with José Antonio Gil, former comandante, Séptima División Militar, February 2010, Cochabamba).

When questioned, every interviewee present for the events in January recalled that participation was not correlated with class.[26] Olivera observed that "even the rich owners of the condominiums in the city of Cochabamba joined" ("The fight for water and democracy: An interview with Oscar Olivera" 2000). Víctor Gutiérrez, PUMA founder but also an upper-class lawyer, explains the participation of his peers: "The upper class joined because it was a problem of dignity. An unjust, antipatriotic contract. They felt solidarity with the people. They identified with the fight of the rest of the people. The government wasn't considering the *patria* of the country" (author interview with Gutiérrez, January 2010, Cochabamba). For Gutiérrez, water created the potential for national associations – solidarities between people who had never met were forged because the concept of *patria* was at stake. One upper-class

---

[26] Some local business associations did maintain opposition throughout the wars ("Cochabambinos protagonizaron un paro cívico contudente" 2000), yet it appears that there were few to whom the movement's goals did not appeal.

participant echoed other interviewees when she recalled, "I joined because this was about defending all of us – water was important to each of us and should not be taken away from any Cochabamban" (author interview, January 2010, Cochabamba). A language of solidarity grounded in region and country permeated interviews and informal conversations. Furthermore, notions of class itself need to be understood in relational terms – even those who may have been of a financially privileged class in the Cochabamban context may consider themselves part of a class ignored or marginalized by national elites. These shared perceptions of marginalization tapped into the imagined communities of nation and region, motivating even Cochabamba's wealthy to participate.

The significance of water to the livelihoods and identities of Cochabambans allowed the Coordinadora to explicitly call on collective Bolivian and Cochabamban identifications, underscoring collective vulnerability without trying to distinguish the needs or interests of distinct groups within a broad framework of citizenship. Regional and national imaginaries did not appear to be in competition with one another. Albro argues that the Coordinadora effectively "acted to create an alternate significance to citizenship in Bolivia around explicitly collective cultural heritage or property rights" (2005, 251). A critical ingredient in the Coordinadora's ability to "deepen citizenship" (Albro 2005) in Cochabamba and, as a result, create a large-scale social movement, was how local residents perceived the threat to water.

However, it was not just imagined communities, but also their face-to-face counterparts that brought people to the streets. For those who seek to explain the water wars simply as a reaction to increased water rates, the participation of those who did not receive municipal water bills at all is even more puzzling than the participation of their wealthy neighbors. As they did not have hookups to the SEMAPA network, none of them had to contend with the increase in water rates that accompanied the switch to Aguas del Tunari. If the increase in prices was all that mattered, we should not have seen individuals without municipal water connections taking to the streets. However, increased rates were not all that was at stake. The contract allowed the company to place meters on community-constructed wells or water networks. These meters would charge for systems that had been privately developed. They would also disrupt the quotidian community structures developed for regulating, maintaining, and charging for water services. Although the company had not yet taken these steps and it was unclear if it would, even those Cochabambans who did not initially receive bills from Aguas del Tunari had to contend with fears that the contract would violate hard-won perceptions of autonomy. While many participants who did not receive water bills also reference national, regional, or ethnic claims when explaining their actions, they uniformly emphasized the perceived violation of the small communities that had developed to facilitate access to water.

Signs held by protesters during the protests in February support the claim that some participants perceived the Aguas del Tunari contract as a threat to local community autonomy and organization. A film of the events shows handwritten placards reading, "Long live the self-organization of the *pueblo* [people/town/community]," "The *pueblo* organizes alone and without parties," and "Popular support can more than any state" (Rioja Vasquez 2002).[27] All three statements are indicative of the perceived divide between "the people" and "the state." But they also reveal water's local connection to self-determination. References to self-organizing, organizing alone, or the effectiveness of popular action without the state speak to pride both in the very protests themselves *and* in Cochabambans' history of providing for themselves where water was concerned. The events of the water wars exemplify the self-reliance invoked in these phrases. But the statements also speak to the perception of the Aguas del Tunari contract as a threat to the local, community-based organizational efforts that dominated *state* relationships with water in both urban and rural areas throughout the Valley.

It is impossible to tell how many people without consistent access to the municipal water system took to the streets; however, it is clear that they participated in large groups and that movement leaders consider their participation critical to favorable movement outcomes (author interviews with Gutiérrez, January 2010, Cochabamba; and Walter Antezana, September 2008, Cochabamba). Residents of Barrio Petrolero, as well as Valle Hermosa, both regions either without SEMAPA hookups or without regular service, recall that "all" of their friends and neighbors joined them in the plaza (author interviews with Águilar, February 2010, Cochabamba; and Oropeza, February 2010, Cochabamba). For Carlos Oropeza, a resident of the Southern Zone community of Valle Hermosa, water "makes the community organized … we had to fight to keep that organization" (author interview with Oropeza, February 2010, Cochabamba). "The water was ours," he recalls. "We had worked for it; it gives us community, dignity" (ibid.). Abraham Grandier, also a Southern Zone resident who went on to found an NGO devoted to water communities in the region, argues that "our social structures were built around water. It was a necessity so we organized for it. We had taken control and it became the foundation of our community. Aguas del Tunari was taking that community away" (author interview with Abraham Grandier, President of ASICA Sur, February 2010, Cochabamba). Something beyond material connections to water was clearly at stake. Through daily practices and struggles, Southern Zone residents imbued water with community-related meanings. It is hard to explain their participation without paying close attention to how these meanings produced political action.

The rapid rise of the Committee for the Defense of Water in June 1999 and the subsequent emergence of the Coordinadora show how micro-level understandings of the ways in which water and community were intertwined coalesced at the meso-level. Contested meanings at the micro-level worked as the foundation for shared meso-level understandings. These broader

[27] In Spanish, the signs read: "Viva la autoorganización del pueblo," "El Pueblo organiza solo y sin partidos," and "La respaldía popular puede mas que cualquier estado."

understandings allowed movement leaders to broaden and strengthen the movement through frames that appealed to imagined communities (e.g., nation, region, and ethnic group), autonomy, and self-reliance. Already established understandings of water made these frames highly resonant. Connections between the Aguas del Tunari contract and threats to nation, region, heritage, ethnicity, autonomy, and a collective "we" had, in Snow and Benford's words, "ideational centrality" (1992, 141); the frames "rang true" in the Cochabamban context.

How and why frames work the ways they do, when they do requires further exploration. Frames are not the product of unbounded creativity – not every frame is available to or appropriate for every movement – and should not be taken as a given or as a product of the ingenuity of one particular leader or another. Indeed, movement leaders will need to capitalize on, and effectively articulate available frames, but frames as broadly appealing and potent as the ones that brought Cochabambans to the streets are not available to every movement. To satisfactorily understand the mechanisms at work in the water wars, we must explain why and how the nationalist appeal and, in particular, its plural nature was possible. We must look prior to the frame to understand the dynamics at work. It is not enough to simply describe and show how framing worked in the Cochabamban case. We must also explain the conditions of possibility for the frame itself.[28]

Here, I argue that we should understand the agency of social movement entrepreneurs as in constant interaction with cultures that are produced through iterative, dynamic, and meaning-making processes. The agency of social movement leaders is "inseparable from the unfolding dynamics of situations" (Emirbayer 1997, 294). Within the social movement literature, framing is often something that is "being done" (Benford and Snow 2000, 614). It is active, signifying work that can generate and challenge dominant meanings

---

[28] I am not proposing that every movement leader or participant mentioned here or in the pages that follow was motivated either partially or entirely by the variety of community-related meanings of water. A host of other factors were undoubtedly at work, as both leaders and participants saw the moment through opportunistic lenses. For some it may have been a chance to finally fight the forces of neoliberalism; for others it may have been an opportunity to demand increased regional autonomy or seek personal recognition. Local leaders had personal interests and investments at stake, and no doubt they kept those interests in mind as they encouraged, discouraged, or participated in the resistance movement. Yet prior to the water wars, these kinds of claims and aggregations of interests had been unable to motivate large-scale resistance to market-driven threats. Water provided the grievance around which various interests could unite, even if leaders or participants understood it as a vehicle and not as an end in itself. Ultimately, as Wedeen (2008) has warned, it is impossible to ascribe intentionality to actors – motivations are never truly known, either because actors do not themselves understand what was behind a particular action or because they may misrepresent, misremember, or embellish their own accounts. Yet we can look to the work performed by the discourses – both the discourses used during moments of protest and those of actors as they recall them – to attempt to make the contours of the movement intelligible.

(ibid.). Social movement entrepreneurs actively create and maintain meanings for participants and nonparticipants throughout the movement process. Yet these entrepreneurs often build on preexisting interpretive frames. Collective action frames can be "the outcome of negotiating shared meaning" (Gamson 1992, 111), but these negotiations will be more successful if the interpretive schema from which they are developed overlap – interpretive processes are at work well before savvy social movement entrepreneurs engage in their own processes of meaning construction. Indeed, while movement organizers in Cochabamba deftly deployed frames that had the "empirical credibility, experimental commensurability, and ideational centrality or narrative fidelity" (Snow and Benford 1992, 140) necessary to resonate, the question remains as to why they were able to develop frames with these characteristics.[29] In short, why was the water movement able to create and capitalize on resonant master frames? Why did frames of regional autonomy and ethnic heritage "ring true" to Cochabambans in the context of the Aguas del Tunari contract? Why did a nationalist frame around water appeal to so many Cochabambans whereas calls to national pride during teachers' marches did little to unsettle the city? Here we must look to meaning-making processes that preexisted the mobilization. Frames mattered, but to understand how and why they worked the way they did we must explore the micro-level process through which Cochabambans made sense of their worlds.

Nationalist, regional, and ethnic frames appealed to a cross-class, cross-sector, cross-urban–rural, cross-ethnic, cross-age, and cross-gender participant base. Movement leaders appealed to both national and regional participant identities, using national and regional symbols and nationalist language to bring people to the streets irrespective of the relative impact of the rate hikes. The flag of the Bolivian nation-state is featured prominently in video footage and photographs of the events, and discourse tapped into Bolivian pride and sense of belonging. Maria Esther Udaeta, who later helped to negotiate agreements with the government in February, recalls that she felt as though to violate water "was to violate our sovereignty" (author interview with Maria Esther Udaeta, Secretaría de Agua de Vivienda Básica, January 2010, La Paz). Nelly Yañez, a member of the Women's Civic Committee and self-defined member of the Cochabamban upper-middle class, says that she participated because "water is *patria*"; to sell it or make it unaffordable for anyone was simply a "violation of the *patria*" (author interview, January 2010, Cochabamba). For Raúl Águilar, protestors took the plaza "in the name of Bolivia ... The state forfeits the flag when they don't do their job. The people raised the flag because they were defending the country" (author interview, January 2010, Cochabamba). In some cases, flags

---

[29] By empirical credibility, the authors refer to the "apparent evidential basis for a master frame's diagnostic claims" (Snow and Benford 1992, 140). Experiential commensurability suggests direct experience with a problem, and ideational centrality refers to how well the frame "rings true" with in a given contextual system.

formed a literal divide between protestors and police. Photographs show the front line of protestors marching toward the plaza wrapped in an extended banner made up of the colors of the Bolivian flag. Other images show groups of protestors standing behind a flag as the police approach.

The highly regional Misicuni myth also took center stage. Placards held by protestors read, "No to the *tarifazo* [rate increase], yes to Misicuni." The Aguas del Tunari contract was perceived as the end to the promise of Misicuni – both the modernization that Misicuni was to bring and the past it was to recall were somehow made impossible with the arrival of Aguas del Tunari. The discourse of protestors throughout the movement invoked a "we" that implied a divide between Cochabamba and La Paz. Cochabambans deserved better and came together to demand it from the central government. Movement slogans and discourse called on Cochabambans to rank their identity as Bolivians or Cochabambans above other affiliations and to take to the streets as individuals whose nation or region was under siege.[30]

But even as Cochabambans invoked national patrimony and promises of regional "progress," they also deployed decidedly ethnic symbols; the indigenous *wiphala*, a flag often used to represent a broadly Andean indigenous category, filled the protests.[31] The perceived threat to water tapped into not only national, but also clearly ethnic identifications. Movement participants performed *k'oas* – a ritual to ask for the blessing of the *Pachamama*, or mother earth – at the end of a day's rally, and students played music commonly associated with Andean *Tinku* fighting as they marched behind a Bolivian flag. Bolivian and indigenous identities were brought together through a single nationalist master frame; the inclusive nationalist appeal was broadly resonant. COD leader Walter Antezana's recollections echo those of other participants. Both the Bolivian flag and the *wiphala*, he recalls, "brought more energy to the streets. They reminded us what was at stake, what we were fighting for" (author interview, September 2008, Cochabamba). For many participants, the *wiphala* appears to have simultaneously symbolized *usos y costumbres*, the Andean cosmovision, and conceptions of regional heritage. One participant who was in his early thirties at the time of the protests told me, "the *wiphala* was about respect; respect for our past, respect for who we are, for our beliefs and customs" (author interview with water war protester, August 2008, Cochabamba). With water at stake, the Bolivian nation and the indigenous nation could be understood as having the same goals and protecting the same rights.[32]

The kind of plural nationalism that emerged during the water wars was available to organizers because the conception of water as national or regional

---

[30] See Gould (1995) for a relevant discussion of "participation identities."

[31] Film footage from *Leasing the Rain* (Finnegan 2002), photographs from CNN.com, BBC.com, One World Communication, and World Forum.

[32] This idea is rooted in Albro's (2005) discussion of citizenship in the water wars. See particularly pp. 251–2.

FIGURE 3.2. A "water warrior" carries a stick with both the Bolivian flag and the *wiphala* attached (photo courtesy of *Los Tiempos* and Carlos López).

patrimony resonated simultaneously with national political and indigenous claims. Furthermore, neither claim competed with the other.[33] Indeed, many interviewees who did not identify as Aymara or Quechua claimed that their heritage was at stake as well. One college student in her mid-twenties who participated in the water wars told me, "*usos y costumbres* can't be lost. They are an important part of where we come from" (author interview with water war protester, August 2008, Cochabamba). Even Antezana claimed that part of what was at stake was *lo andino* (author interview, September 2008, Cochabamba). To defend water was to defend the country, the region, and cultural practice. Nationalist and ethnic imaginings came together, in addition to associations with region, alongside one another without conflict. Water had tapped into powerful imagined communities that were, for this moment, able to bring people to the streets and to exist together without conflict. See Figures 3.2 and 3.3 for images of the *wiphala* and the Bolivan flag appearing side by side during the water wars.

---

[33] In some cases, as I am arguing here, national patrimony may overlap with indigenous patrimony. Others may consider their national and indigenous roots as highly distinct – they are at once Quechua and Bolivian but do not consider the two identities as overlapping. Albro (2005) suggests that the water wars brought indigenous and Bolivian conceptions of nation together under the banner of "popular 'citizenship.'"

FIGURE 3.3. *Wiphalas* and Bolivian flags appear side by side in the crowd (photo courtesy of *Los Tiempos* and Carlos López).

Movement leaders helped facilitate these feelings of shared community. The oft-repeated phrase "*Nosotros Somos la Coordinadora* [We Are the Coordinadora]" was invoked by leaders at rallies, by protestors during interviews with the press, and by participants more than eight years later. It appeared spray-painted on buildings and went on to be used as the title of a collection of essays on the events (Olivera and Gutiérrez 2008). The phrase indiscriminately gave community members not only membership in the movement, but a sense of leadership in the events. "We were all making it happen," one participant said more than eight years later. In a statement reminiscent of the title of the book on the events mentioned earlier (*Nosotros Somos la Coordinadora* – We Are the Coordinadora), the participant continued: "Really, we all were the Coordinadora" (author interview, February 2010, Cochabamba). In reflecting on the protests, a middle-aged male from Pagador (a Cochabamban *barrio* in the Southern Zone), stated, "We were no longer irrigators or factory workers, residents of Pagador or the center. We all had the same problem and came together to fix it" (author interview, February 2010, Cochabamba).

Water itself was also explicitly evoked in ways that called a people of Cochabamba into being. Throughout the protests, signs included slogans: "The water belongs to the people of Cochabamba," and "The water is ours, Damn it!" (Olivera 2004). These frames portrayed water in a particular way – something that belonged to the community but could not be owned. At the same time as the slogans challenged liberal conceptions of individual property, they also brought concepts of community and belonging to the fore. The discourse did not single out particular groups, but rather called on Cochabambans' sense of collective unity to protect something that was not theirs or mine, but belonged to everyone.

These frames captured the imagination and drove the participation of many of the protestors. Whereas previous fiscal and monetary reforms took a significant immediate toll on the livelihood of the poor, few could be framed in such starkly nationalist, regional, or ethnic terms.[34] Water could be described as belonging to Bolivians, as a particular right of Cochabambans, or as a reflection of perceived Andean or regional customs in ways that cuts in teachers' salaries or decreased provision of social services could not.

The power of the frames deployed in Cochabamba suggests that we would do well to continue to explore how emotional processes influence social mobilization. Frames resonate precisely because they tap into or evoke particular affective states. In addition to incorporating the importance of process benefits into our analysis (e.g., see Wood 2001; Gould 2009) or the role that fear or hope may play in the dynamics of contention (Pearlman 2013), we should continue to explore how affective ties to community are produced and reproduced and what role those ties may play in our understandings of why some citizens are emboldened to protest at particular times and places. When we connect the materiality of subsistence with the insecurities produced by markets, meaning-making practices, and political resistance, we can better understand how national, regional, and ethnic imaginings worked alongside direct, personal relationships to create ties across a variety of income levels in Cochabamba. Powerful connections to neighborhood, region, nation, and ethnicity helped to define perceptions of what was at stake, heightening feelings of group belonging and shared fate. These may be precisely the kinds of processes that work to create the "cognitive liberation" that McAdam (1982) wrote about when political process theory first took hold or the emboldening that Pearlman (2013) more recently argues is central to any analysis of contentious processes.

Throughout the January protests, Cochabambans appeared as a single group in the streets, their connection to country, region, and local community heightened by the perception of a shared threat. Regardless of the kinds of challenges individual Cochabambans faced as they sought to access water daily, or the personal or spiritual connections they claimed with the good, many Cochabambans understood the Aguas del Tunari contract as a threat to the collective. Movement slogans such as "*nosotros somos la Coordinadora* [we are the Coordinadora]," "*El agua es del Pueblo* [the water is of/belongs

---

[34] This book does not take a position on the long-run outcome of neoliberal reforms on economic growth. It is not controversial, however, to assert that many of them had immediate negative consequences for Bolivia's poor. Whether the reforms will prove a "good" decision for economic growth is heavily contested.

FIGURE 3.4. "THE WATER IS OURS, DAMN IT!" The sign hung outside of the Fabriles offices in April, but it illustrates a slogan used throughout the water wars (photo courtesy of Tom Kruse).

to the people/town/community]," "*El Pueblo decide y no necesita órdenes* [the people/town/community decides and doesn't need orders]," and "*El agua es nuestra ¡Carajo!* [The water is ours, damn it!]" summoned a collective "we" into being in the very moments in which they were uttered or written. Cochabambans became a group in the streets, brought together as members of a *pueblo*, as members of the Coordinadora, as part of a "*nuestra* [ours]" to which they all could collectively belong. While the larger collective was created in these moments, it grew from preexisting perceptions of other categories of belonging. During the final days of protest in April 2000, graffiti had crossed out "Aguas del Tunari" on a company sign and replaced it with "Aguas del Pueblo." See Figures 3.4 and 3.5 for images of the slogans appearing during the water wars.

On January 13, at the end of the third day of protests, government representatives and movement leaders were ready to sit down to negotiate. The archbishop agreed to mediate and participants left the streets. Although there was much more to come, the water wars had undoubtedly begun. The disparate identities and interests that protested the water contract had become part of what Bustamante, Peredo, and Udaeta call "a single group in the streets" (Bustamante et al. 2005, 80), difficult to isolate, divide, or undermine. It is hard to understand how and why Cochabamba erupted when it did without specific attention to the mobilizing power of the meanings with which water was

FIGURE 3.5. "THE WATER IS OF THE PEOPLE, DAMN IT!" The image comes from the final days of protest in April 2000, but, again, the slogans were deployed throughout the water wars (photo courtesy of Tom Kruse).

imbued. Cochabambans took to the streets because they understood far more to be at stake than simply their material relationship with water – local communities and regional, national, and ethnic identifications were perceived to be at risk. Whereas other dynamics took hold as Cochabambans took to the streets again in February and April, what water meant sheds light on the mechanisms at work as they came together to form a movement in late 1999 and early 2000.

EXPLORING ALTERNATIVES

There are, of course, many approaches to understanding social mobilization. I have tried to address a few throughout this text, showing how an account that pays attention to water as a symbol complements our understandings of political opportunities, resource mobilization, and framing processes. But other alternatives remain. I cannot fully address each but offer thoughts on threshold and demonstration effects, the power of charismatic leaders and political entrepreneurs, as well as the size of the rate hikes in the following sections.

Threshold effects

Threshold effects provide a potentially attractive approach to thinking about the events in Cochabamba. As Pierson (2004, 83) reminds us, tipping points can be critical in the development of social movements; a slow buildup of stress can lead to a "rapid 'state change' once some critical level has been reached." His argument implies that privatization of water in Cochabamba may have been the proverbial straw that broke the camel's back after many years of economic hardship. The water agreement might have pushed Bolivians over the threshold, the argument might go, but any other reform that imposed economic hardship could have done the task equally well.

Two components of the Cochabamban case suggest that threshold effects were not at work. First, organizers' and protestors' language rarely suggested that the movement was concerned with more than the case at hand. Leaders referenced the country's history of neoliberal policies, but earlier reforms rarely played a prominent role in public discourse. Second, in the time that led up the water wars, there was small-scale protest activity throughout the country. Just as the Aguas del Tunari contract was being discussed, signed, and implemented in 1999, teachers' unions marched and transportation workers struck. Yet neither of these protests took on the scale or caused the disruption of the water wars. The threshold effect cannot explain why the water wars became a large-scale movement whereas protest activities at the same time around different issues did not.

Demonstration effects

A second alternative hypothesis rests on the premise that local occurrences are often informed by global events. For example, it is difficult to explain the emergence of revolutionary movements throughout Central and South America in the 1960s and 1970s without some reference to a successful revolutionary movement in Cuba in 1959. A historical timing approach to protest in Cochabamba would look to other instances of global or regional protest in the mid- to late 1990s to understand whether they influenced the local decision to protest. A successful rejection or reversal of a government reform in a neighboring country through local protests may have led some Cochabambans to believe that protest was a potentially useful tool. With other conditions in place (e.g., strong local networks), a successful protest nearby (or perhaps on the other side of the globe) may have provided the "cognitive liberation" (McAdam 1982, 1999) necessary to overcome the collective action problem in Cochabamba in 2000.

A general survey of anti-neoliberal or antiglobalization protests in the late 1990s suggests that a demonstration effect was not at work. Events in neighboring Ecuador offer what is perhaps the most plausible possibility for a demonstration effect. In May and July 1999, the *Confederación de Nacionalidades Indígenas del Ecuador* [Confederation of Indigenous Nationalities of Ecuador] (CONAIE) mounted large demonstrations against national austerity measures.[35] Yet there appears to be little link between the events in Ecuador and those in Cochabamba. Anti–World Trade Organization protests in Seattle

[35] On January 21, 2001, popular forces went on to bring down the Ecuadorian government.

in late 1999 are another plausible source of influence on the Cochabamban activities. Yet the movement was already well organized by the time the events in Seattle occurred, and it is difficult to imagine that the "success" of largely northern protestors in a northern context (even if they were trying to give voice to southern issues) would inspire protests in Cochabamba. Perhaps most importantly, my extensive analysis of newspaper coverage of the events in Cochabamba, speeches given as the movement unfolded, video clips of the protests themselves, as well as post hoc interviews did not unearth any mention of events in Seattle or Quito (or other contemporary social movements).[36]

In fact, the water wars themselves served as a catalyst for later social protest, at least within Bolivia's borders, and have been hailed as the inspirational "first victory" against neoliberalism worldwide. Since April 2000, Bolivia has experienced an "almost continuous process of mass mobilization" (Petras and Veltmeyer 2005, 179).[37] We find leaders during the water wars at the helm in 2003 during the gas wars where similar organizational structures and slogans were deployed. The 2005 movement against Aguas del Illimani in La Paz–El Alto also had roots in the water wars, with leaders there using similar language to discuss the company's ouster. It is hard to believe that the explanation for the timing or composition of the water wars rests with larger trends in global social mobilization.

Past mobilization

When conducting large-N analyses of political protest, social scientists often want to know if previous histories of mobilization have any effects. Is a region particularly prone to contentious episodes and might this proclivity help explain the mobilization at hand? Cochabamba does, indeed, have a reputation in Bolivia for social protest. The valley was home to peasant mobilizations under the Banzer regime but remained relatively quiescent throughout the neoliberal period. It was certainly home to no more mobilization than La Paz–El Alto during the years prior to the water wars. Although it may not be surprising that Cochabamba was the site of Bolivia's first major anti-market contentious episode since neoliberal reforms began, the region's contentious history cannot tell us why it was that Cochabambans organized to oppose this particular reform when earlier reforms had passed with little unrest.

→ *lack of substantiation*

Charismatic leadership and political entrepreneurs

The "individualist dimension of inquiry" (Katznelson 2003, 279) offers another potential alternative explanation. Although Oscar Olivera quickly emerged as

---

[36] See *Presencia* and *El Diario* January 1999–May 2000. See also Olivera (2004) and "The fight for water and democracy" (2000).

[37] For example, in October 2000, Aymara leaders organized and forced the government to submit to a broad range of demands, including reverting water rights back to the Indians.

the spokesman for the movement and received significant personal attention in the aftermath, process tracing of the events themselves suggests that neither his role nor his presence was pivotal. Olivera's leadership did not seem to hinge on his personal attributes. Protestors rarely appeared to be in the streets at Olivera's behest. Rather, the leaders of the component organizations – FEDECOR, neighborhood organizations (*juntas vecinales*), and so on – did the organizing critical to getting so many groups and people involved. In fact, it was only in the aftermath of the April protests, as international NGOs and news organizations took an interest in the events, that Olivera emerged as the apparent "leader" of the movement.

It is also critical that we consider the potential role of local political entrepreneurs. What were the stakes of local politicians in the continued existence of SEMAPA or in the adoption of the Aguas del Tunari contract? Presumably a number of local figures benefited from SEMAPA corruption, receiving considerable political rents in the form of patronage positions or even direct financial payouts. At the same time, we can also assume that a number of local political leaders had personal incentives to see the contract implemented. Indeed, movement rhetoric often evoked the ways in which corrupt local political officials might benefit from the new corporate partnership. Leaders of *juntas vecinales*, leadership of FEDECOR and the local unions, and the organizers of CODAEP do not appear to have been benefiting from SEMAPA's patronage networks. In fact, irrigators' interest in the status quo was exactly the opposite – SEMAPA left them alone. Similarly, many of the participating members of *juntas vecinales* did not have SEMAPA connections. They might have thought that it would be easier to pay the necessary bribes to SEMAPA officials to get connections than to pay the large sums stipulated in the Aguas del Tunari contract, but it is also clear from interviews that many claim to have thought that Aguas del Tunari would never expand connections into Cochabamba's poorer neighborhoods. Participants in the water wars were not mobilizing to preserve political rents from the status quo.

The problem of prices

Did the increase in water rates simply hit Cochabambans harder than any previous reform? Is the mobilization purely a reflection of the dramatic price increases? There are three ways to address this alternative explanation. The first recalls the standard social movement theory critique: grievances are everywhere and constant and therefore cannot explain the relatively limited amount of social mobilization to address them. If prices are the problem, why, we might ask, do comparable price increases spark mobilization only some of the time? Second, we might look to other reforms with comparatively similar monetary impacts on Bolivians. For example, the tax burden on Bolivians rose from an annual average of 5.6 percent of GNP prior to the imposition of the New Economic Policy in 1985 to 14.2 percent in the early 2000s (Arze and Kruze 2004, 24). Similarly, whereas state income from taxes on profits and incomes represented an average of 69 percent of revenue in the late 1980s, by the early 2000s that figure had been fully eclipsed by revenue from consumption, reaching 77 percent (ibid., 24). The tax burden had shifted decidedly to Bolivia's poor, who were subsidizing increasingly meager social services spending through their own tax payments. Yet protests around the changing dynamics of redistribution were few and far between, even among Bolivia's poorest who were both hit the hardest and might have the least to lose by mounting organized opposition. Finally, a focus on prices also leaves us unable to explain the participation of both members of Cochabamba's wealthier classes and residents who did not have municipal water connections. If mobilizations were purely a response to the dramatic increase in the price of the good, why would individuals for whom the new rates had little material impact – those who could afford them as well as those who never got a water bill – also take to the streets? A focus on prices alone leaves the story incomplete at best.

CONCLUSIONS

The events in Cochabamba from June 1999 through January 2000 offer evidence that the meanings with which grievances are imbued can play an indispensable explanatory role in our understandings of social movement origins and composition. For many Cochabambans, water indexed the communities of region, nation, ethnic group, and neighborhood. As a result, many understood the Aguas del Tunari contract as a threat to community – to long-standing traditions, to established communal systems, to expectations for and of the Cochabamba region, to Bolivian *patria*. The notions of "us" that emerged bridged traditional regional divisions, bringing professional workers, unions, rural communities, and previously unorganized Cochabambans together to fight for a common cause. I have argued in this chapter that the meanings water took on helped to enable the diverse participation in the water wars and help us to understand why this broad-based coalition was possible when water was at stake.

Throughout this chapter, movement resources and frames surface continually as critical components of the water wars.[38] Indeed, the movement relied heavily on the already organized *regantes*, the power of organizations and connections created by *juntas vecinales* and community water cooperatives, and many of Cochabamba's professional organizations. None of these resources was new. Yet, prior to the signing of the Aguas del Tunari contract, they had not worked together to affect political outcomes. CODAEP and then the Coordinadora brought many of these organizations together, creating, in turn, new resources to bring to bear on the issue. We cannot explain the water wars without understanding the roles that

---

[38] In these concluding remarks, I do not address political opportunity structures directly, as there is little new information or analysis introduced in this chapter that is directly related to the framework.

CODAEP, the Coordinadora, and each of the individual organizations involved in the movement played. But to understand why these organizations and individuals brought their resources to bear on this particular issue, and not any number of other, earlier reforms, we must look prior to the organizations and individuals. What explains the availability of the *juntas vecinales*? Of the professional sector? Of the *regantes*? Why were they able to come together to form CODAEP and the Coordinadora? The community-related meanings that water took on, the ways in which a threat to water was perceived as a threat to multiple notions of a collective, explain why residents of the Southern Zone mobilized for the same cause as condominium owners and engineers, *regantes* and economists.

The frames deployed throughout the course of the movement's early organization and initial protest activities are also inextricably tied to the movement's early development. With frames depicting water as *patria* and as something that was *nuestra* ("ours"), frames helped to produce the unity that appeared in the streets in January 2000. The frames were inclusionary and could appeal to any Cochabamban with national, regional, or communal pride. To understand how and why these frames worked the way they did, however, we must understand the work that a market-driven threat to water was able to do in the Cochabamban context.

Without variation over time in the frames deployed (e.g., with one set of frames deployed in one period with little success, and a different set of frames deployed in a later period with different results), the water wars are a particularly difficult case for disentangling the frame from the grievance.[39] Was it the description of water as a communal good and a threat to it as a threat to community that galvanized widespread participation in the movement? Or was the frame incidental, as the grievance did not need to be described in particular ways to motivate the participation that it did?

The relationship between the grievance and the frame can never be fully disentangled; once frames are deployed they can imbue grievances with new meanings. Indeed, part of the point of this research is to show that to understand how and why frames work the ways they do you must understand how they interact with meaning-making processes around the grievance. Yet

---

[39] We can only understand why frames work the way they do when we pay attention to the grievance (see Simmons 2014). However, there are some instances when a variety of frames is possible for a particular grievance and, if they are deployed at different moments during a movement's development, we can begin to discern the effect of one frame or another. Part of the challenge in disentangling the grievance from the frame in the case of the water wars is that the movement did not simply use new frames for old problems – the problem itself was new. See Snow and Benford (1992) for an example of an analysis that brings to the fore how new frames for old problems can influence a movement's development. Gould (2009) is able to show how the same frame for mobilizing against the AIDS epidemic was not effective early in the movement and became effective later on. In line with the argument that grievances and frames can never be fully disentangled, however, I would posit that, at least in part, the meaning of the grievance had shifted. With the *Bowers v. Hardwick* decision the failure to address the epidemic took on new meanings.

the attention paid to sequencing in this chapter, combined with the evidence offered both here and earlier in this book, shows that the meanings water took on in Cochabamba in 1999 and 2000 were not a product of any frame deployed by savvy social movement organizers as the movement was getting off of the ground. We cannot understand why the frame is able to do the work that it does without looking to the meaning-making processes around water as the movement began to take hold. Water was "ours" and "of the people" long before leaders such as Oscar Olivera described it as such.

This speaks directly to the question of frame availability. The frames that dominated the water movement were both unifying and urgent. The Aguas del Tunari contract was portrayed as threatening core conceptions of community, with the whole region incorporated into conceptions of "us" or "we." But what made these frames both possible and potent were ways in which water already symbolized community to many Cochabambans. As this chapter and the previous one have shown, the particular meanings that water took on for Cochabambans made frames of neighborhood autonomy, region, country, and ethnicity both possible and credible. They also made the frames broadly resonant, appealing to the interests of Cochabamba's middle class as well as its poorest populations, to urban and rural communities, and to those who identified with indigenous communities as well as those who did not. The evidence suggests that we must look prior to the frames deployed during movements, specifically to the community-related meanings with which the grievance itself was imbued, to understand the broad-based coalition that was at the core of the water wars; it was these meanings that made the frames themselves possible.

4

Corn in Mexico

Patria, tu superficie es el maíz.

Homeland, your surface is corn.

        – *Suave Patria* by López Velarde

El maíz significa nuestra vida y la vida de dios…
Maíz es nuestro padre y nuestra madre.
El maíz es también nuestro hijo,
El maíz somos nosotros y nosotras.
Es nuestro y nuestra madre
Porque nos da la vida, nos da la unidad y la identidad,
Como hijos de una misma familia y un mismo pueblo
Nos hace amar a nuestra madre tierra
Y no abandonarla…
Hijo mío: respétalo porque ahí
Están tus abuelos, estás tú.

Corn signifies life and the life of god…
Corn is our father and our mother.
Corn is also our child,
Corn is each of us
Corn is our mother
Because it gives us life, unity and identity
Like children from the same family, the same town
It makes us love our mother earth and not abandon her…
My child: respect corn because there
Are your grandparents, there you are.

        Excerpted from a poem written by a community in
        the Sierra Norte in Puebla
        Printed in Hernández García (2009)

The La Roma neighborhood in Mexico City is a popular, trendy spot. It is not the fanciest neighborhood in the city, but it is certainly an affluent residential area, boasting a plethora of neighborhood bars, restaurants, and coffee shops. Mansions built at the turn of the century line central avenues, many converted into restaurants and offices. But residents can now also find the clean lines of modern architecture throughout the neighborhood, often in the form of residential apartment buildings. Upon entering one such building on Avenida Tabasco, visitors and residents are greeted by an open courtyard with stairs in the center, leading to the apartments above. The courtyard is filled with small stones and green foliage. A single stalk of corn emerges conspicuously from among the stones and tropical plants. The stalk does not appear to be in keeping with the aesthetic design of this modern apartment building's courtyard. The gardener responsible for planting and tending to the courtyard explains that he chose to put the corn there because he thought it was a critical element of any Mexican courtyard, that it would both bring luck and firmly situate the space as Mexican.

The courtyard in La Roma is not the only place in Mexico City where you can find corn growing. It appears in parks and alongside highways, inside other courtyards in other neighborhoods, and in the gardens of private homes. The image of the La Roma cornstalk, however, is particularly emblematic. As the pages that follow will show, the stalk marks the modern building in the middle of the world's most populous city as distinctly Mexican. It reminds residents of Mexico's origins and heritage, of the countryside that has been mythologized and made sacred. In the midst of a "modern" world, the stalk ties Mexico to its history while serving as a reminder that the present can never be fully pried from the past.

There is no one mythology of corn in Mexico. Corn has multiple meanings throughout the country – these meanings coexist within individuals, cities, and towns, as well as within the borders of the Mexican nation-state. According to the Mayan legend of the *Popol Vuh*, man was forged from corn. The variety of stories and legends, symbols and sayings related to corn in Mexico is overwhelming. The thread that connects them is that they exist and continue to work to make corn a symbol of "*lo mexicano*," which translates loosely to "the Mexican way." Even though corn has been mythologized and ritualized in a variety of ways throughout Mexico, there is a sensibility across the country that it is imbued with special meaning, making the grain into a national symbol – a tie that binds a political community of more than 40 million people and spans more than 760,000 square miles. For many Mexicans, corn serves as a signifier of the Mexican nation.[1]

---

[1] Interestingly, although the Mexican flag contains images of objects from Mexican mythology, corn is not among them. An eagle, a serpent, and a cactus appear on the flag, recalling the legend of the founding of Tenochtitlán (the Aztec city built where Mexico City stands today). Although a powerful national symbol, the emblem with the eagle, serpent, and cactus appears far less

For only a very few Mexicans, however, does life today revolve around corn to the extent that it is said to have done 50, 100, or 500 years ago. Even though corn continues to dictate daily rhythms in some of Mexico's most rural communities, it rarely does so in the cities. And even in rural areas, increasing mechanization frees many from the hours spent tilling a field or grinding corn on a *metate*.[2] Corn remains a focal point for meals, and a morning visit to a *tortillería* may drive morning routines for some, but the ease with which corn and tortillas can be purchased means their production no longer structures city life. Yet when many Mexicans speak of *lo mexicano*, among the other images conjured up are those of endless cornfields, harvest dances, a *campesino* with his cowboy hat tending to his *milpa* (a small plot of land where corn is grown alongside a variety of other crops), or a woman leaning over her *metate* grinding dried corn kernels into *masa*. These iconic images of Mexico continue to reflect daily practices in many communities. But it is the way in which the images pervade Mexican imaginaries, the way in which the preservation of "the" *campesino's* rituals and way of life has become synonymous with preserving Mexico, that works to make corn something worth defending, even for many Mexicans who have never personally witnessed a *campesino* working the field or a woman bent over a *metate* grinding corn for the day's tortillas. These rituals are part of what many participants understood to be at stake during the *tortillazo* protests, for the rituals are at the heart of what many think Mexico is, and often what they think it should be.

Even as corn has come to mean a connection to an idealized past, it is also symbolic of Mexico's progress and accomplishments. Corn and Mexico have grown together, adapted together. Scholars, activists, politicians, and "ordinary" people describe corn as both human-made and something that makes humans. Anthropologist Bonfil Batalla (1982) wrote that, "in cultivating corn, human beings also cultivated themselves." Activist and former *Partido de la Revolución Democrática* [Party of the Democratic Revolution] (PRD) politician Víctor Suárez called corn "an amazing accomplishment. It came from us and now makes us who we are as Mexicans" (author interview, February 2009, Mexico City). Many hold corn up as a proud symbol of what Mexico can accomplish – the domestication and cultivation of an essential foodstuff. Humans' ability to domesticate corn elevates them, they claim, serving as a reminder that humans are superior to animals. But, as many are quick to remind me, corn continues to need man to survive, as it cannot reproduce on its

---

frequently in daily life and practice than do corn and tortillas. The emblem recalls one founding myth, whereas corn plays a role in a number of Mexican myths, conceptions of development and "progress," and contemporary daily life. Corn's absence from the national flag should not be read as a suggestion that corn is any less important (indeed, it is arguably more important) to Mexican national identity than the images that do appear.

[2] *Metates* are large stone tools used largely by rural Mexican women both to remove dried corn kernels from the cob and to grind the kernels into the paste (*masa*) from which tortillas and tamales (as well as other staples) are made.

own. In this, corn represents a symbiotic relationship between man and nature, a balance, a reflection of how they are interdependent. But it is also a symbol of humans' ability to mold nature to their needs, a symbol of advancement. These claims exemplify the ways in which corn in Mexico works as both a symbol of modernity and a link to the past.[3]

Furthermore, many Mexicans understand corn as a reflection of their own adaptability as a people. It is a national symbol because it has, with the help of the farmers who actively select for particular traits, adapted to grow in almost any climactic condition. Mexicans successfully cultivate corn in every region of the country, from the mountains, to the coasts, and to the deserts. The oft-heard phrase "we live, thanks to corn" speaks to the past and the present, the ways in which corn helps inform notions of what Mexico was and the ways in which it works every day to produce and reproduce notions of what Mexico is.

The analysis that follows cannot do justice to the variety of semiotic practices relating to corn in Mexico. Through a limited treatment of history and mythology, as well as urban and rural practices, this chapter offers the broad contours of some of the meanings that corn takes on in Mexico. The following questions motivate the discussion: How does corn take on meaning in contemporary Mexico? What are those meanings and how might they help us better understand resistance in the face of market-driven threats to corn? To answer these questions, I look to Mexican history, mythology, cuisine, and daily life and argue that corn's role as a subsistence good has worked to imbue the grain with community-related meanings of family, neighborhood, and nation. This chapter pays particular attention to the ways in which corn helps to produce and reproduce imagined and quotidian communities. It also focuses largely on imaginings and practices in urban Mexico. While there is some discussion of rural life, the experiences of urban Mexicans are most relevant to questions of participation in the *tortillazo* protests. The movement spanned urban–rural divides but the participation of the urban and socially unattached subject is part of what is most puzzling.

The substance of the imagined and quotidian communities discussed in the analysis of the Mexican case – in particular an emphasis on family that appears throughout – differs from the ones analyzed in the Cochabamban case. Yet they work in similar ways to shape daily life and perceptions of communal belonging. By understanding ways in which corn is both a foundation of daily

[3] Corn's link to modernity is produced and reproduced through its symbolic connection to progress. Even though Mexico's corn production now lags behind that of the United States in efficiency (U.S. producers are able to grow more corn per hectare and at a lower cost per kilo than their Mexican counterparts) and, some would argue, quality (although this is highly contested), corn still serves, for some, as a symbol of progress. The grain represents what Mexican creativity and ingenuity can accomplish. At the same time, given the industry's inability to compete on an international scale, conceptions of corn as progress are fraught with tension. Some Mexicans see corn production as something that should be relegated to the country's past; as Mexico does not have a comparative advantage, it should stop producing corn all together.

ties and has come to mean Mexico, we can begin to understand why a threat to corn might motivate political resistance.[4]

HISTORY OF CORN IN MEXICO

A discussion of the history of corn in Mexico does not merely serve as background to the analysis of practices in contemporary Mexico that follows. Instead, the ways in which history is told and retold by scholars, schoolteachers, and activists, as well as at the dining room table, continue to situate corn squarely at the center of contemporary understandings of "Mexican-ness." During a conversation over Sunday lunch an affluent Mexican friend in his forties stated that corn was indispensable to the growth and success of the communities of people who populated the area before the arrival of Spanish explorer Hernán Cortés in 1519. Scholars seem to largely agree (e.g., Thompson 1964). But it is not only corn's centrality in the growth of these early populations that places it squarely at the center of contemporary conceptions of Mexican heritage. Mexico as the literal place of the origin of corn – the region in which humans engineered the growth of the first cornstalk – has taken on enormous weight in the imaginary of many Mexicans. It pervades newspaper coverage of the grain, government publications, and everyday discourse, firmly embedding corn as an indispensable element of Mexican history.

Determining the scientific history of corn has sparked a veritable cottage industry among archeologists and paleontologists, particularly in Mexico. Pinning down the exact place and date of the first domesticated corn has proven, at least to date, an impossible task (Warman 2003). But the scientific community overwhelmingly argues that Mexico is, indeed, the center of origin of corn and that sometime by before 3500 BC, populations in south-central Mexico had successfully modified a grassy stalk called *teocinte* into an early variety of domesticated corn.[5]

A few recent examples of newspaper articles on corn offer an illustration of the ways in which it is covered by the Mexican media. When *Science* Magazine ran an issue on the corn genome, the Mexico City news magazine *Milenio* published a feature article on the issue, including an interview with the director of the Mexican National Genome Laboratory for Biodiversity, which had contributed to the research (Salazar 2009). Coverage of corn, including references to Mexico as corn's center of origin, appears frequently in the Mexican daily newspaper *La Jornada*, including everything from recipes that "celebrate"

---

[4] The evidence that appears in this chapter comes from print media, Mexican film and television, and the author's personal experiences.

[5] Although archeologists cannot date the first tortillas to the origins of corn, remains of *comales* (the griddle used to make tortillas) that date to 2,300 years ago have been found in the Valley of Mexico. As a result, tortillas are said to have more than 2,000 years of history in present-day Mexico.

corn, to articles on the threats from genetically modified corn, to coverage of the annual "*día del maíz*" (day of corn) festival in Mexico City.[6] That an article in *La Jornada* on genetically modified corn begins with a reiteration of claims that "Natural corn, of which Mexico is the center of origin, where we find 59 of its varieties, is not just the most important crop in the world, and part of the cultural and nutritional patrimony of humanity, but it will also serve to guard against climate change and hunger" (Enciso L. 2011) suggests that corn's history in Mexico is widely celebrated. The article describes corn as a foundation for both contemporary culture and the future of the earth. *La Jornada* is not alone in its coverage of corn as part of Mexico's heritage. After the first approval to grow experimental plots of genetically modified corn in Chihuahua, a number of major Mexican papers, including *Reforma, Excélsior, El Diario, El Universal*, and *El Financiero*, ran stories on the officially sanctioned arrival of genetically modified corn in Mexico.[7] The evening news on at least two major channels, TV Azteca and Televisa, covered the story as well and *Aristegui*, a popular interview program on CNN en Español in Mexico dedicated more than ten minutes to the topic shortly thereafter.[8]

Furthermore, references to Mexico as the center of origin of corn pervade government declarations, press releases, and publications. The Mexican undersecretary of agriculture's comments at an international meeting on grain production in Washington, DC, are not unique.[9] The undersecretary stated that, for Mexico, the relevance of the crop goes much further than economic and commercial aspects, as it has come to represent the country's cultural values (SAGARPA 2011). These kinds of claims – routinely incorporated into public comments, press releases, or published documents – produce and reproduce a conception of corn as central to Mexican culture. A quick Google search of the website of the Ministry of Agriculture, Livestock, Rural Development, Fisheries, and Food [*Secretaría de Agricultura, Ganadería, Desarrollo Rural, Pesca, y Alimentación*] (SAGARPA) produces more than 100 links that reference Mexico as the center of origin of corn. One document on the Aserca website (a subdivision of the Ministry of Agriculture) is specifically dedicated to telling the history of the domestication of corn from *teocinte* in southern Mexico (Aserca 2010).

That corn quickly became a staple of Mayan and Mexica (Aztec) cuisine, ritual, medicine, and construction seems to be well known among contemporary

---

[6] *La Jornada* is widely understood to be a "leftist" newspaper in Mexico. In the course of my research, I reviewed a wide variety of Mexican newspapers, chosen to represent the range of the ideological spectrum. Newspapers cited include *Reforma* and *El Universal*. I also read *Milenio* and *Proceso*, two news magazines.

[7] There is evidence that genetically modified corn had arrived in Mexico prior to the approval for planting in Chihuahua. These claims, however, remain controversial.

[8] Mexican journalist Carmen Aristegui, who anchors the program, is considered by many part of the Mexican left.

[9] At the time, the undersecretary was Mariano Ruiz-Funes Macedo.

Mexicans. This history is routinely invoked both as a rationale for defending the continued cultivation of Mexican corn and simply as a part of everyday life. Without intending to suggest cultural coherence, the critical place of corn in the history of the region that is present-day Mexico and the region's role in corn's origins seem to serve as "common knowledge." I first heard the expression "*maíz, nuestra carne*/our flesh is corn" when I lived in Mexico in the summer of 1994. I have heard it again and again over the years, in both urban and rural settings, and when I inquired about it during fieldwork in 2009 people often told me that the phrase has Mexica origins. In using the phrase, the importance of corn is reproduced in the present, while that importance is located in a connection to the past. A participant in the *tortillazo* protests claimed during one of our conversations, "It [corn] is as much in our flesh as it was in the Mexicans who stood in this very spot thousands of years ago [we were near the Zócalo in Mexico City, the location of Tenochtitlán, the former Aztec capital]" (author interview, March 2009, Mexico City).[10] The expression locates the critical role of corn in constituting present-day Mexican-ness, while connecting corn and contemporary Mexicans to a past. Corn helps construct conceptions of "Mexican-ness" today, in part, by connecting Mexicans to powerful notions of communal heritage. Corn is "our" flesh – it is something that "we" (Mexicans) share with one another.

The stories of corn's importance in the founding and growth of the Mayan and Mexica empires are told and retold. They appear in elementary and high school textbooks and are peppered throughout the National Museum of Anthropology (considered a critical Mexico City landmark and a must-see for any visitor or elementary or high school class within driving distance).[11] Indeed, much of the National Museum of Anthropology is dedicated to corn – to the tools used to cultivate it, grind it, and cook it and to how it dictated the layouts of early towns and cities. Exhibits describe corn as what made these early civilizations possible, signaling corn's critical role in enabling Mexico to be what it is today. The late Carlos Monsiváis, a prominent public intellectual, wrote of the National Museum of Anthropology, "if the indians of today are invisible, the indigenous past dazzles" (2008, 25). Mexico's pre-Columbian past, with corn as a focal point, is made dazzling in the present through these exhibits. The celebration of corn's role in the past through displays experienced in contemporary Mexico brings corn-as-cultural-heritage into the present.

Even though it is possible to describe the museum's exhibits as "official government propaganda," this does little to take away from what the exhibits reveal

---

[10] Some of the interviews were conducted in confidentiality and the names of the interviewees are withheld by mutual agreement.

[11] For example, the fourth-grade history textbook published by the Ministry of Education dedicates a section to the importance of corn cultivation, including assignments that ask students to reflect on the question "why is corn important to Mexicans?" and to "research with your family the food and drink made from corn that they eat frequently and make a list of them in your book. Pick one and bring an example to class. Ask your teacher to comment on the importance of corn today" (Dirección General de Materiales Educativos 2010, 35–6).

and the work they do in contemporary Mexico. If we think of the museum as a site of government propaganda, we might understand corn as something that government officials actively chose to highlight in the telling of Mexican history. Corn's place in national culture would be the result of what Hobsbawm and Ranger (1983) have called an "invented tradition." However, *why* corn has come to be imbued with national meanings is not the key question for this chapter. Corn might be an "invented tradition" and it might not – the answer is irrelevant to the purpose at hand. Instead, we need merely establish that those meanings are continually produced and reproduced in the present. The museum, regardless of the purpose of the exhibits, becomes one site of production. It is the work the exhibits do in contemporary Mexico, not their origins, that matters.

Corn is given top billing not only in official government venues, but also in decidedly academic settings. In a volume containing a collection of presentations given during a conference on corn sponsored by the Anthropology Department at the Autonomous University of the State of Mexico [*Universidad Autónoma del Estado de México*] (UAEM) in June 1999, one essay claims that what gives Mexicans their identity is the

undeniable pre-hispanic presence and cultural heritage ... Within this heritage, what stands out are the uses our ancestors gave to corn and everything included in the process of obtaining it, from the selection of the seeds to the planting and the harvesting, to its consumption and sale; this heritage was not lost with the intervention of the Spanish culture, instead it adapted and consolidated itself within the different groups that formed the country, showing corn to be an important product within the diet and life of those groups that together achieved the creation of that identity that today we call national. (Valdez Ruiz 1999, 18)

That the UAEM conference on corn happened at all suggests that corn has played a particularly important role in the production and reproduction of Mexican culture. The title of the volume, *Corn: Sustenance of the Past and Present in National Popular Culture*, highlights corn in late twentieth-century Mexico as an indispensable element of "national popular culture" specifically through its role in shaping Mexico's past. The passage quoted here clearly spells out the imagined link.

Other scholars offer more explicit accounts of how corn defined pre-Columbian life and, as a result, continues to define the present. British anthropologist Eric S. Thompson (1964, 280) writes, "Corn, strictly speaking, constituted much more than the simple economic base of the Mayan civilization. ... Without this grain, the Mayas wouldn't have had sufficient time nor would they have enjoyed the prosperity that allowed them to build their pyramids and temples." In this telling, corn becomes what made the achievements of Mexico's ancestors possible. Without it, the Mexican nation-state could never have emerged. Thompson's reflections on attitudes toward corn in Mexico during his own fieldwork in the 1940s and 1950s are revealing. "Even today," he writes, "after four hundred years of Christian influence, corn is spoken of with reverence. … It is corn, then, that is the supreme gift that the gods gave man, and for the same reason, it must be treated with great respect and more than a little humility" (ibid., 280). Whether Thompson's words reflect everyday practices during the period he studied is of little consequence to the arguments advanced here. What is important are the ways in which, by writing about corn in the ways that he did, Thompson situated corn as a central, sacred component of daily life in Mexico. Thompson connects the Mayas and 1950s Mexico through corn. The republication of his words in the late twentieth century in scholarship on Mexican culture does the same in contemporary Mexico.[12]

Everything from historical scholarship to contemporary children's books tells us how corn structured space, time, and social status in pre-Columbian Mexico. Anthropologist Bonfil Batalla (1982) describes how gardens determined the layouts of houses, which were built around places to shuck and cook corn. A children's book called *Como lo Usamos* (*How We Use It*) contains colorful illustrations of small homes with adjacent *milpas* and women bent over *metates* (Beas 1982). More than one street vendor, two taxi drivers (both middle-aged men), and multiple activists around corn-related issues recalled for me how "before Cortés," a woman would not become a worthy bride until she had mastered the *metate* and could produce quality tortillas. Whereas the accounts of historians (e.g., Clendinnen 1991; Pilcher 1998) offer ample evidence to suggest that corn served as a centerpiece to daily life in pre-Columbian Mexico, what is most important is the work that the telling of these histories does to locate corn in contemporary Mexican imaginaries.[13] In recounting how corn organized the past, it is reproduced as critical component of Mexican heritage and, as a result, is revered in the present.

Even as corn's imagined role in Mexican history looms large, the entwining of the life cycles of corn and humans continues in contemporary Mexico. In some rural communities, adults are still called *mazorcas* – the corncob when it is dried and matured–whereas children are *elotes* – the young, tender cob. *Pinole*, the coarse flour made from toasted corn kernels, is the end of the life cycle. It is a sign of maturity and age. From the streets of Mexico City to the Sierra Juárez of Oaxaca, "*Somos gente del maíz/* We are people of (the) corn"

---

[12] For example, see Zorrilla (1982).

[13] Historian Wendy Waters argues that even until the 1940s, many Mexicans considered tortilla making so essential that members of some communities did not think women eligible for marriage until they had developed the skill (cited in Pilcher 1998). Historian Jeffrey Pilcher describes wedding ceremonies at which the mother-in-law fed tamales to the bride and the bride then fed tamales to her new husband. Corn served as a central link, the crucial sustenance for daily life that bound mother to daughter and wife to husband; corn connected families and served as the symbolic and physical foundation for marriage. Pilcher (1998) also describes how babies were called "maize blossoms" and girls were "tender green ears," whereas warriors in their prime were "Lord Corn Cob." Corn became so entwined with life that the Mexica used the phases of corn's growth to describe phases of human development and accomplishment. Historian Inga Clendinnen argues that for the Mexica, corn was considered "our sustenance, our flesh" (Clendinnen 1991).

is an oft-repeated refrain. Many phrases that recall the reportedly Mexica saying noted earlier, "our flesh is corn," fill everyday discourse. "Our bodies are of corn," "corn is our strength," "corn is our blood," "corn is our father/mother" are statements that appear not only in conversation, but also in advertisements, billboards, and political speeches. Humans created corn, but corn also fashions humans – these two ideas exist side by side in the Mexican imaginary. An elderly female tamale vendor on the streets of Mexico City remarked, "when we eat corn, we're eating our own flesh. Corn is our blood, our sweat, our tears" (author interview, June 2009, Mexico City). The tamale vendor's allusion to cannibalism aside, corn becomes deeply entwined with conceptions of self that are both individual and rooted in broadly shared understandings that corn serves as a common foundation for many Mexicans.

It is not surprising that scholars have linked corn to moments of political resistance in both New Spain and the early Mexican republic. In particular, historians have traced a number of rebellions during the period of Spanish rule to increases in the price of corn. Historian Gibson (1964) describes two uprisings against the Spaniards in the seventeenth century, crediting, at least in part, elevated corn prices for both. Historian Florescano (1969) draws connections between corn scarcity, high corn prices, and the beginning of the war of independence in 1810. Corn was also purportedly at the root of the nineteenth-century Mayan rebellion, the "*guerra de castas*" (caste war) in Yucatán. According to a volume written for the inauguration of the Museum of National Popular Culture (which opened with an exhibit dedicated to corn), corn became both a rallying cry and the dictator of the rhythm of the attacks – when planting or harvesting season arrived, rebels suspended their fighting until the corn was properly cared for (Zorrilla 1982, 36). There is some evidence that similar patterns emerged during the rural fighting in the early twentieth-century Mexican Revolution. Historian Tutino (1986) ties increasing restrictions on *campesinos'* ability to farm corn at subsistence levels to the roots of the revolution itself.

But in spite of corn's central place in Mexican life and livelihood (or perhaps because of it), it was not always revered by the country's elites. Convinced of the superiority of wheat, the sixteenth-century Spanish missionaries tried, largely in vain, to convince *campesinos* in New Spain to make the switch. The beginning of the twentieth century brought what became known as the "tortilla discourse" – a concerted effort by national political elites to replace corn with wheat throughout the country. Conventional wisdom among elites held that corn was responsible for the country's underdevelopment. Low yields, combined with supposedly poor nutritional content, made corn an inferior product, and its prevalence was holding Mexico back from greatness. During Porfirio Díaz's (1876–1911) reign in the late nineteenth century, corn-based pre-Columbian foods were stigmatized as low class and backward. Yet the tortilla discourse gained little traction among the key target population. Mexican *campesinos* were slow to replace corn with wheat, either in their fields or at the table. Pilcher argues that the discourse of the Mexican elites "did recognize the deep significance of maize, both as a subsistence crop and as a source of identity," but was nevertheless fated for failure (1998, 85). The campaign survived the revolution, peaking in the 1930s under Lázaro Cárdenas, but then quickly faded.[14]

Yet even as the push for wheat reached its climax in the early years of postrevolutionary Mexico, the state implicitly acknowledged the central role of corn in both rural and urban communities. In 1938, the government created the Regulating Committee for the Subsistence Good Market, which was charged with ensuring affordable corn in the cities and fair prices for *campesinos* selling their harvests. Although it had multiple names over the years, and its charge expanded dramatically, some version of the Regulating Committee continued to play a critical role in the distribution and subsidization of Mexican corn until the end of the twentieth century. On January 1, 1999, however, the committee met its official end when, in keeping with widespread market-oriented economic reforms, President Ernesto Zedillo announced the closing of the National Company of Popular Subsistence [*Compañía Nacional de Subsistencias Populares*] (CONASUPO).[15] The final remaining CONASUPO program sold subsidized corn to *nixtamaleros* (producers of the corn *masa* with which tortillas are made) and offered cash subsidies to corn millers (corn flour producers), both of which, presumably, worked to bring the final purchase price of tortillas lower than it would have been without government intervention.[16] With CONASUPO's end, tortilla subsidies ended as well.

It is no coincidence that the last CONASUPO program standing offered indirect consumer subsidies for tortillas.[17] Tortillas were, and continue to be, the vehicle through which much of Mexico's corn is consumed. The process of making tortillas by hand can last much of the day, even if one is only making tortillas for a single family's mid-afternoon meal (*comida*). To make tortillas by hand, one must first grind corn kernels in a *metate*; then mix them with lime in a *cazuela* (a large clay pot); pat the balls of dough into small discs; and, finally, cook the tortillas quickly on the *comal* (a large, flat griddle). Each stage in the process is usually a gendered task, performed largely by women. The first step

[14] Interestingly, there appears to be little evidence of an effort to associate wheat with a now discredited aristocracy. Perhaps this is because, in spite of the revolution, few national political leaders could claim humble beginnings. Some historians do link a poor corn crop to the timing of the revolution (for example, see Tutino 1986), but corn itself does not appear to have become a symbol of the revolutionary backlash.

[15] The committee had been known as CONASUPO since 1965 when the government created the organization in an effort to consolidate a number of food regulatory programs under one roof. At CONASUPO's elimination, Diconsa and Liconsa continued to operate but were moved to the Ministry of Social Development.

[16] In the final years, Aserca actually administered the subsidies.

[17] An indirect tortilla subsidy targets the *maíz*-tortilla chain prior to consumer purchase. For example, an indirect subsidy might allow *nixtamaleros* to purchase corn flour at below-market prices or *tortillerías* to purchase *masa* at similarly discounted rates. The subsidy is not for the tortilla itself but rather for a necessary input in the product.

is the most labor intensive. Hand-grinding corn can take hours, particularly if a woman needs to be prepared to serve large quantities of tortillas for the *comida*. The arrival of corn mills, however, slowly changed the rhythm of the daily tortilla-making ritual. Commercial *nixtamal* mills began to take root in rural Mexico as early as the 1920s. Pilcher argues that early resistance to corn mills "demonstrated the importance of tortilla making to traditional domestic culture," but (and despite technical problems with taste and texture) communities gradually succumbed to the convenience (1998, 106).[18]

The quest to build a fully mechanized tortilla maker proved challenging, but by the 1960s, the machines dotted the Mexican countryside. The invention of dehydrated corn flour and the growth of large-scale commercial flour companies such as Maseca and Minsa brought machine-made tortillas into many households. But the moniker "La Malinche," reportedly given to one of the first of these machines, is revealing (Abarca 2006). La Malinche is the nickname for the Nahua woman who served as advisor and lover to Hernán Cortés during his conquest of New Spain. She serves as a symbol of the ultimate betrayal – the word *malinchista* is now used to accuse others of treason. Like La Malinche, a tortilla machine was understood to betray the fundamentals of the Mexican way of life. It was progress, but dangerous and corrupting. Without the discipline of the daily process of tortilla production, rural Mexican women would undoubtedly become lazy and undisciplined (ibid.). Yet tortilla mechanization is also held up as an example of Mexican progress and ingenuity. It is an example of "creativity and inventiveness, of the development of our own technology in fitting with the needs and possibilities of the country" (Zorrilla 1982, 81). As a result, the tortilla simultaneously symbolizes modernization and tradition. It is a reflection of Mexico's past, on one hand, and a symbol of Mexico's adaptability, on the other.

As a result of the mechanization of the tortilla-making process, the handmade tortilla has become a marker of both the Mexican elite and of rural life. Ironically, besides only the most rural of communities, wealthier families were the ones who ultimately stuck to the *metates*. Home-ground corn began to serve as a marker of social status – eating "better" tortillas was equated with having a "better" life (Pilcher 1998). This continues to be the case in Mexico City. The least expensive tortillas are usually found at Wal-Mart or other large supermarket-like stores. *Tortillerías* produce fresh, albeit mechanized, tortillas and can charge 30–50 percent more than their supermarket competitors. In Mexico City, one finds handmade tortillas at the fanciest restaurants or homes with enough kitchen staff so that someone can dedicate a few hours daily to tortilla production. Handmade tortillas are now a delicacy to be relished. Even

---

[18] Pilcher notes that in the mid-twentieth century, these mills served as the center of political conflicts; local *caciques* (political bosses) often dictated the terms and location of a mill's development and operation, and regional politicians used them as forms of political patronage (1998, 109).

in rural Mexico, one must travel far off the beaten path to find homes where handmade tortillas are a staple of daily life. Yet even if machines now make most tortillas, the corn discs still serve as a connection that helps to produce and define membership in the Mexican nation.

The parallels between the ways in which perceptions of the histories of corn in Mexico and water in Cochabamba worked to produce imagined communities might not be immediately apparent. The account of corn in Mexico just offered is tied at almost every stage to conceptions of national history and belonging in ways discussions of water in Cochabamba are usually not. But there is a parallel, if we think of the history of water in Cochabamba as tied not necessarily to Bolivian but rather to regional and Andean histories. Pride in regional cultivation and agriculture most certainly make water a part of conceptions of regional growth and success. And the telling and retelling of the critical role irrigation played in the expansion of early Andean empires ties the flourishing of Andean communities directly to their relationships to water. Contemporary understandings of how water and corn played critical roles in the past helps to tie both goods directly to national, regional, and/or ethnic imaginings.

CORN AND MEXICAN MYTHOLOGY

Whereas the daily production and procurement of tortillas produces an imagined community of Mexicans, corn's prominent role in Mexican mythology firmly situates the grain as a critical component of Mexican heritage. Through these myths, the origins of the Mexican people are intimately intertwined with the discovery and use of corn. The number of stories told and retold that include the grain precludes the retelling of all of them here. The myth of human creation through corn is perhaps the most pervasive of all the stories I heard. My own personal friends and their family members, activists, government officials, and street vendors with whom I developed relationships and even elementary schoolchildren attending the school down the block from where I lived in Mexico City all alluded to or fully recounted the tale. But even absent its full telling, the myth has worked its way into daily life through everyday discourse, including sayings and advertisements. Although arguably few Mexicans believe that the events depicted in the story actually took place, the myth continues to shape daily life and understandings (López-Austin 1996). With every telling, the story serves to establish and reestablish the centrality of corn in conceptions of *lo mexicano*.

As noted earlier, the story comes from the *Popol Vuh* – the Mayan myth of creation. Although interviewees did not always identify the *Popol Vuh* as the origin of the myth, they confidently recounted the importance of corn in Mexican life because of how "god made man with corn." The story as told in the *Popol Vuh* (Tedlock 1996) details how humans were originally made from corn. There are multiple versions of the story, but the basic contours outlined here generally hold. The tale proceeds as follows: After numerous failed attempts to fashion man with clay or wood, the Creator finally turned to corn. The Creator ground the corn into flour and mixed the flour with liquid. From this dough, he fashioned the flesh and blood of humans, ultimately creating four men and four women. Their descendants populate the earth today.

The myth works to connect corn to what it means to be Mexican in the most physical of ways – Mexicans are literally made of corn. But it also establishes corn as a critical piece of Mexican heritage by locating it prominently in Mayan mythology. Corn thus connects Mexicans to a precolonial heritage that is elevated and idealized in the telling of the creation story. In doing so, the myth helps produce imaginings of a shared national experience. A shared mythology of common origins in corn is part of what makes a Mexican a Mexican. Interestingly, the myth does not produce exclusionary notions of who is, or is not, Mexican. The *Popul Vuh* tells the story of the origins of all humans – each of us is said to be a product of the Creator's efforts to forge man out of corn. As a result, anyone can claim the myth as the story of his or her own ancestry. Yet when friends, colleagues, and interviewees told the tale, the language was decidedly focused on its Mexican-ness. Mexicans were made from corn, or the story is of "the beginnings of the Mexican people." Thus, the myth is decidedly Mexican, but it still works to create an inclusionary imagining of who might be Mexican. Someone of, for example, European ancestry is not precluded from claiming his or her origins in corn, and the claim works to "make" them Mexican.

When myths are presented in classrooms and living rooms, they need not be understood as "true" to produce an understanding of shared identity or particular connection to a place or thing. Contemporary Mexicans do not need to believe in the legend of the five suns, an Aztec creation myth in which corn plays a central role, or the story of human creation as told in the *Popol Vuh*. But by telling and retelling these stories, the centrality of corn in Mexican identifications continues to be produced and reproduced. The myths serve to place corn at the center of imaginings of what it is to be Mexican today while imbuing the grain with a deep connection to Mexican history. Corn becomes a part of Mexican heritage; it can be connected to the "true," precolonial Mexicans, reflecting something pure and uncompromised. Corn becomes a direct link to the past that, through the very connection it creates, serves to produce contemporary imaginings of Mexico and Mexican-ness.

It is not, however, just through a link to the past that corn's role in daily life finds its way into household tales; corn has also found its way into contemporary children's stories. I heard a variety of stories recounting how children left paths of corn kernels to keep from losing their way in the forests. Unlike their European counterparts, these children often found that edible paths left perfectly reliable trail markers. One story I heard explains the appearance of the night sky through corn – each star is said to be a kernel of corn that lights the sky and shows people the way home through the constellations. These stories show how corn remains an active part of present imaginaries. Corn serves as a navigational device that helps show the way. It is almost as if, without corn, Mexico would somehow be lost.

The ways in which stories of corn are evoked in contemporary Mexico put corn at the center of imaginings of *lo mexicano*. They connect Mexicans to a highly accomplished past, to ancient, advanced civilizations that dominated the region that is Mexico today. Some also artfully incorporate Christian imaginings through tales that recognize elements of what is conceived of as a pre-Columbian version of events while placing Christian figures such as the Virgin Mary on center stage. Corn becomes a touchstone for children, something that helps locate them geographically to find their way "home."

CORN IN RURAL LIFE

Even as references to corn evoke images of tortillas, tamales, or a myth of human creation, they also conjure pictures of *campesinos* and the Mexican countryside. "*Lo campesino*" is both revered and derided as emblematically Mexican. The ideas and images tied to the *campesinado* are fraught with tension. For some Mexicans, these images evoke nostalgia for the past, a notion of an imagined "essence" of what it is to be Mexican, and a connection to ancestors who are imagined to have cultivated the same land in the same way centuries before. It is a heritage of which to be proud, representing the very "best" of what Mexico is, or perhaps what it should be. This pride becomes clear in countless books, magazines, and documentaries dedicated both to corn specifically and to the *campesino* more generally (e.g., see Morales Valderama and Lazcano 2009).[19] A large art-like print magazine, *Diario de Campo* (*Daily of/from/about the Countryside*), comes out approximately every two months, and the newspaper *La Jornada* includes a supplement called *La Jornada del Campo* (*La Jornada of/from/about the Countryside*) every two weeks. Some of the classics of Mexican literature, found in high school and college Mexican literature classes, also adopt *campesinos* as the central and often heroic, if tragic, characters.[20] Even Mexican feature films have celebrated "the" Mexican *campesino*. From *Macario* (1959) to *El Violín* (Vargas Quevedo 2006) or *Los últimos cristeros* (2011), *campesino* life is both essentialized and revered.[21]

---

[19] Whereas the 2002 film *Los últimos zapatistas, héroes olvidados* (Tabone 2002) is most directly a celebration of the members of Zapata's army during the revolution, it is also an excellent example of how *campesinos* are revered and idealized in contemporary Mexican imaginaries.

[20] For example, see Juan Rulfo's works *Pedro Páramo* (1955) and *El llano en llamas* (1986). Even though the countryside is often a desolate place for Rulfo, it remains celebrated, largely through Rulfo's characters. More recently, Cristina Pacheco's works offer a critique of rural–urban migration (e.g., 1983).

[21] Mexican actor Mario Moreno Cantinflas became an iconic national figure in the early 1940s and remained one even after his passing in 1993. Cantinflas's characters offer a particularly good example of how Mexico's *campesinos* are at once revered and derided. Even though Cantinflas's

The rapid decline of a *campesino* way of life, idealized in the image of farmers cultivating corn on small *milpas*, guided by communal expectations of reciprocity, is, for some, something to regret. For others the image of the *campesino* plowing a field of corn behind an ox and plow or planting corn kernels by hand evokes embarrassment. The *campesino* becomes what is wrong with Mexico, an impediment to progress. Tied to old ways and old values, Mexico is held back by these idyllic notions. The country does not, after all, produce corn as efficiently as the United States. The *campesino* is emblematic of the nation's stubbornness and backwardness.

These two images of the *campesino* do not exist separately. Although some statements appear to fall on one side or the other, the ideas are complex and claims can seem contradictory. Both imaginings are often intertwined in reflections by single observers, observers for whom *campesinos* are both a critical piece of Mexican heritage that must be preserved and a frustrating instance of the country's failure to become a "modern" nation.

Unabashed celebration of the Mexican *campesino* appears not only in conversation, but also in places dedicated to deciding what counts as Mexican culture. A volume developed for the opening of the Museum of National Popular Culture titled *El Maíz* (The Corn) is emblematic of how corn and *campesinos* are treated in much of Mexican popular history.[22] The volume remarks that "the resistance of the *campesinos*, their extraordinary capacity to hold on to their customs and traditions, without doubt will bring the miracle of recuperating for everyone a way of living and dying, of working and celebrating, that was defined over centuries by them and by corn" (Zorrilla 1982, 109). *Campesinos* have, in this telling, preserved customs and traditions over centuries – even though these customs may offer little actual resemblance to those of previous centuries, in performing their daily rituals, *campesinos* are offering an imagined connection to Mexico's past. Yet they are also an idealized future. Only through attention to the *campesino* traditions can Mexico return to a hallowed way of "living and dying" (ibid., 109).

A collection of essays on corn published by the National Autonomous University of the State of Mexico offers an additional illustration of unambiguous celebration of *campesino* life.[23] An essay on corn and agricultural diversity

campesino (or urban poor) characters were almost invariably the heroes of his films, they were often comic or "backward" figures.

[22] The entire inaugural exhibit of the museum was dedicated to corn and was titled "*El maíz, fundamento de la cultura popular mexicana*" ("Corn, the foundation of Mexican popular culture"). The museum mounted another exhibit dedicated to corn for the celebration of its tenth inaugural. This second exhibit was titled "*Sin maíz no hay país*" ("Without corn, there is no country"). This phrase went on to become a slogan during the *tortillazo* protests and the name of an ongoing campaign to protect Mexican corn.

[23] The collection cited here is one of many books, essays, magazine issues, and edited volumes that reify and celebrate corn and *campesino* life in the ways outlined here. I have chosen to focus on the volume from the Museum of National Popular Culture and the collection of essays from the

begins, "Campesino agricultural production is a synthesis of the interaction between man and nature. Their practices are based in knowledge of the natural setting, in the satisfaction of family needs and the availability of resources" (Chávez et al. 1999, 69). The claims reflect an idealization and reification of *campesino* life as the embodiment, everywhere and always, of a balance between humans and nature where family is most important, and practices are a response to the natural environment. A later essay in the collection claims that *campesinos* have "perfect knowledge of the conditions of their product, the land, [the] agricultural cycles, and the weather" (González Martínez 1999, 97). Throughout the volume, *campesinos* are not only treated as if they are a coherent, static group, but also as if their behaviors, knowledge, and preferences somehow reflect an ideal, unadulterated, and at times perfect and uncomplicated slice of Mexico.

Corn plays a central role in many of these imaginings that reify and elevate *campesino* life; whereas Mexican *campesinos* cultivate far more than corn, corn is the quintessential crop. As the Museum of National Popular Culture volume cited earlier outlines, corn has come to define "what is understood as well-being, especially *campesino* well-being," in Mexico (Zorrilla 1982, 85). According to the volume, corn helps define and organize the past, dictate the use of space, mark the passage of time, and serve as a foundation for community. Corn continues to be a fundamental element of the rural economy, the base of the social system, and the way of regulating the activities of daily life. With corn, "we fix the sequences of history, the central points on the calendar, the hours of the watch" (ibid., 31). The volume suggests that without corn, Mexico's past would lose its chronology, and the country would be unable to mark time in the present.

The ways in which *El Maíz* and similar volumes describe these systems of reciprocity as producing uncomplicated, ideal, harmonious communities both reflects the elevated status of and works to further elevate *campesino* life in the Mexican imaginary. The descriptions exalt the simple, rural life, where communities revolve around cultivation and cooperate to produce a common good.

Yet even as the *El Maíz* text focuses on the past, it also describes many of the ways in which corn continues to inform the Mexican present. In many rural communities, corn cultivation does, indeed, continue to help locate seasons of the year and structure the time of day. Planting signals the arrival of spring, the height of the stalks marks the progress of the summer months, and the corn harvest indicates the arrival of fall. Chores relating to the cultivation and consumption of corn structure the day – women in many rural communities grind (whether by hand or at a mill) in the mornings, make *masa* midday, and cook tortillas in the early afternoon, just in time for the *comida*. See Figures 4.1 and 4.2 for images of women engaged in cross-generational corn-related tasks.

UAEM as one was produced with an eye toward popular consumption and the other appears to have been generated for more academic audiences.

FIGURE 4.1. A woman and her granddaughter hand-forming tortillas in Munérachi, Chihuahua (photo courtesy of David Lauer).

Although the knowledge that corn structures life in similar ways throughout Mexico helps produce the imagined Mexican community, the routines themselves also produce the quotidian communities that serve as a central foundation for the arguments advanced here. In helping organize communal life, corn produces and reproduces local communities based on routine, face-to-face interactions. Corn-related ceremonies are one of the ways in which quotidian communities are made and remade. Throughout Mexico, residents of small towns and villages come together for elaborate ceremonies to ask for a good harvest or give thanks for one that has passed. As they do the Virgin of Guadalupe, Mexico's quintessential religious symbol, many communities treat corn as though it were a divine phenomenon (de Orellana 2006). The cycle of planting, growth, and harvest relies on an alliance with gods from another world. The alliance must be cultivated, celebrated, and revered. Descriptions of the alliance can also be humanized, with the relationship between the planter and the corn itself depicted as a marriage, both a deep bond and a fragile relationship that must be treated with respect (Neurath 2006). Even though the relationship between a farmer and his field is a deeply personal one, it also works to connect a farmer to his or her neighbors, both through the imagining of similar practices reproduced elsewhere and through the personal connections cultivated when farmers aid one another during planting or harvest seasons.

Whether corn is treated as human, divine, or both, elaborate ceremonies that celebrate the relationship continue to take place throughout rural

FIGURE 4.2. A woman showing her granddaughter how to make *pinole* in Urique, Chihuahua (photo courtesy of David Lauer).

Mexico (see e.g., Alvarez 1982; Díaz León 2003; Imaz and Lipkes 2003). Countless books, magazines, and documentaries describe rituals from corn-blessing ceremonies to corn dances (e.g., see Alvarez 1982; Huasteca 2000; Díaz León 2003; Imaz and Lipkes 2003). The spirit of corn is blessed, protected, and revered during these events, which are often heavily infused with Christian symbols and rituals. Children often have particular roles to play, leading processions or offering gifts. Adults gather to dance, offer blessings, and provide food to both participants and the gods.

Elements of the corn plant are used not only for food, but also to adorn altars, to fashion headpieces, or to make dolls. In their study of Huasteca fiestas, two anthropologists note that during these rituals, corn "represents the Virgin, the mother of God, and Jesus Christ on the cross" (González Aktories and Camacho Díaz 2006, 18).[24] At the end of the harvest, *campesinos* select seeds from the stalks with the best performance during the prior year or

[24] In some communities, white corn is the flesh from the body of Christ, yellow corn is his fat, the blue kernels are his bruises, and the white with the red stripes are his blood (Morales Valderama 2009).

those that exhibited other characteristics beneficial for strong harvests. These seeds are kept in a sacred space through the winter – often an altar of sorts in a family's home – so they can be used for the next year's planting (Gallegos Devése 2009).

These rituals are communally produced, with particular families or individuals making themselves responsible for individual components (food, music, flowers, candles, corn kernels, etc.). Both the preparations for and the celebrations themselves produce and reproduce direct connections with other community members. During the preparations for a corn celebration in rural Michoacán in 2001, I watched neighbors cooperate on the construction of an altar and fight about who was responsible for providing alcohol. At the event itself, they gossiped, told childhood stories, inquired after the health of relatives and friends, talked about their own children, and danced late into the night. One can imagine the same kind of event – where small communities spend time together both preparing for and participating in a corn-related celebration – taking place in rural areas throughout Mexico.

But it is not only through these ceremonies that corn helps produce and reproduce quotidian communities. The small-scale cultivation of corn continues to be based on systems of reciprocity, with labor at the center of the exchange. As in irrigators' local governance organizations in peri-urban and rural Cochabamba or through water cooperatives in urban areas, collaboration around corn cultivation in rural Mexico can require high levels of social coordination. Neighbors unite for the planting and the harvesting, offering their labor on a neighbor's plot in exchange for help when their own time to plant or harvest comes. These systems of mutual help have developed throughout rural Mexico. Just as the *usos y costumbres* of water governance vary in Cochabamba, the practices surrounding corn cultivation vary throughout Mexico. But each reflects a set of communal expectations of reciprocity to ensure that each member has a successful harvest at the end of the season. The need to plant or harvest corn or make *masa* and tortillas can include communal routines and responsibilities. This ideal of cooperation is most certainly not how each harvest season takes place in every *campesino* community. As with Cochabamban *regantes*, individuals fail to live up to their responsibilities by stealing or simply not doing their share. While the idealizations of *campesino* relationships discussed earlier are part of national imaginings, the relationships themselves – with all of the challenges that come with human interactions – are the basis for quotidian communities in places where small-scale corn-based agriculture continues to dominate daily life. These quotidian communities work to produce perceptions of belonging in ways that are similar to those of irrigators and members of water governance groups in Cochabamba.

More formal *campesino* cooperatives, associations, and unions also exist throughout Mexico and help to produce quotidian communities similar to those that emerge through FEDECOR in Cochabamba. While the national union – the

Confederación Nacional Campesina [National Peasant Confederation] (CNC) – structured most of these relationships for more than fifty years, independent unions can now not only mobilize large numbers but also provide places to meet, connect, and organize. Some deliver social programs and others offer services to help *campesinos* expand production and distribute their harvest. For example, regular meetings of members of the *Asociación Nacional de Empresas Comercializadoras de Productores del Campo* [National Association of Commercial Businesses from the Countryside] (ANEC) in Mexico City helped to forge connections between *campesino* leaders from all over the country, creating networks that spanned geographic divides. Many of these associations played key mobilizational roles in the *tortillazo* protests.

Corn may be "life, sustenance, and hope" (Zorrilla 1982, 93) for those who cultivate it. But it is also highly symbolic for those who do not – the idea that *campesinos* are preserving sacred rituals offers hope that an idealized notion of what Mexico "really" is continues to survive. These images of *campesino* life as sacred live side by side in many Mexican cities with conceptions of "backwardness" and "underdevelopment." Whether negative or positive, these images have become emblematic of Mexico even in the country's largest cities, where daily contact with corn usually comes in the form of consumption.

CUISINE AND NATION

The role cuisine can play in helping produce and reproduce national identifications has not gone unnoticed by scholars.[25] Pilcher reminds us that "cuisine and other seemingly mundane aspects of daily life compose an important part of the cultures that bind people into national communities" (1998, 2). Anthropologist Arjun Appadurai (1988) shows how cookbooks helped forge a national cuisine in India, and Pilcher describes a similar process in Mexico. According to Pilcher, the increasing use of cookbooks in 1940s Mexico helped dissolve regional and ethnic boundaries. Dishes distinct to Veracruz became national delicacies, and moles became "national" cuisine. The same "interplay of regional inflection and national standardization" (Appadurai 1988, 6) that Appadurai identifies in India both forged a national menu and made regional cuisines sources of national pride in Mexico. The nationalism that emerges

[25] Whether "traditional" Mexican cuisine is a tradition conceived of and propagated by government officials, business leaders, or perhaps even cookbook publishers, is irrelevant to the questions explored here. How corn came to take on the meanings it has today is a secondary concern to what those meanings are and what work they do to produce and reproduce Mexican culture. See Zolov (1999) for a discussion of how Mexican "national" music was largely invented by Mexican government officials in the 1930s and 1940s who promoted music largely from Jalisco as a national tradition. Whether corn is an "invented tradition" (see Hobsbawm and Ranger 1983 for more on invented traditions) matters little when the central question focuses on the contemporary work corn does to produce and reproduce notions of Mexican-ness.

through food reflects an almost inclusive ethnic nationalism – regional traditions are affirmed but subsumed into a national conception of *lo mexicano*. Foods can be hailed as reflecting particular regions, but they can, at the same time, be understood as consummately Mexican.

Similarly, a willingness to celebrate *campesino* food at the national level has helped blur regional boundaries and forge a sense of shared national experience. The interplay between regional and national, *campesino* and haute cuisines highlights commonalities that already exist while working to make common cuisines that have not always been enjoyed throughout the country. Cookbooks published from the mid-twentieth century through today make the prominent role of corn in the Mexican diet clear while elevating particular corn dishes, most notably tamales, as a marker of the Mexican nation.

Corn-based foods, whether prepared at home or consumed on the streets, have become a critical ingredient in *lo mexicano*, in part because of the proliferation of cookbooks. These foods connect Mexicans across space and time, as one can imagine the production and consumption of similar foods not only across regions in contemporary Mexico, but also in a Mexican past, present, and future. In her introduction to the reprinting of a cookbook first published in 1831 called *Cocinero Mexicano*, Mexican researcher and journalist Cristina Barros writes that the clearest "Mexican presence" in the cookbook is in the section on "light lunches prepared with tortillas or corn masa" (Anonymous 2000, 1831, 10). Even the book's own description of these meals describes them as "truly national" (ibid., 149). Perhaps what is most interesting, however, is that it is not only the original authors', but also Barros's comments written in 2000 that highlight the role of corn in Mexican cuisine. Literacy rates alone suggest that it is unlikely that the books were widely read in Mexico in the mid-1800s. As a result, they are not interesting for the work they did in producing national imaginings at the time, but rather as a reflection of consumption patterns. That the books were republished speaks to the importance of food in contemporary Mexican culture and conceptions of Mexican heritage; that Barros and the original authors draw our attention to the link between corn and nation suggests that corn was central to Mexican daily life in 1831 and in 2000.

As cookbooks became more widely read in the mid-twentieth century, they bridged regional and temporal boundaries, making dishes such as tacos, enchiladas, and tamales into symbols of national unity. Marketed to Mexico's urban middle classes, the cookbooks may have played a role in the highly critiqued process of "homogenization" that weakened regional particularities. But they also helped create a common national conversation through food. This forging of a national cuisine not only gave corn a particular place in Mexican national imaginings, but also helped generate an awareness of the grain's importance throughout the country. Knowledge of other regional cuisines and the elevation of those cuisines into national symbols supported an awareness of corn's importance throughout the country. Mexicans in Sonora could

FIGURE 4.3. Grilling *elotes* on the street in Mexico City (photo courtesy of Bonjwing Lee).

imagine Mexicans in Oaxaca making not simply similar dishes, but meals with a similar foundational ingredient – corn. It was not only the sharing of recipes that forged a sense of connectedness within the boundaries of the Mexican nation-state, but also the use of common ingredients – corn generally and tortillas more specifically. See Figure 4.3 for a style of corn preparation common on Mexico City streets.

With or without cookbooks, the specific genre of the taco has established a particularly strong presence throughout Mexico. Academic and public intellectual Sergio Aguayo (2007) wrote during the *tortillazo* protests that tacos in particular were the central ingredient in the Mexican diet, and a symbol of national "identity and diversity." "With the exception of the tortilla," he goes on to write, "what do the lobster tacos with rice and beans of Baja California have in common with pork tacos from Arandas, Jalisco, or those from the basket of the Federal District?" At the small taco stands that pepper the street corners in Mexico City, you can see men and women in business dress standing next to construction workers as they eat tacos of almost every variety. I passed a taco stand just off of Insurgentes in the La Roma neighborhood almost daily. The vendors – a husband-and-wife team, often accompanied by their small son – knew customers by name and often chatted with them about politics or family as they prepared their orders. Urban life does not eliminate daily routines or local ties that revolve around taco consumption.

Not surprisingly, corn is the central ingredient in many of Mexico's other national dishes as well. Yet even for those in which corn is absent – mole poblano, for example – tortillas are a critical accompaniment. Baskets of tortillas arrive with almost any order at restaurants throughout Mexico. Day-old tortillas find their way into tostadas, totopos (corn chips), soup, or chilaquiles.[26] Whether they are eaten immediately or stored in the refrigerator or freezer, tortillas are often treated with extra care. At the home of a friend, a household employee warned me not to drop a tortilla on the floor or I would be cursed with hunger until I could prove that I truly valued my food. This particular superstition is, according to Mexican anthropologist Miriam Bertrán Vilá, widespread, particularly among indigenous communities (2005, 66).

Approximately 80 percent of the corn consumed in Mexico finds its way into hungry mouths via the tortilla. The Mexican government estimates that a million tons of tortillas are produced per year in Mexico. Of those, 29 percent are made with *nixtamal* (the traditional method), 30 percent with plain corn flour, and the remaining 41 percent with a mix of the two. An estimated 50 percent of the calories in the Mexican diet come via the tortilla, and the percentage rises for the poorest of the population (Instituto Nacional de Salud Pública 2006). The price of tortillas clearly matters on a material level. But, as I argued earlier, the material and the ideational cannot be pried apart. Tortillas became and remain important symbolically precisely because of their material role.

But it is not just through eating the corn discs that tortilla-related practices can forge feelings of national belonging. The process of producing tortillas can work in similar ways. Whether in a home in the Sierra Juárez of Oaxaca or a *tortillería* in the center of Mexico City, every stage in tortilla making broadcasts membership in Mexican culture and signifies a respect for Mexican heritage and tradition.[27] In these moments, the self may be a "performed character" (see Goffman 1959), but the performance does not imply that the nation produced in those moments is experienced as anything less than authentic. Whether a Mexican dedicates a full day to the grinding of *masa* and the forming of tortillas, goes to a local *tortillería* to procure the day's supply, or buys premade, prepackaged tortillas at Wal-Mart, he or she can imagine other Mexicans throughout the country performing the same ritual. Purchasing supermarket tortillas may seem very different from making them at home with a *metate*. Yet the tortillas still serve to connect their purchaser to a past, to a mother or grandmother who also ensured that tortillas were on the table for every *comida*, or perhaps to an imagining of colonial or precolonial

---

[26] Chilaquiles are usually a breakfast dish made from fried tortilla chips and salsa. Eggs and chicken are often included as well.

[27] Interestingly, anecdotal evidence suggests that this is just as powerful, if not more so, for many individuals of Mexican origin residing outside of the country as it is for those within Mexico's geographical boundaries.

practices. In the hours it takes to produce handmade tortillas or the seconds required to purchase them at a supermarket, the practice of making or buying tortillas creates imagined connections among Mexicans – connections that signify membership in the Mexican nation.

But the imagined community of nation is not the only community produced by the process of making or procuring tortillas. Quotidian communities also emerge in the daily tortilla routine. The process of hand grinding corn can bring small groups of women together for a number of hours, sharing stories and gossip as they work. In a small town in rural Oaxaca, I watched as five women ground corn for two hours – talking, laughing, and bickering as they passed the time. This daily ritual, however, largely takes place only in particularly remote areas. Yet even in rural or peri-urban areas where corn is rarely hand ground, the process of tortilla production helps create and sustain quotidian communities. Whereas their dynamics differ from hours together at the *metate*, corn mills also work as social centers. Groups of women gather in the mornings to catch up on the community news while waiting in line for their corn to be ground.

One sees similar dynamics in urban Mexico, although they are one step further removed from the production process. *Tortillerías* fill Mexico City and many families (or their household employees) buy fresh tortillas daily from the same spot. During the *tortillazo* protests, *Reforma* reported that more than 87 percent of Mexicans who purchased tortillas (as opposed to making them at home) bought them at local *tortillerías* (Alatorre 2007a, 2007b).[28] Two or three people usually staffed the *tortillería* that I visited regularly. They made the *masa* and pressed the tortillas with small, hand-operated presses throughout the day. Other *tortillerías* use a more mechanized system to press each tortilla. *Tortillerías* can serve as a routine meeting place where neighbors say hello, share local gossip, and produce and reproduce communal ties.

The daily tortilla purchase shares some features with the semi-weekly wait for water in cooperatives in Cochabamba's Southern Zone. The local *tortillería* can be a routine meeting spot where community connections are established and reestablished. I watched patrons in line at *tortillerías* throughout the city as they greeted the employees by name, often struck up conversations with other regulars, and ran into acquaintances. As with the routine practices of water procurement in Cochabamba, these exchanges might include questions after the health of a grandparent, the school accomplishments of a child, or local politics. Each individual encounter, as well as the repetition of these morning encounters over weeks, months, or years, forges and sustains connections within a city of more than 20 million people (see Figure 4.4 for images of neighborhood *tortillerías* in Mexico City).[29]

---

[28] The data in *Reforma* is based on the 2005 *Encuesta Nacional de Ingresos y Gastos de los Hogares*.
[29] Some dynamics are different between *tortillería* encounters in Mexico City and those at community wells in Cochabamba. *Tortillería* customers are overwhelmingly women, and many are purchasing tortillas not only for their own families, but also for the families of employers.

FIGURE 4.4. Two neighborhood *tortillerías* in Colonia Narvarte in Mexico City (photos of courtesy José Luis Enríquez).

Although daily trips to the *tortillería* in Mexico City and routine visits to the community well in Cochabamba might work similarly in how they help to produce quotidian communities, there is one particularly marked way in which the Mexican and Bolivian cases differ with respect to face-to-face communities. Family figures prominently in the discussion of the Mexican case and appears little, if at all, in the discussion of water in Cochabamba. Families are most certainly quotidian communities, but they differ from the other kinds of quotidian communities discussed in this book. The quotidian community produced by family would continue to exist even without corn. Unlike the other quotidian communities discussed, like, for example, the Cochabamban *regantes* that appear in Chapters 2 and 3, the purpose of the family community is not likely to be corn related. Whereas *regante* associations could actually disappear were water to be regulated in particular ways in Cochabamba, even the elimination of corn from the Mexican diet is unlikely to eliminate the Mexican family. But this is not to say that perceptions of what family is and family means couldn't have been perceived to be at risk when corn and tortilla prices rose. Critical imaginings of family – of what mothers and fathers cook for their children, of the kinds of foods made by grandparents, of the meals made during regular Sunday lunches – were rendered insecure. Families may continue to exist without corn, but family practices – those routines and rituals that help to construct understandings of what family is – would most certainly be altered.

The practices described here – family and otherwise – not only produce and reproduce both imagined and quotidian connections to other Mexicans, but also conceptions of who or what a Mexican should be. Mexican anthropologist Valdez Ruiz writes that as many in Mexico like to take as "fact" that everyone thinks alike and shares the same customs throughout the country, "corn moves from being a cultural element to something that is seen as ours, or as a symbol of Mexican identity, including the supposition that all Mexicans, or at least 'a good Mexican' that appreciates being Mexican, should eat tortillas, beans and chiles, that they should love to drink mescal, tequila, or pulque" (1999, 19).[30] "Proper" Mexicans are expected to consume and enjoy tortillas and other corn-based foods. And they reaffirm their identity as Mexicans while doing so. Mexico's political elites are no exception, as tortillas, tamales, and other corn-based foods often appear at campaign events or political rallies (see Figure 4.5).

Yet even as many Mexicans identify corn-based cuisine as a marker of *lo mexicano*, these understandings are not without tension. As the preceding analysis of corn and rural Mexico addressed, how corn is understood to

---

[30] Pulque is a fermented drink made from maguey. The drink reportedly dates back to pre-Columbian Mexico and was heavily consumed throughout the country until the early twentieth century. One can still find pulque in Mexico City, but it is rarely on menus, appearing most frequently in the small restaurants that fill large markets.

FIGURE 4.5. Tamales and politics. PRI presidential candidate Enrique Peña Nieto is served tamales (which he is pictured here on the right enjoying) after giving a press conference (photo courtesy of *La Jornada*, February 11, 2012).

tie Mexico to a rural, often distinctly indigenous past can make corn-based, *campesino* foods into a symbol of failure to modernize. The associations with national cuisine are not unambiguously positive. Instead, there is a tension, a sense, for some, that particular dishes, while undoubtedly continuing to signify "nation," do so in ways that signal a slice of Mexico of which some are not proud. Here some dishes are not a component of Mexican heritage that is to be revered, but rather a part of a *campesino*, indigenous, and "backward" Mexico.

In spite of this, cooking itself is a ritual that reinforces national bonds. The production and reproduction of Mexican recipes – whether written in cookbooks or passed orally down from one cook to the next – in households throughout the country can, in and of themselves, serve as instantiations of patriotism. The routines and practices of cooking in everyday life have become national symbols, imbued with political meanings.[31] As cookbooks proliferated, women became aware that other women thousands of miles away were making tortillas in similar ways, preparing pozole with the same kind of corn (even if the particulars of the recipes differed), and serving their families tamales (even if the particular fillings differed) for special occasions. The very idea of imagining other women engaged in similar daily routines and

[31] See Hobsbawm (1992).

FIGURE 4.6. Preparing quesadillas and quecas on a *comal* in a market in Puebla (photo courtesy of Bonjwing Lee).

other families sitting down to similar meals helped to put cuisine, and corn in particular, at the center of how imaginings of the Mexican nation are produced and reproduced.

As the anecdote on La Roma that opened this chapter makes clear, cornstalks are no strangers to city life. Yet most urban Mexicans encounter corn on a daily basis through their prolific consumption of the grain. You can find something made with corn prepared and sold on almost any block in Mexico City and in most cities throughout Mexico (see Figure 4.6 for an image from Puebla). "Fast food" in Mexico includes not only the street vendors described earlier, but also national chains that offer sit-down service. One such chain is exemplary of how corn and tortillas appear even in the most generic culinary environments. Vips is a national chain with at least one location in every state.[32] It is a popular spot for business breakfasts or lunches, to meet friends for a meal, or even for a family gathering. The ambiance is relatively bland with booths covered in faux red leather, and nondescript chairs and wall decorations. The menu includes offerings familiar to any American – pancakes and waffles as well as a cheeseburger, pepperoni pizza, or even a philly cheesesteak for lunch or dinner. But chilaquiles are also an option during the morning hours, and eggs are always

---

[32] Sanborns offers a similar, generic experience, with slightly more "Mexican" decor. A restaurant/store combination (you can buy everything from batteries to perfume after or before your meal), Sanborns has locations throughout Mexico as well (although its reach is not quite as far as Vips's is) and offers menu items that, like Vips, range from hamburgers to moles.

served with corn tortillas. For lunch or dinner, a host of options includes enchiladas, tacos, and tortilla soup, and the "Mexican" salad comes with tortilla strips. Tortilla chips arrive at every table before you order, whether you're eating breakfast, lunch, or dinner, and tortillas are always available upon request if they don't come with your meal.

Corn is also a centerpiece of cuisine at more exclusive urban venues. The Club de Industriales (club for industrialists or businesspeople) is a private club catering to businessmen and businesswomen that "promotes good eating and great style" and has locations in a number of the country's biggest cities.[33] The Mexico City venue changes its menu regularly, but the host suggested that tortillas were almost always served with the main course, and that the offerings usually include something "traditionally Mexican." At an equally upscale venue in Mexico City, a breakfast for Finance Minister Augustín Carstens, hosted by friends of the University of Chicago, eggs, fruit, and coffee came with tortillas and tortilla chips.

It goes without saying that at the top Mexican restaurants in Mexico City, corn is included in every meal, even if it comes only in the form of homemade tortillas. El Cardinal, just off of the Zócalo, is about as "traditional" as it gets and handmade white corn tortillas come with nearly everything. At Pujol and Izote, both located in the upscale neighborhood of Polanco (in 2014 Pujol was number twenty on the list of the top fifty restaurants in the world, a group compiled annually by The Diners Club®), the fare won't likely look like what your Mexican grandmother made, but corn appears throughout both menus and the Mexican-ness of the venues is signaled, in part, through these reinventions. Even "modern" Mexican cuisine doesn't do without corn.

CELEBRATING CORN

Corn is part of daily life in both urban and rural areas, and it is also the explicit focus of special events. In communities where agriculture remains the center of daily life, these special events may look like the planting and harvest festivals already discussed. In more urban areas, *ferias* or *festivales* (both translate most closely to "festival") of corn provide moments to come together as a town or neighborhood and celebrate food, family, community, and almost anything else. In larger urban areas these events do not require the kind of high-level social coordination and initiative necessary in rural communities. Instead, they are often coordinated by municipal councils. In Xochimilco, a Mexico City borough famous for its waterways, the neighborhood of Santiago Tepalcatlalpan hosts an annual Festival of Corn and Tortillas, usually in the late spring. Even though Xochimilco is undoubtedly an urban area, many residents continue to cultivate their own corn and make tortillas by hand. The festival serves as an opportunity to celebrate and promote the

[33] www.club.org.mx/. Viewed March 7, 2012.

corn-based cuisine that the neighborhood's residents produce. In 2009, the festival included musical performances at night and various cultural events during the day. Attendees could watch women make dolls from cornhusks; browse a photographic exhibition focusing on corn and the Xochimilco neighborhood of Santiago Tepalcatlalpan; listen to a variety of lectures on corn-related topics; watch pre-Columbian dances; view *tapetes* made of corn; and, of course, try a wide variety of corn-based foods.

To encourage residents from throughout the city (and perhaps any visiting foreigners) to attend the festival, the local government developed a variety of promotional materials, each of which sheds light on the ways in which corn is part of the contemporary Mexican imaginary. The festival is, according to the borough's promotional website, "an homage" to the women who cultivate and cook with corn (Xochimilco 2012). These women, the website argues, "have taken great pains at every stage of development, from the cultivating, to the way they create the *nixtamal*, grinding it in the *metate* to make masa; moving their hands with different gestures to make tortillas that are oval or round" (ibid.). The website goes on, entreating the reader to "come and taste" the various goods on offer. "To know Mexico and love Mexican culture it is necessary to taste the different products made with corn flour," the materials argue.

The poster advertising the twentieth annual festival (pictured in Figure 4.7a) announces the dates and location, advertising that there will be "history," "culture," "art," "food/cooking (*gastronomía*)," and "entertainment." The only other words on the poster state, "A Living Tradition." Whether corn is the living tradition or the referent is the festival itself is ambiguous. The phrase can be read as referring to both – the traditions of cultivating, cooking, and consuming corn continue to "live" in Mexico while corn itself is also both a living plant and a part of a living Mexico. It isn't immediately clear what all of the images on the posters' artwork symbolize, but a rendering of a presumably pre-Columbian woman is most prominent. She holds something glowing in her hands (corn?) and wears a skirt decorated with images of corncobs. The buildings behind her appear pre-Columbian as well, but buildings to her right recall a colonial aesthetic. The art firmly places corn as part of Mexico's precolonial heritage, while also drawing corn into colonial times. The poster appears to pull corn into the present through the festival itself.

Interestingly, although the language on the poster advertising the previous year's festival remains exactly the same, the image could not be more different (see Figure 4.7b). A bright yellow corncob, half shucked, appears simply against a black backdrop. The attention is on the corn itself, lending new emphasis to the phrase "a living tradition." Instead of evoking connections to Mexican cultural history, the poster suggests a different connection to Mexico's past. The kernels themselves, as products of generations of *campesino* selection and cultivation, serve as containers of Mexican history. The poster draws our attention to the value of the kernels, making it difficult to avoid thinking of

(a)

(b)

FIGURE 4.7. Posters from the 2008 and the 2009 Xochimilco corn and tortilla festivals.

the threat to Mexico's "criollo" corn from genetically modified varieties. The perceived threat to Mexican culture here comes not from changing practices in how corn is used in daily life, but rather from the possibility that centuries of knowledge, embodied in the corn itself, might be lost with the arrival of genetically modified organisms (GMOs). Both posters depict a living tradition, if in very different ways.

Corn festivals take place annually throughout Mexico and can look very different from place to place. The festival in Xochimilco consciously roots itself in Mexican history; others seem less intent on celebrating corn as an element of Mexican heritage. Instead, many of the festivals appear to function like a big town party, bringing residents to the streets to listen to music (everything from Mariachis to local rock bands), share food, play carnival-like games, and watch fireworks.[34] These festivals take place throughout the country and at various times of year, some of which appear to have been chosen for their connection to planting; the harvest; or the celebration of the birth of Christ. For example, the festival in Ocampo, Tamaulipas, coincides with the Christmas holiday, kicking

---

[34] The Xochimilco festival is among many that emphasize corn's role in Mexican heritage and culture. Among other such festivals I found what appeared to be similar events in Ixtenco, Tlaxcala; Amantlán, Tepotzlán, Morelos; San Cristóbal de las Casas, Chiapas; and Teotitlán del Valle, Oaxaca.

FIGURE 4.8. A sign displayed at the 2011 National Day of Corn in Mexico City (photo credit: AFP).

FIGURE 4.9. Promotional posters for the 2009 National Day of Corn celebrations.

off on December 24 with music, dancing, and fireworks, and lasting through the 28th. Corn festivals in Jalisco and Aguascalientes include a Western-style beauty pageant where the "Queen of the Corn Festival" is chosen.

These festivals, where the focus is less on celebrating corn as heritage and more on celebrating contemporary life, help locate corn in the Mexican present irrespective of a connection to Mexico's past. As teenage girls put on evening gowns and makeup and parade in front of audiences cheering their names in the hopes of being named Queen of the Corn Festival, they are at once a part of a pageant culture common throughout Mexico and a reminder of the centrality of corn in daily life.

A relative newcomer to the scene of Mexican corn festivals is the "National Day of Corn," a celebration held annually throughout the country on September 29. U.S. Spanish-language television channel Univision covered the third annual celebration of the National Day of Corn, which had taken place the previous day. Coverage included a clip on the evening news and photos on the channel's website.[35] The images on the website were accompanied by the caption "More than a culinary object, corn is a fundamental part of the Mexican culture" (Univisión 2011). One of the photos reproduced here shows the shadow of a man dancing next to an image of a corncob that has been altered to make it appear like a heart, with large arteries protruding from the top of the corncob (see Figure 4.8). The words "*maíz y libertad* (corn and freedom)" circle the top. The image has appeared repeatedly during this annual celebration, both at the events themselves and in promotional materials. A promotional poster for the 2009 National Day of Corn includes the image printed on a stack of tortillas (see Figure 4.9).

In addition to recalling the myths of the *Popul Vuh* and the statements that "corn is our flesh" or "corn is in our blood" discussed earlier in this chapter, the images are visual representations of the idea that corn is what keeps Mexico alive – that *sin maíz, no hay país* (without corn, there is no country). Corn flows through the blood of Mexicans because it is the basic element in the daily diet, but it is also, as the slogan suggests, a critical component to maintaining Mexican independence. "Freedom" in the phrase "corn and freedom" evokes concerns around national sovereignty; to turn to other nations to supply Mexico's "blood" would foster dependence and undermine independence. The heart image, in particular, connects the themes of this chapter into one clear visual – corn as the heart of Mexico.

CONCLUSIONS

In *The Labyrinth of Solitude* (1985), Mexican author Octavio Paz argues that Mexicans spend much of their lives living behind masks, putting a face to the

---

[35] TV Azteca and Televisa were among the other news stations to cover the National Day of Corn.

world that is not reflective of who Mexicans "truly" are.[36] One of the few moments in which these masks disappear, he argues, is during fiestas, when Mexicans can reveal their "real" identities. Food is at the center of these events. Even though Paz's formulation is problematic (How can a public persona ever be pried apart from a "true" self? How can we even begin to imagine what a "true" self is?), that he turns to the moment of fiesta as a place where Mexican-ness is revealed is itself revealing. Fiestas are about more than the tacos or tamales that are consumed, but food is at the center of any Mexican party, helping to construct communities as small as a family or a neighborhood or as large as a nation.

But it is not just through food that corn continues to be a part of urban Mexican identity. The telling and retelling of founding myths and historical legacies and the ways in which corn has worked its way into everyday sayings are also part of why corn is so intimately tied to notions of what it means to be Mexican. The imagined notion of the essence of Mexico somehow surviving on a *campesino's milpa* is also particularly powerful within urban communities. Pilcher notes that corn has become "a symbol of nostalgic nationalism for the urban middle class" (1998, 121). To burn a tortilla on a *comal* is still considered bad luck in many households; corn should be revered, treated with respect. Corn cultivation and consumption is both part of an ancient tradition that must be protected to ensure that being Mexican still means something and simply a description of what "we do" as Mexicans.

But these kinds of imaginings of national belonging are not the only conceptions of community produced through relationships with corn; this chapter has shown how, throughout Mexico, corn works to create face-to-face, quotidian communities. The quotidian communities produced and reproduced around corn are in some ways very similar to those that emerged around water in Cochabamba. Connections among people form and are reinforced through the ways in which corn and water are at the center of daily practices and livelihood strategies. But the extent to which those relationships do not require high forms of social coordination and collaboration, particularly in urban Mexico, differs from the Cochabamban connections forged through communal efforts to obtain water in urban neighborhoods or to regulate irrigation in peri-urban and rural areas.

The kinds of quotidian communities exemplified by *regantes* or local water cooperatives in Cochabamba did exist in many rural agricultural areas in Mexico dominated by corn farming. But the high levels of social coordination required for water use and consumption in much of Cochabamba is largely unnecessary in order to access corn or tortillas in urban Mexico. Daily conversations at taco stands or with tortilla vendors may help to create perceptions of shared experiences and belonging, but they are unlikely to produce the kinds of

---

[36] Although the first edition of this book came out in 1961, I would argue that the observations drawn on here remain relevant in contemporary Mexico.

ties that emerge through shared labor and communal reciprocity. Acts of cooking and consumption shared in a family kitchen, around a family dining table, or at a community celebration may create different types of quotidian connections than those that emerge through practices of communal water governance.

The emphasis on the quotidian community of family is also a difference between the two cases. The ties between corn and the domestic sphere and the ways in which family relationships are produced and reinforced through corn that are so prevalent in Mexico do not have an immediately apparent parallel in the Cochabamban case. And these differences may have played important roles in the kinds of resources and frames available to the two movements. The community autonomy and self-governance concerns that were front and center in Cochabamba were largely marginal during the *tortillazo* protests. Independence emerged as a theme but it largely invoked desires for national independence as opposed to autonomy or self-governance at the neighborhood or regional level. Yet while the types of quotidian communities playing dominant roles in the social mobilizations may have differed, it is clear that, in both cases, relationships to goods at the center of life and livelihood produced routine connections built on face-to-face interaction and that these relationships mattered in the mobilization process.

Link to corn & national identity but not link between NI & contention

- Quotidian communities rely on culture rather than necessity.

5

Sin Maíz No Hay País: the Mexican
tortillazo protests

In the fall of 2006, corn and tortilla prices rose throughout Mexico. In January 2007, a protest movement emerged. The claims revolved around access to affordable, Mexican corn and tortillas and the discourse was firmly rooted in connections between corn and community in Mexico. Key demands revolved around subsistence concerns, setting in motion causal processes and generating movement characteristics reminiscent of those of the water wars. The *tortillazo* protests did not grow to the size or strength of the protests in Cochabamba. The movement never gained momentum and quickly collapsed. Yet while the outcomes were decidedly different, some of the mechanisms at work in Cochabamba and Mexico look remarkably similar. In Wittgenstein's (1973) language, the cases bear a "family resemblance" that creates the opportunity to think about how subsistence-related protests might share similar character- istics across space and time. When I look at the two cases together, I can push my theoretical model beyond water to speak to the ways in which the market- ization of other kinds of subsistence concerns might be related to mobilization. Analysis of resistance to the marketization of corn in Mexico allows us to explore how corn and water might work in similar ways in different times and places and why they work similarly when they do.

The comparison also allows me to exploit the tensions that come from study- ing movements in different political contexts and with different trajectories. The *tortillazo* protests of 2007 were neither the first nor the most dramatic instance of popular resistance to market reforms in Mexico.[1] Political mobilizations are nothing new in the country. In particular, unions and *campesino* organizations

---

[1] The protests that grew out of rising tortilla prices in the winter of 2007 undoubtedly drew on the networks and connections developed during the course of both the now well-known indigenous movement that began in Chiapas in 1994 and the sustained efforts of Mexican farmers during the *El Campo No Aguanta Más* [The Countryside Can Bear No More] (ECNAM) movement – a national effort to secure various agrarian reforms – in 2003.

are capable of rallying large numbers of their members to participate in demonstrations in the nation's capital. The existence of previous, larger, explicitly
anti-neoliberal movements sets the Mexican protests surrounding the tortilla
crisis strikingly apart from the water wars in Cochabamba. Furthermore, while
the water wars transformed Bolivian politics and gained international attention as the "first victory" of the larger anti-neoliberal movement, the *tortillazo*
protests arguably have largely been forgotten.

Yet even as the protests emerged in distinct contexts and took different
paths, similar dynamics were at work in the early mobilizing moments of the
tortillazo protests and the water wars. The *tortillazo* protests brought together
individuals across occupational and regional divides and in spite of internal
sectoral squabbles. *Campesinos*, union members, civil society organizations,
a largely unorganized urban consumer base, and political leaders from every
major party came together around a common concern.[2] Furthermore, many
of the participants did not belong to a formal sectoral organization or union.
Whereas the urban unions' and *campesino* organizations' abilities to mobilize
their own members is not surprising, the participation of individuals without
membership in a sectoral group or union is noteworthy. Many of these people
were participating in their first political mobilization, and were not in attendance at the behest of a union official or with the expectation of material compensation (author interviews with *tortillazo* protest participants, January–July
2009, Mexico City).[3] The perceived importance of corn – both to quotidian and
to imagined communities – dominates movement rhetoric and media coverage.

[2] The coalition that emerged on the streets defied historical expectations. Cooperation between
unions and farmers' organizations evidenced in January 2007 is not routine. Furthermore, splits
within the *campesino* movement, particularly in the aftermath of ECNAM, have hindered coop-
eration between organizations with large membership bases such as the *Asociación Nacional de
Empresas Comercializadoras de Productores del Campo* [National Association of Commercial
Businesses from the Countryside] (ANEC), the *Central Campesino Cardenista* [Cardenist
Farmers' Union] (CCC), and the *Unión Nacional de Organizaciones Regionales Campesinas
Autónomas* [National Union of Regional, Autonomous *Campesino* Organizations] (UNORCA).
Indeed, the post-ECNAM splits in the *campesino* movement have been the subject of significant
scholarship (in particular, see Sánchez Albarrán 2007). The extensive cooperation both within
the *campesino* movement and between *campesinos* and urban workers that took place around
the *tortillazo* requires explanation. Equally worthy of note is how political cooperation crossed
party lines, with each of Mexico's three major parties calling on the Calderón administration
to take action, and leaders of Calderón's own *Partido Acción Nacional* [National Action Party]
(PAN) endorsing, if not participating directly in, the protest events.

[3] This citation is meant to indicate that the evidence for the preceding claim came from multiple
interviewees during the course of research. Variations on this citation appear throughout the
text. I try to be as specific as possible in each of the citations. The type of mobilization is also
puzzling. The mention of dramatic food price increases often precedes images of riots. Food
prices hit a record high in the summer of 2008 and riots in Cote d'Ivoire, Mozambique, and
Haiti made front-page news across the world. Yet the mobilizations in response to rising tortilla
prices in Mexico were most certainly not riots. Protest events were planned, coordinated, and
consistently peaceful. What emerged was a cross-sectoral, cross-class, and urban–rural peaceful
social movement demanding access to affordable tortillas.

This chapter serves this book's argument by making a case for the gener-
alizability of the theoretical propositions – this chapter shows that the subsistence arguments advanced here should not be limited to water. The evidence
presented in the following pages suggests that the events in Cochabamba were
not epiphenomenal and that a theoretical focus on the connections among
marketization, subsistence resources, and political protest is warranted. We see
similar mechanisms – subsistence-related communal identifications producing
cross-cleavage solidarities – working to mobilize political protest around a perceived market-driven threat to corn in Mexico as we did when privatization
threatened water in Cochabamba. The comparison between the water wars in
Bolivia and the tortilla crisis in Mexico highlights how different goods can be
understood in similar ways and, as a result, work similarly to produce protest.
Analysis of the Mexican case is critical for both the development of the analytical category and for the refinement of the mechanisms at work. This chapter
also shows how the theoretical arguments play out in strikingly similar ways
in different times and places.
   We can best explain the emergence of a broad-based movement during the
tortillazo protests by understanding how the perceived vagaries and vicissitudes
of the market interacted with the meanings that corn took on in the Mexican
context. As with the water wars, how the good at stake symbolized community helps us to better understand the alliances that emerged. To threaten corn
was to threaten family, community, and nation in the ways that threats to
other basic foods did not. An activist affiliated with a *campesino* organization
remarked, "corn is a *tema aglutinador* [theme that ties things together]. We are
all made with a base of corn. We knew there was incredible potential to bring
all of Mexico together in a fight against so many years of neoliberal techno-
crats" (author interview, June 2009, Mexico City). Many understood corn to
be critical to life and livelihood. It symbolized both the imagined community
(Anderson 1991) of the Mexican nation and the quotidian communities of
family and neighborhood.
   An analysis of the discourse and symbols deployed by protest leaders and
participants, as well as the media and other analysts, during the *tortillazo* protests shows how these meanings powerfully shaped political resistance. When
markets created perceived insecurities around access to corn – when individuals
imagined that they or other Mexicans might not be able to consume a good at
the center of daily life and imaginings of nation – unexpected alliances formed
and people voiced opposition in the streets. To explain why so many different
organizations came together during the *tortillazo* protests and why their message resonated so widely, we must look to the ways corn as perceived material
necessity and as symbol is intertwined in the Mexican context and how these
meanings intersect with expectations of the state, communities, and markets.
   Because of the rapid rise and fall of the corn movement, as well as the similar ways in which meanings worked across sectoral divides, this chapter is
structured slightly differently from the one on the Cochabamban water wars.

This chapter begins with a discussion of the political and economic context of marketization in Mexico followed by a brief narrative of the events surrounding the tortilla crisis. The core is structured around four discursive themes: domesticity, class, security, and nation. The discourse used and symbols deployed during the *tortillazo* protests show how conceptions of family, domestic life, and class (understood not only in reference to income, but also to occupation) intersected with conceptions of security and nation to help generate this episode of contention. The themes cannot be neatly pried apart – much of the discourse and many of the symbols analyzed in the pages that follow are relevant to all four rubrics. However, by structuring the analysis around them, I show the ways in which corn worked as a symbol for family and nation and how those meanings help explain the broad-based mobilization in Mexico in January 2007.

CORPORATIST LEGACIES AND MARKET REFORMS

Central to movement organizers' ability to mobilize so many people so quickly in January 2007 were the legacies of a politics of "inclusionary corporatism" (Stepan 1978). To understand how the *tortillazo* protests unfolded we must place them in the context of the legacies of corporatist governance. For more than seventy years Mexico's labor, peasant, and popular sectors were directly integrated into the *Partido Revolucionario Institucional* [Institutional Revolutionary Party] (PRI) – Mexico's ruling party – through overarching federations that penetrated deeply into Mexican civil society (Knight 1991). When independent labor and *campesino* organizations began to emerge in the 1970s and 1980s they created new opportunities for social mobilization and challenged traditional corporatist organizations to adapt to a changing political climate.

But corporatist legacies were not so easily dismantled. Independent organizations drew on the preexisting formal sectoral networks and organizations for much of their strength. Even the PRI's defeat in the 2000 presidential elections did little to reshape the fundamental dynamics of corporatist-style political organization and participation (Bizberg 2003). During the *tortillazo* protests independent unions and *campesino* organizations played prominent roles – both in mobilizing their own members and in issuing the calls to protest that brought unaffiliated consumers to the streets. However, the mobilizational know-how and structure developed over decades of corporatist rule, as well as the legacy of a culture of sectoral political participation, helped to create a strong foundation on which these new organizations could draw.

Yet even as the legacy of corporatist incorporation helped to enable large-scale participation in the *tortillazo* protests, it cannot explain the broad-based, widespread composition of the movement. Independent *campesino* organizations had been plagued by internal divides and urban union and *campesino* organizations often found themselves at odds over policy issues. Furthermore, the cross-sectoral horizontal ties evidenced during the *tortillazo* protests showed a capacity to overcome the sectoral isolation that was a hallmark of the PRI's corporatist strategies. The strong mobilizing structures in place in 2007 played a critical role in bringing people to the streets, but they cannot explain why we saw such extensive cross-sectoral, cross-party collaboration when it came to protesting rising corn and tortilla prices in January 2007.

Attention to mobilizing frames helps to answer the question. Calls to defend national patrimony and heritage functioned as powerful master frames (Snow and Benford 1992) and played an important role in bridging divides and mobilizing across classes and sectors. These frames explain the broad-based appeal of the movement, and the participation of previously unorganized communities in particular.

Even so, attention to frames alone misses a critical piece of the story. We must understand why and how the frames worked as they did. Why were such powerful master frames available to this particular movement at this particular moment and why did they resonate so broadly? Why were political actors with diverse individual agendas able to rally their constituencies to work together when corn was at stake? To answer these questions, we must look to perceived vulnerabilities created by markets and how those vulnerabilities intersected with what corn meant in the Mexican context.

Reforms and reactions

Like Bolivia, Mexico is considered a poster child for market-oriented economic reforms (e.g., see Lustig 1998). Yet Mexico's narrative of reform and resistance follows a more complex trajectory than does Bolivia's. In addition, a variety of policies played an important role in the politics and economics of corn production and consumption. Corn and tortilla policies evolved across presidencies and were born and changed in a number of government institutions and ministries.

Many analysts date the beginning of Mexico's commitment to marketization to 1982 with the onset of the debt crisis. After announcing that it would no longer be able to service its international debt, the Mexican government sought stabilization and growth through orthodox economic approaches, including a large devaluation of exchange rates and the implementation of drastic fiscal austerity measures.[4] However, government officials deemed these first efforts unsuccessful (Lustig 1998), and increasingly radical programs, reflecting a return to increased government involvement in economic planning, gained favor in mid-1985. An oil price shock that sent prices falling in 1986 further complicated the government's ability to successfully implement orthodox reforms, and 1987's Economic Solidarity Pact reflected a return to a number of more heterodox measures, including wage and price controls, exchange rate freezes, and tight fiscal and monetary policy. However, not all orthodox

---

[4] For a thorough account of Mexican economic adjustment from 1982 to 1991, see Lustig (1998).

policies were discontinued. Mexican governmental officials pursued privatization with increasing vigor and free trade remained on the agenda.[5]

By the early 1990s, efforts to negotiate the North American Free Trade Agreement (NAFTA) were under way, and in January 1994 implementation began. Although NAFTA's reach was broad, Mexican negotiators explicitly lobbied for and ultimately included provisions designed to ease the transition for some of Mexico's most crucial agricultural sectors. Tariff-free imports of corn, beans, sugar, and powdered milk were to be phased in over more than fifteen years, with tariffs completely eliminated by January 2008.

In spite of these gestures, the agreement provided an opportune moment for the emergence of opposition to the Mexican state. On January 1, 1994, the world woke to news of insurrection in Chiapas. In Mexico's southernmost state, a small army calling itself the *Ejército Zapatista de Liberación Nacional* [Zapatista National Liberation Army] (EZLN) seized towns in eastern and central regions of the state and proclaimed the beginning of a revolutionary movement. Although the timing of the first offensive connects NAFTA to the EZLN, the movement had been growing for decades and its claims initially focused on rural livelihood and governance. Neoliberal reforms, particularly as they changed the dynamics of relations between citizen and the state (see Yashar 2005), played a role in the emergence of the EZLN, yet the 1994 uprising should be understood as part of a longer history of economic change and the relationship between the center and the periphery within Mexico itself.[6]

Even as NAFTA's negotiators sought to include some protections for Mexican agriculture, other arms of the Mexican government began to eliminate programs for food subsidies and price guarantees. For many agricultural products, the government had guaranteed a purchase price for farmers and heavily subsidized the ultimate price for the consumer. In accordance with broader structural adjustment efforts (many linked to NAFTA), Mexico began to slowly dismantle this system. However, policy makers added new programs to support farmers and consumers during the transition.[7] Farmers received direct payments determined by the size of their landholdings, subsidies by the ton to support prices during periods of world market drops, and incentives to improve yields and invest in advanced technologies. Most of the programs, however, were designed to meet the needs of large commercial farmers (Appendini 2008). Consumer food subsidies took longer to dismantle, with

---

[5] Between 1982 and 2003, the number of state-owned enterprises in Mexico dropped from 1,155 to 210 (Chong and López de Silanes 2004, 9). President Carlos Salinas de Gortari (1988–1994) spearheaded the most intense period of privatization, creating an Office of Privatization of State Owned Enterprises and overseeing more than 96 percent of the total conversions (ibid., 10). From 1994 to 2003, the government consolidated previous reforms and successfully privatized airports, telecommunications, ports and toll roads, among others.

[6] For analysis of the events in Chiapas, see Harvey (1998), Womack (1999), Higgins (2004), Bob (2005), Collier and Quaratiello (2005), Yashar (2005), and Jung (2008).

[7] These included *Procampo*, *Aserca*, and *Alianza para el Campo*.

tortillas presenting the biggest challenge. By 1998, however, even tortilla subsidies (*tortibonos*), which reached 1.2 million of Mexico's poorest families, were eliminated (Appendini 2001).[8]

The 1994 peso crisis complicated continued reform efforts.[9] With a massive devaluation in December 1994, middle-class families watched their savings evaporate overnight.[10] In spite of the extraordinary toll the crisis took on Mexican families, however, popular resistance was muted. Strikes were limited and other popular mobilizations were largely absent.[11]

The lack of widespread resistance to Mexico's economic reforms (the EZLN rebellion remained largely contained to Chiapas, although there were sympathetic marches in Mexico City) and the peso crisis in particular is notable. However, small groups of farmers throughout the country did not let increased exposure to international markets and the dismantling of the system of price guarantees pass without some opposition.[12] Strikers in late 1982 and early 1983 demanded a 100 percent increase in the guaranteed price for corn, and farmers throughout the country refused to sell their grain (Appendini 2001). Most of the resistance, however, was regional and focused on demands specific to local or organizational needs.[13] As a result, the government was able to reach local and organization-by-organization agreements, partially meeting the needs of each group while weakening the movement as a whole. Salinas's establishment of the Permanent Agrarian Congress [*Congreso Agrario Permanente*] (CAP) – a government advisory council of twelve of the most powerful farmers'

---

[8] In 2000, the Fox administration implemented a *programa tortilla* that gave a kilo per week of tortillas to Mexico's poorest families. The program lasted until 2003.

[9] In mid-1994, in the face of a 31 percent decrease in capital reserves, Mexican authorities raised internal interest rates, and the popularity of *Tesobonos* (instruments to raise short-term debt that are denominated in pesos but redeemable in dollars) skyrocketed. The presidency changed hands on December 1, with Ernesto Zedillo replacing Carlos Salinas, and the new administration faced an immediate crisis. Capital reserves had continued to drop precipitously while more than $29 million in outstanding *Tesobonos* threatened to collapse the Mexican financial system. On December 21, Mexican authorities switched the peso to a floating rate and a meltdown ensued.

[10] The causes of the 1994 peso crisis are many, including Salinas's refusal to risk political favor through earlier devaluations, but the increasing deregulation of banks and the weak oversight that accompanied this shift clearly bear some of the blame (Lustig 1998).

[11] The incidence of strikes declined dramatically throughout the implementation of market reforms. Between 1980 and 2001, rates declined from more than 1,400 strikes per year to fewer than 60 (Kurtz 2004).

[12] Other small pockets of resistance also emerged. An organization of debtors – largely farmers and small business owners – that had begun in Chihuahua and Sonora and took hold in Nuevo León in the fall of 1994 gained momentum. The movement set up roadblocks but never grew to capture the national imagination or the attention of regional or federal governmental officials.

[13] By 1986, resistance strengthened as farmers occupied CONASUPO stores, offices of the Ministry of Agriculture and Water Resources [*Secretaría de Agricultura y Recursos Hidráulicos*] (SARH), and the Panamerican Highway, demanding subsidies for fertilizers, decreased interest rates, and higher guaranteed prices. Fights continued to be largely regional in nature, however, with little national coordination.

organizations – after his inauguration further served to undermine conditions for national, intraorganizational cooperation; giving independent farmers' organizations a foothold within the governing structure decreased the likelihood of more contentious political activities.[14]

It was not until the early 2000s that farmers were able to organize a sustained, collaborative movement to protest the preceding twenty years of market reforms. In the fall of 2002, three of Mexico's largest independent farmers' organizations, the *Asociación Nacional de Empresas Comercializadoras de Productores del Campo* [National Association of Commercial Businesses From the Countryside] (ANEC), El Barzón, and the *Unión Nacional de Organizaciones Regionales Campesinas Autónomas* [National Union of Regional, Autonomous Peasant Organizations] (UNORCA), joined with nine other farmers' groups to launch the *El Campo No Aguanta Más* [The Countryside Can Bear No More] (ECNAM) movement.[15] The movement's formation coincided with NAFTA's ten-year anniversary and the continued implementation of the agreement's agricultural provisions. The movement proposed a moratorium on the implementation of NAFTA's agricultural chapter, as well as increased government spending on rural agricultural programs and reform of the rural finance system. It was a decidedly rural, farmer-driven initiative.

After a formal declaration of demands in November, the movement proceeded to organize mobilizations throughout December and January, culminating in a march to the Zócalo (main plaza) in Mexico City on January 31, 2003. A reported 100,000 people attended the march (Rubio 2007), putting the renegotiation of NAFTA, as well as the concept of food security and sovereignty, onto the national political agenda. The government responded by organizing eight "*mesas* [tables]" of dialogue. The result was the National Agreement for the Countryside [*Acuerdo Nacional para el Campo*] (ANC), which included commitments to involve farmers in the design of rural policies, form new agreements with rural producers, and modify existing rural policies. Missing from the ANC were the movement's principal demands, including the exclusion of corn and beans from NAFTA. Three participating organizations chose not to sign the agreement, arguing that doing so was a betrayal of the movement's goals and principles. These disagreements left the participating organizations firmly divided, with conflict reaching a highly personal nature. A number of leaders on the opposite sides of the ANC signing continued to

---

[14] Nevertheless, in September 1990, CAP member organizations marched from various regions throughout the country, intending to end in Mexico City, demanding increased protection for the countryside. The government agreed to a series of meetings with the participating organizations, negotiating agreements with individual groups in separate discussions. The government agreed to maintain price guarantees for corn and beans and the march never made it to Mexico City.

[15] Farmers began to formally organize outside of the official PRI farmers' organization the *Confederación Nacional Campesino* [National Peasant Confederation] (CNC) in the 1970s.

refuse to participate in shared conferences or forums, in spite of shared goals.[16] In addition, the agreement itself was poorly implemented, as a number of the agreed-upon changes never resulted in concrete policy reform. The farmers' movement was effectively demobilized without having accomplished comprehensive reforms. It was not until the *tortillazo* protests in January 2007 that the ECNAM movement organizations made a second attempt to work together, this time in close coordination with citizen organizations and a number of Mexico's strongest urban unions.

The *tortillazo*

As tortilla prices began to inch up in the fall of 2006, the Mexican media gave only sporadic coverage to the increases; Mexican daily newspapers *Reforma* and *La Jornada* drew attention to the issue in scattered articles during October. By December, however, high tortilla prices were making front-page news. According to Profeco, a Mexican government consumer organization, residents of some states were paying as much as 15 pesos/kilo in early January – more than double the price reported the previous August.[17] On January 9, prices in Mexico City reached 10 pesos/kilo – 20 percent of a daily minimum wage (*La Jornada*, January 10). The increase reflected a rise of more than 66 percent since the previous September (Profeco 2007).

A coalition of Mexico's urban unions and *campesino* organizations quickly formed to voice opposition to the price increase and demand government intervention. The groups coordinated across urban–rural divides and in spite of internal divisions that plagued *campesino* organizations in particular. A number of previously unmobilized citizens, including housewives, domestic workers, and businessmen and businesswomen, also joined the protests. By the second week in January, members of each major political party – including members of Calderón's conservative *Partido Acción Nacional* [National Action Party] (PAN) – and leaders of prominent civil society organizations joined the *campesinos'* and workers' unions to demand government intervention.

As January wore on, protests took place throughout Mexico. On January 12, Calderón traveled through the states of Mexico and Veracruz, where calls for subsidies greeted him at each stop. Luis Hernández Navarro (2007), a columnist for *La Jornada* and prominent leftist intellectual, wrote that Mexicans were living a "tortilla war ... pitting big agro-business against the poor population." By mid-month, the Mexican daily *El Universal* reported that tortillas ranged from 10 to 17 pesos/kilo in Mexico City and had reached 20 pesos/kilo

---

[16] This information comes from more than ten interviewees, all of whom were promised confidentiality. Participation in corn-related events during fieldwork confirmed the interviewees' observations.

[17] Tortilla prices vary not only by region, but also by distributor; the extent of the price rise differed throughout the country. On average prices in *tortillerías* rose from 30 to 100 percent.

in the states of Durango and Tamaulipas. Daily protests continued and plans for a *megamarcha* on January 31, the fourth anniversary of the ECNAM mobilization, began. Mobilizations throughout the country brought citizens from a variety of social and economic groups to the streets. Continuing price increases could very well have kept them there.

Calderón's team, however, moved quickly. Inside the administration, concern over the price increases began almost immediately.[18] Calderón called on close advisors within Los Pinos, as well as the *Secretaría de Hacienda y Crédito Público* [Ministry of the Treasury and Public Credit] (Hacienda), the *Secretaría de Economía* [Ministry of the Economy] (Economía), and the *Secretaría de Desarrollo Social* [Ministry of Development] (SEDESOL) to explore his options. The group came up with few potential solutions – it was left with finding some way to stabilize prices, instituting immediate subsidies, or letting the price increase run its course. Administration officials saw the risks of allowing prices to continue to rise as enormous (author interviews with members of the Calderón administration [see fn. 18], May–July 2009, Mexico City). Mobilizations were already beginning, and Calderón's advisors anticipated that opposition would intensify if it became clear that the government wasn't going to act. As they sat in early meetings, two administration officials recalled an extended discussion of the French Revolution. Tortillas, they claim to have thought, could very well be for Mexico what bread was for the French. Calderón did not want to be responsible for turning the country upside down. Furthermore, the administration worried about its continued ability to implement its policy program. If Calderón could not effectively control a price rise for something so important and so basic to Mexicans as tortillas, he would lose the confidence of the people and be unable to implement his policy agenda. Internal public opinion polls reinforced the fears of Calderón's closest advisors; not only was the president's popularity plummeting, but Mexican citizens blamed him and his team personally for allowing international openness to interfere with domestic prices of such a critical good. External polls validated the internal conclusions. According to *El Universal*, Calderón's popularity fell 15 percent in a week as a result of the *tortillazo* (Riva Palacio 2007). To all of the administration officials interviewed for this research save one, action was considered a "no-brainer."[19]

The question, however, was what to do. A price freeze was not an option. The concept ran up against principles central to the administration's economic policy platform, which adhered closely to a traditional neoliberal agenda.

---

[18] Information on discussions inside Calderón's administration comes from more than twenty interviews with members of the Ministry of the Economy, Ministry of Agriculture, and Ministry of Development, as well as policy advisors to the president inside Los Pinos. All asked not to be quoted directly. All information included here was confirmed by at least two interviewees.

[19] Only one interviewee insisted that he had argued that the best course of action would have been to let the market run its course. Others did not even seem to question the need for action – the issue for them was consistently not "if" but "what."

Publicly, the government refused to explore the possibility of the reintroduction of subsidies. On January 8, Eduardo Sojo, Calderón's minister of the economy, declared that subsidies were off the table (Posada and Pérez 2007). Increasing corn imports emerged as an option as it offered a vehicle for bringing prices down without violating the administration's economic platform. Calderón's first public response was to move up the date for the quota for increased corn imports – a move that neither helped control prices nor addressed the more fundamental demands around food sovereignty that had begun to surface.[20]

The administration worked behind the scenes to put other options in place, while tensions continued to rise on streets and in homes throughout the country. By January 18, the government had talked large-scale distributors and producers into a "voluntary" price pact; participants agreed to keep prices at or below mutually agreed-upon, predetermined levels at stores across the country. Five million (of the existing 65 million in the country) *tortillerías* committed to sell tortillas at no higher than 8.5 pesos/kilo through April 30. Supermarkets agreed to sell tortillas at 6 pesos/kilo, and the government distributor, Diconsa (responsible for selling goods largely in rural communities other vendors did not reach), agreed to sell corn at 3.5 pesos/kilo and corn flour at 5 pesos/kilo. The *Confederación Nacional Campesino* [National Peasant Confederation] (CNC) – the "official" peasants' union and a hallmark of PRI-style corporatist politics – also signed the agreement.

The pact – officially called the Agreement to Stabilize the Price of the Tortilla – had been in progress for more than a week.[21] The pact was voluntary, with no actual method of enforcement, leaving Sojo's promise not to control prices intact; administration officials insisted that the pact did not constitute a price freeze. Yet the incentives for businesses to participate were many. First, a number had provided significant support to Calderón's campaign. To see his administration falter so early in its tenure could translate into future losses for their interests. Second, a number of participating store owners reasoned that they could use low tortilla prices as a hook – people would come into their stores for tortillas but pick up a number of other items with higher margins while in the store. Finally, a number of businesses may have understood that by participating in this voluntary agreement now, there would be a payoff down the road. Among many stores the pact functioned effectively as any price freeze would – even those that had not signed onto the pact could not maintain high prices if they were faced with nearby competition from a pact participant. As its first major policy decision, and in response to its first crisis, the Calderón administration had acted contrary to its most fundamental principles of economic policy.[22]

---

[20] There was not enough corn available in world markets, let alone available at prices that would help bring down the cost of tortillas, to have a notable impact.

[21] SAGARPA put together extensive briefs on prices and production while analysts at Economía and Presidencia took the lead on formal policy development.

[22] What makes the decision even more noteworthy is that it happened with little internal debate. Not only did most advisors think that government action (as opposed to letting the market

After the pact, prices throughout the country stabilized relatively quickly. Although 8.5 pesos/kilo was more than most had been paying in November, and not all retailers brought their prices down to the pact-determined levels, the fear that prices would continue to rise was now largely quelled, and the pact sent a strong signal that the government was willing to respond quickly to citizens' concerns. The pact fundamentally changed the dynamics of mobilization and participation. It appears to have relieved perceptions of insecurity by demonstrating that the government would not let the crisis pass unaddressed. Nevertheless, movement leaders were able to mount one final large-scale march on January 31.

The *megamarcha* on January 31 brought union, *campesino*, and other civil society leaders together, shutting down Mexico City's central thoroughfares for much of the afternoon. "Ordinary" Mexicans were no longer the driving force of the mobilization – consumers who were unaffiliated with a union or civil society organization largely stayed at home. Yet participation in the movement remained broad based. More than 150 organizations, including unions, *campesino* federations, civil consumer organizations, and members of political parties, filled the Zócalo on the afternoon of January 31 (Muñoz et al. 2007). Union organizations mobilized their members in large numbers. The Electrical Workers' Union [*Sindicato Mexicano de Electristas*] (SME), the National Workers' Union [*Unión Nacional de Trabajadores*] (UNT), the social security workers' union, the telephone workers' union, and the pilots' union were among the participants (Muñoz et al. 2007). The National Agrarian Congress, a grouping of twelve organizations representing rural workers, and the CNC also mobilized their members. The caption for a photo of the event in *La Jornada* reads: "The march against price increases and for *soberanía alimentaria* achieved the union of traditionally antagonistic sectors." The same paper went on to report that this was the "first time in the recent history of the country" that unions, farmers' organizations, social organizations, and political parties had come together to make demands on the government, fighting "the crisis of the [current] economic model" (Muñoz et al. 2007). Groups

determine prices) was necessary, few opposed a price intervention. A failure to act could have meant disaster not only for this administration, but also for the Mexican government as an institution. Out-of-control tortilla prices would have labeled this administration as incompetent during its second month in office. When asked why the government acted the way it did to stabilize only tortilla prices, while other prices were also rising dramatically at the time, administration officials offered quizzical looks and smiles. Of course they intervened when the tortilla was at stake – not only was it a central component of the Mexican diet, it was also a fundamental component of daily life and cultural identity throughout the country. These comments reflect portions of every interview with government officials, save one, conducted for this project. The lone dissenter, who argued that it was necessary to act because Calderón cared deeply about Mexico's poor and wanted to be sure they could afford a critical component of their daily diet solely for humanitarian motives, was a young member of his cabinet of policy advisors and was said to have personal political ambitions. See Simmons (2011) for further discussion of the Calderón administration's responses to the *tortillazo*.

that often fought one another, disagreeing fundamentally on tactics or particular policy outcomes, pitted against one another in a battle for government resources, worked together that day and an estimated 50,000 to 75,000 people filled the Zócalo.[23]

The remainder of this chapter shows how corn's symbolic role in Mexican lives and livelihoods helped to shape the response to the *tortillazo*. By understanding corn both materially and ideationally, we shed light on how conceptions of family, class, security, and nation came together to help mobilize Mexicans from a variety of regions, sectors, classes, and political affiliations. To understand both why so many organizations and individuals were available for mobilization as well as the resonance of the frames deployed, we must look to the ways in which corn's meanings produced resistance. Regardless of the interests or strategies of movement leaders, corn provided a grievance around which various interests could unite.

The mobilizations in Mexico dominated national headlines for only a month. Yet they can tell us much about conceptions of Mexican-ness, and how those conceptions might clash with the politics and policies of a neoliberal state. A threat to corn heightened expressions of national belonging by creating perceptions that what it meant to be Mexican might be at risk.[24]

DOMESTICITY AND NATION

The home – a critical site for the production and reproduction of Mexican national belonging – was one of the central sites of perceived vulnerability during the *tortillazo* protests. Corn-based foods, whether prepared at home or consumed on the streets, have become a critical ingredient in perceptions of *lo mexicano*.[25] During the protests, domestic concerns intersected powerfully with a sense of national belonging as it was not simply "my family" but also "Mexican families" that were understood to be at risk.

Initial protests

The first signs of the mobilizing power of connections between domesticity and tortillas appeared soon after the price hikes began. Many of the initial protest participants were women. Women in Mexico are often charged with ensuring a family's food security; their immediate response is not particularly surprising. Yet the language they used and the tools they deployed as they took to the streets clearly situated the tortilla crisis as a threat to both family and

[23] Many splits in the farmers' movement are rooted in disagreements over tactics (e.g., Rubio 2007; Sánchez Albarrán 2007).
[24] See Brubaker (2004) and Wedeen (2008) for discussions of moments in which feelings of "groupness" are heightened.
[25] See Pilcher (1998) and Chapter 4.

FIGURE 5.1. Protesters in Acapulco, Mexico on January 12, 2007. Two signs read: "If you aren't in agreement with the price increase of tortillas! Sound your horn!" and "Tortibonos, now!" (photo courtesy of *La Jornada* and J. Guadalupe Pérez Pérez).

conceptions of national belonging; these first mobilizations were gendered but also inclusive.[26] Furthermore, the issues at stake cut across urban–rural and class divides that had previously created tensions in discourse in women's movements in Mexico (see Hernández Castillo 2010).

As Calderón traveled to the states of Mexico and Veracruz in early January, angry residents greeted him. On the streets of Chalco in the state of Mexico, groups of women welcomed Calderón with shouts of "*¡Que baje la tortilla!* [That tortillas come down!]" "*¡y la leche!* [and milk!]." In Veracruz, housewives met Calderón with signs and chants: "*Sí a la tortilla, no al PAN!* [Yes to tortillas, no to PAN/bread]" and "*¡soberanía ya!* [sovereignty now!]." They demanded the return of *tortibonos* and the end of the monopolies that controlled the production and distribution of corn flour (Núñez and Vega 2007). See Figure 5.1 for an image of protests in Acapulco.

Calls of "yes to tortillas, no to bread/PAN" speak to the lack of substitutability of tortillas in Mexico.[27] The slogan, of course, also highlights the ways

[26] If we define a women's movement as one in which "women engage to better the circumstances of their lives" (Ray and Korteweg 1999, 48), both the *tortillazo* protests and the Cochabamban water wars can be understood as such.

[27] The "tortilla discourse" discussed in Chapter 4 is an excellent example. Even when national-level politicians implemented policies, Mexicans were largely unwilling to replace corn and tortillas with wheat and bread.

in which Calderón's party, the PAN, was immediately blamed for the tortilla crisis. PAN was at once an inferior good – bread – and a political party responsible for making a part of what it is to be Mexican – the tortilla – increasingly inaccessible. The comments of a tamale vendor interviewed by *Reforma* later in the month speak directly to perceptions of substitutability. "The tortilla is the most important thing on any family's table," she claimed, "but it looks like they [government officials/business owners] want to kill us with hunger.... They know that what they want goes up but one has to buy it anyway." The imperative – *having* to buy corn – seems clear. And perhaps for a tamale vendor, there is, indeed, no substitute for corn. But many of her clients for whom other options are available will continue to buy tamales, even if they buy fewer, or sacrifices are made elsewhere.

That sovereignty also emerged in these early protests is unsurprising, but only when the ways in which corn and tortillas work as symbols of the Mexican family and nation are taken into account. On one hand, calls for sovereignty speak to the domestic sphere. The demand for "sovereignty now!" can refer to the ability to decide what to buy based not on unpredictable markets but rather on a family's individual assessment of its wants and needs; a family should be sovereign over its own kitchen. On the other hand, these calls also register at the national level. High corn and/or tortilla prices suggested somehow that officials entrusted to manage the Mexican state could not control something of critical importance. The references suggest both that Mexico should not have to rely on foreign markets for its supply of corn and that it should not simply accept market prices for something as critical to the nation as corn. Sovereignty – of both family and nation – was at stake.

These demands echo the discourse of regional and neighborhood autonomy that appeared throughout the water wars. A desire both to be able to plan for tomorrow and to decide consumption patterns and levels for yourself infuses the language in both protest events. A *campesina* woman who had traveled from Morelos to march on Avenida Juárez, a main street near Mexico City's historic center, on January 14 invoked both of these expectations in an interview two years later. "Corn," she claimed, "has maintained us in our families, it has maintained us in our communities … we have to defend corn because through defending it we defend our autonomy and independence" (author interview, May 2009, Mexico City). Through her defense of corn she is simultaneously defending individual autonomy and independence – her personal ability to purchase the foods she wants to cook and consume – and that of the imagined community of the Mexican nation.

But even as corn is about independence on an individual and national level, it is also about independence at the level of the familial unit. The protester claims to perceive rising corn prices as a threat to this most intimate of quotidian communities. High tortilla prices relocate decision making from mothers or fathers shopping for the day's meal to the abstract, invisible hand of the market, challenging a family provider's ability to decide for him- or herself what to cook in his or her own home and what to feed his or her own family. Family routines and perceptions of welfare needs are rendered insecure by the unpredictable forces of the market and the expectation that the state can no longer be counted on to intervene.[28] Furthermore, these domestic practices cannot be pried apart from conceptions of, and desires for, national belonging. The family kitchen is one of the places in which nationalism is produced and the nation is brought into being (see Appadurai 1988). Family and nation work together to make a threat to tortillas more than a financial hardship. ⟋ *MILK*

The reference to milk – "*¡Que baje la tortilla!* [That tortillas come down!]" "*¡y la leche!* [and milk!]" – in these early protests is particularly illustrative of the mobilizing power of a market-driven threat to corn and tortillas and how tortillas worked to symbolize the intersection of family and nation, whereas milk did not. According to the 2005 National Survey of Household Income and Spending, 6 percent of spending in an "average" Mexican household is dedicated to tortillas.[29] Whereas this surpasses many other oft-consumed items (e.g., sugar, fruit, eggs, and chicken), it is roughly on par with average spending on milk. In purely material terms, a similar percentage increase in milk and tortilla prices should have a similar impact on household spending. Although milk is clearly a critical part of the diet in Mexican households, it plays little (if any) role in conceptions of Mexican heritage or in contemporary food culture outside the home. For many, milk seems to mean family and nourishment, but in a way that fails to index the broader community or evoke connections to the nation. Milk is about taking care of one's own family; it is neither about patterns of communal rituals of consumption and celebration nor about pride in nation or conceptions of Mexican-ness.

Of course, it is rare that world events unfold in such a way as to create conditions that align perfectly with a social scientist's object of inquiry – in the years surrounding the tortilla crisis, milk prices did not undergo a spike equivalent to those of tortillas in January 2007. However, the price of milk sold through the Leche Liconsa (government-run) stores did rise in the fall of 2006.[30] After maintaining a 3.5 peso/liter price for five years (a price that was, notably, about half that of major commercial brands), Liconsa increased prices to 4.5 pesos – a 28.6 percent increase – on November 17. National newspapers covered the increase but only briefly, with four articles appearing in *El Universal* during the month of November and coverage dropping off entirely after the director of Liconsa publicly defended the increase and stated that he would not reverse

---

[28] See Ray and Korteweg (1999) for analysis of women and mobilization in response to structural adjustment policies in the third world more broadly.

[29] *Encuesta Nacional de Ingresos y Gastos de los Hogares* 2005. The poorest 10 percent of the country spends 9 percent of its income on tortillas; the richest 10 percent spends only 2 percent of its income on the staple.

[30] At the time, Leche Liconsa served approximately 6 million Mexicans, 80 percent of whom resided in Mexico's urban areas.

or temper the policy change. The increase received attention on the floor of the legislature (Gómez 2006), but there was little, if any, social movement organizing.

With the tortilla crisis, however, protesters brought the recent increase in milk prices to national attention. As in the previous quote, milk was often tacked onto the end of a declaration or comment about tortillas. Milk was not quite an afterthought, but not enough to serve as the central focus of a banner, slogan, statement to the press, or recollection during an interview two years later. The comments of a domestic worker in her twenties in Tlalpan resemble those of other protest participants. When asked why she chose to mobilize against rising tortilla prices but had stayed home when milk prices rose, she responded: "Of course I was upset with what happened with milk. It became harder to feed my kids overnight. But tortillas felt different. They are part of who we are. I don't know" (author interview with *tortillazo* protest participant, March 2009, Mexico City). Many interviewees identified a "feeling" around tortillas and invoked the notion of tortillas being a part of a "we" or an "us."

Deborah Gould's (2009) concept of emotional habitus sheds light on these professed feelings around tortillas, as well as how many interviewees concluded their interviews with an ambivalent statement like the "I don't know" quoted here. Drawing on Bourdieu (1990, 1977), Gould argues that, "Operating beneath conscious awareness, the emotional habitus of a social group provides members with an emotional disposition, with a sense of what and how to feel" (2009, 34). Gould's concept "locates feelings within social relations and practices" (ibid., 35), which helps us understand why the socially produced meanings tortillas take on can evoke such strong emotional reactions. The concept also elucidates the seemingly unconscious, natural qualities to those feelings. Attitudes toward tortillas were so deeply engrained through habitus that it was often difficult for sources to explain where the feelings came from or why they were experienced so powerfully.

It is not surprising that these feelings become attached to or manifested themselves as feelings of national belonging. When pressed further on who was included in the statement "tortillas are part of who we are," the extent to which answers did not differ was surprising. Almost invariably, "we" was meant to refer to "Mexicans." Tortillas symbolized nation in ways that milk did not – as a result, a threat to them was perceived differently. No one said he or she failed to protest the milk price increase because it was comparably smaller than the increase in tortilla prices.[31]

While increasing milk prices failed to translate into national mobilization, resistance to rising corn prices quickly spread; protests in the states of Mexico, Guerrero, and Veracruz were not isolated incidents. Simultaneous mobilizations took place in front of the Ministry of Economy in the Federal District, and the comments of participants offer additional insights into how

[31] The limited reach of Leche Liconsa might be another explanation for the relatively muted reaction, but this also failed to surface during interviews.

corn, family, and nation can be intimately intertwined in Mexico. *El Universal* quoted a Mexico City resident present during a January 12 mobilization in Mexico City as saying, "if you don't eat tortillas, nothing else fills you up" (Simón 2007). Tortillas do, indeed, satisfy caloric needs. But they also satisfy appetites for national belonging and domesticity, for family and community. Tortillas nourish conceptions of what it means to be a "good" Mexican mother or provider, reminding consumers of both their heritage and contemporary national practices.

Citywide *cacerolazos* (an oft-used repertoire of contention in Latin America involving the banging of pots and pans on the street) on January 17 offered a glimpse of the potential for widespread participation of previously unmobilized Mexicans and the ways in which domesticity continued to surface as a tool of political protest. That afternoon, Mexicans from a variety of occupational and social classes left their places of work and homes to meet on corners throughout the city. Participants banged pots and pans and carried signs that read, "*Abajo el PAN, viva la tortilla* [Down with the PAN/bread, long live the tortilla]," "*En defensa de la economía popular* [In defense of the popular economy – also understood to mean 'family' economy, or economy 'of the people']," "*Sin Maíz No Hay País* [Without Corn There Is No Country]," and *Sin Maíz No Somos País* [Without Corn We Aren't a Country]." Cars honked their horns as they passed, and the protests stopped traffic in the upper-class neighborhood of Coyoacán and its more middle-class neighbor, Tlalpan.

Residents of Gustavo A. Madero, one of Mexico City's northernmost and poorest regions, also staged a *cacerolazo*, blocking traffic and demanding protection from tortilla price increases. *La Jornada* quotes a participant in the Gustavo A. Madero *cacerolazo* as saying, "this doesn't have to do with any political party related movement, instead it's social, because it affects all of us in the *bolsillo* [pocket/wallet]" (Gómez Flores 2007). According to *La Jornada*, housewives in Gustavo A. Madero claimed they were taking to the streets "because this is what the federal government needs [to see for them] to put a stop to the situation" (ibid.). Responsibility for solving the situation was located squarely within the Calderón administration. The quote clearly communicates how expectations of the state and tortillas were intertwined.

In spite of the familiarity of the tactics involved, the *cacerolazos* are illustrative of how the *tortillazo* protests stand apart from "the usual" where contentious politics are concerned in Mexico. Union, *campesino*, other civil society organizations, and political parties issued the call for the *cacerolazo*. Yet reports suggest that as many as half of the participants were unaffiliated with any of Mexico's highly organized sectors (author interviews with *cacerolazo* participants, January–July 2009, Mexico City). When I spoke with people unaffiliated with union or *campesino* organizations who protested that day they invariably told me they came out because they heard about the mobilization from a neighbor or family member or on the radio (author interviews with *cacerolazo* participants, January–July 2009, Mexico City). Union and *campesino* leaders claimed during interviews that efforts to reach beyond highly organized sectors were intentional and motivated by the sense of possibility created by the issue at stake (author interviews with union and *campesino* leaders, January–July 2009, Mexico City). The claim – often leveled at protesters in Mexico City – that participants were only there because the union would pass out favors (something I heard repeatedly from government officials) cannot explain the participation of unaffiliated Mexican citizens from a variety of class backgrounds in the protest action that day.

As people were beginning to organize in the streets, the *tortillazo* also occupied increasing amounts of ink in Mexico's print media. One early column is particularly illustrative of the intersection of domestic and national issues. *Reforma* columnist Armando Fuentes Aguirre (known by his byline, Catón) put it directly: "In Mexico, man's basic nutrients are Coca-Cola, beans, and corn. Any elevation in price of these elemental nutrients shakes the social structure of the nation." Catón goes on to argue that the markets are supposed to function like nature, but before corn is used to make motors run, it should be used to feed humanity (2007). His allusion to ethanol and the United States through the comment about "making motors run" is veiled, but clear. Corn should be reserved for a "higher" purpose – it is meant to feed humanity (literally and figuratively), not serve Mexico's northern neighbor's need for fuel. Markets, here, clearly cannot get it right.

These kinds of comments were not limited to newspaper columnists or to tamale vendors or housewives – the latter being people we might imagine with daily, physical connections to Mexican kitchens as part of their lives and livelihoods. The archbishop of Tuxla Gutiérrez, Rogelio Cabrera López, echoed the sentiments of newspaper columnists, social movement leaders, and ordinary Mexicans when he stated that "the tortilla is the bread of the poor, and we are worried that it is not arriving to Mexican families" (Jiménez et al. 2007). In addition to highlighting the importance of tortillas to Mexican families, the archbishop also indicated another theme of the *tortillazo*: class. An analysis of how issues of class and nation intersected in the *tortillazo* appears later in this chapter. With the archbishop's statement, however, it is worth noting how corn, family, nation, and class are intimately tied. In calling tortillas "the bread of the poor," Cabrera makes clear that tortillas are a staple of daily life for Mexico's poor and a threat to them is an issue of concern. But accessing tortillas is not just about feeding the poor, it is about feeding Mexican families, intertwining the concept of family in Mexico with the idea that tortillas are what feeds it. Tortilla, family, and nation become inseparable.

Party politics

As members of the clergy added their voices to those of protesters and newspaper columnists, politicians were not going to be left out of the conversation. The central role of tortillas in conceptions of domestic life and the intersection of domesticity and the Mexican nation surfaced strikingly in the responses of elected and appointed politicians to the crisis. Using rhetoric that called for the defense of the Mexican family and/or a defense of Mexico, politicians from every major political party worked across party lines to respond to the crisis – a spike in tortilla prices offered them something around which they could easily agree, at least about the need to take some action, if not on the action itself. Political officials began to speak out as soon as prices spiked.

What is most striking about political leaders' initial reactions to the *tortillazo* is that calls to action came from voices representing all three of the country's major political parties. Representatives from the *Partido de la Revolución Democrática* [Party of the Democratic Revolution] (PRD), the PAN, and the PRI – as well as many smaller parties – the *Partido Verde Ecologista de México* [Ecologist Green Party of Mexico] (PVEM) and the *Partido del Trabajo* [Labor Party] (PT) – all began to call on Caderón to take action and leveled critiques of the administration's limited efforts. Political opposition was most vocal among members of the *Frente Amplio Progresista* [Broad Progressive Front] (FAP), which included the PRD and PT. But that members of Calderón's own PAN called for action is noteworthy, particularly in a country with a relatively disciplined party system.[32]

On January 9, legislators from the PAN, PRD, and PRI "demanded" intervention to stabilize the price of tortillas. Not surprisingly, representatives of the PRD called for subsidies and social mobilization. But the PRI and the PAN did not let the PRD dominate the discourse. PRI deputies, making the more modest demand for negotiation with distribution firms, joined the call for a government response. PAN officials also entered the fray, with the party's *Comité Ejecutivo Nacional* [National Executive Committee] (CEN) vaguely calling on the government to act (Guerrero et al. 2007b). The multiparty Permanent Commission of the Congress of the Union called for interventions to stop the price increases (Hernández and Estrop 2007) and deputies from the PRI, the PRD, and the PAN called for price stabilization. Governors from across the country and all major political parties joined in lobbying Calderón to take action.[33]

That the PRD was quick to respond to the *tortillazo* is not surprising. However, the policy changes and actions for which party leaders advocated

[32] Among the PAN members lending their voices to the need to take action were Héctor Larios (PAN coordinator in the *Cámara de Diputados*), Juan José Rodríguez Prats, and Manuel Minjares. Some opposition leaders may very well have been capitalizing on the issue to undermine the PAN's – and Calderón's – credibility. But that calling attention to this issue could damage the ruling party's standing at all speaks to how the issue itself was understood. Regardless of what tortillas meant to them as individuals, many politicians appeared to know very well that tortillas were a critical issue for voters, and they reacted accordingly.
[33] Among those calling for Calderón to take action were the governors of Colima (Jesús Silverio), Veracruz (Fidel Herrera), and Zacatecas (Amalia García).

and the language they used highlight how the central role of tortillas in conceptions of community generally, and the Mexican family in particular, was at play in perceptions of the tortilla crisis. PRD senator Ricardo Monreal explicitly advocated social mobilization to ensure a decrease in tortilla prices, stating that the government had a week to handle the situation before people would start to take to the streets: "We should call a mobilization because we can't accept that a political crime against the domestic economy and the family economy is growing" (Guerrero et al. 2007a). Monreal's language offers important insight into rising tortilla prices in the Mexican context in early 2007. He describes the price increases as criminal, and references to the "domestic economy" and "family" suggest that a threat to corn was also a threat to the national community and the basic familial unit.

His words are part of a political performance. But the performance only makes sense if we know what he is referring to and understand how and why the words resonate. When we understand these words as a performance they offer insight into why opposition was not limited to the left.[34] Monreal ties corn and tortilla prices to valence issues – issues where voters share a general common preference, like support for family or national independence – in the Mexican context. One can safely assume that political figures did not want to find themselves appearing to be against the domestic economy or the Mexican family.

As the crisis continued, gestures moved from rhetoric to legislative action. PRD legislators presented an initiative to create a legal fund to subsidize corn and tortilla consumption for poor families in areas with more than 15,000 inhabitants (Ramos 2007). The initiative also directly denounced Maseca and Gruma – two large corn flour companies – for establishing a quasi-monopoly over the corn flour industry and offered support to the theory that the administration's proposed increase in imports would do little to ameliorate the situation. When asked if there was a risk of large-scale popular mobilization, PRD leader Javier González Garza responded that "it's not a risk, it's a necessity" (Garduño and Pérez 2007). The debate did not remain confined to the halls of Congress. On the afternoon of January 17, more than 150 FAP members marched, pots and pans in hand, to the offices of the Ministry of the Economy to continue to make their voices heard (*El Universal* 2007). Tools of the kitchen were not reserved for Mexican housewives as implements of protest. Protecting family was a national issue.

But Mexico's leftist parties were not alone in their denunciations and proposals for action. During the second week of January, the Permanent Commission

---

[34] The PRD mayor of Mexico City, Marcelo Ebrard, also weighed in, calling on Calderón to reinstate the "*programa tortilla*" established under Fox, which provided a kilo of tortillas per week free of charge to Mexico's poorest families but lasted only until 2003. The price increases, he argued, were having a "devastating effect" on the popular economy in Mexico City (Martínez 2007). For Ebrard, along with many others, the long-term answer lay in investing in the countryside so that Mexico would no longer depend so heavily on foreign imports and foreign prices.

of the Congress of the Union unanimously proposed that the ministers of economy and agriculture investigate the causes of and punish those responsible for the increase in tortilla prices. PRI legislators added their voices to the calls for action, summoning the ministers of economy, agriculture, and development, among others, to the Congress to discuss amending NAFTA's agricultural section. PRI deputy César Duarte called for immediate subsidies and in the Senate, members threw blame in every direction (Guerrero et al. 2007a). There was also cross-party support for a formal denunciation of Calderón's economic minister, Eduardo Sojo, and cross-party agreement that the responsible parties should face sanctions.

Ultimately, appeals to domesticity may very well have been a smart political strategy for members of every political party in Mexico. Concerns for the day-to-day needs of Mexican families no doubt played well with voters. But that the strategy and the discourse bridged party divides speaks to how tortillas served as a unifying force in the Mexican context. Speaking out against the *tortillazo* seemed like the only logical move in a political arena where defending family and nation appears to be an obvious necessity.

CLASS, SECTOR, AND NATION

The events surrounding the *tortillazo* brought class to the fore through both the composition of the protests themselves and the language participants and analysts used to describe the crisis. Unlike the water wars in Cochabamba, where urban and rural organizations gradually joined the movement over the course of nearly six months, cross-sectoral, cross-class, and cross-urban–rural cooperation dominated the response to the *tortillazo* from the outset. Union members joined *campesinos* and a largely previously unorganized base of urban consumers to mobilize against rising tortilla prices. But the language they used to voice their opposition often invoked not personal or sectoral interests, but, rather, conceptions of national responsibilities and aspirations. The protests became a fight for "the people" and "the poor." In particular, the crisis suggested an expectation that the poor reaffirm and reproduce their national belonging through tortillas. During the *tortillazo* protests, a column in the Mexican daily newspaper *Reforma* called a packet of tortillas "one of the most sacred patriotic symbols" (Dehesa 2007). The protests also became a fight for the countryside, as if, embodied in the "right" to consume tortillas, was an effort to preserve the rural Mexico that, for many, worked to signify the nation itself. Notions of class, occupation, and countryside intersected in conceptions of what it meant to be Mexican.

El pueblo Mexicano

From the first protests that greeted Calderón as he traveled the country, the declared universality of the claim to affordable corn and tortillas was readily apparent. Protesters were defending something conceived of as a widely shared "right." This was not about transportation workers or coffee farmers, but rather about a threat to "the people." The threat called that "people" into being through the very claims themselves. One participant called the protest a "defense of her rights" (Ledezma 2007). Another added, "we did not come to talk about an individual or party problem: it is a problem for all of the people (*pueblo*)." Access to affordable tortillas is simultaneously an individual right and a "problem for all of the people." Individual, personal relationships with the good and a far broader set of responsibilities to "all of the people" are both sacrosanct. The use of "*el pueblo*" simultaneously evoked a community of all Mexicans, irrespective of class or occupation, and a notion of something understood to be truly Mexican. Even though it is a frame often deployed by the left, the concept of "*el pueblo*" carries an unimpeachable authenticity – becoming something to be esteemed and protected.[35] In claiming to defend *el pueblo*, protesters situated themselves as defending something "quintessentially" Mexican.[36]

One after another, letters to the editors of the country's major newspapers called for action in response to the price increases. Letters requested that Calderón respond and encouraged fellow citizens to join the protests. We can read the letters as a reflection of middle- and upper-class engagement – precisely the demographic that would be able to bear the increase in tortilla prices with little hardship. We are hard pressed to explain their interest without paying attention to how corn was perceived as fundamental to producing and reproducing notions of what it meant to be Mexican.

"A thing on which we could agree"

The uncommon alliances that characterized the *tortillazo* appeared not only among Mexico's politicians but also among its sectoral organizations. As with the water wars, the *tortillazo* protests brought together organized groups – most notably *campesino* and urban workers' unions that were often on opposite sides of a given issue. Furthermore, the protests helped to bridge divides

[35] *El pueblo* is often a frame specific to protest on the left, but in ordinary language use, it does not carry leftist connotations.

[36] The cardinal and archbishop of Mexico City, Norberto Rivera, chimed in with a decidedly different perspective. Responses to his comments offer evidence of how conceptions of class, community, and nation are intertwined in tortillas. When the cardinal stated, "Tortillas won't set off a social war," on January 14, he set off a virtual firestorm. "Many Mexicans will suffer, but that isn't the tragedy, it isn't the limit, it isn't the end of history in Mexico" (Gómez et al. 2007). Letters to the editors of Mexico City's major dailies accused the cardinal of being removed from the people, privileged, and too good to eat tortillas with the rest of the Mexican people (*Reforma, El Universal, La Jornada*, January 17–20). In suggesting that the tortilla price increases were not a cause for major concern, the cardinal set himself outside of the Mexican community.

within sectors, bringing together *campesino* organizations plagued by personal and political animosities since the signing of the National Agreement for the Countryside in 2003. But the protests also brought unexpected participants to the streets – urban consumers without formal sectoral affiliations.

Campesino organizations were the first to talk about working together to demand government action. The structure of the Mexican corn market meant that the increased prices benefited farmers marginally, if at all.[37] However, the price increases did hit farmers as consumers. Although many produce their own tortillas, few do so year round. Seasonal production forces many farmers to consume what they can of their harvest and sell the rest. The remainder of the year, these farmers purchase corn and corn products. Large *campesino* organizations, including the CNC, the *Central Campesino Cardenista* [Cardenist Farmers' Union] (CCC), the *Confederación Revolucionaria de Obreros y Campesinos* [Regional Confederation of Workers and Farmers] (CROC), and the ANEC, joined forces to rally their membership base.

Urban union members, beginning with the metro workers' union and the umbrella transportation union, organized shortly after their *campesino* counterparts. Having only just negotiated a minimum wage agreement for the year, union leaders argued that the increase in tortilla prices made a mockery of their small wage gains and undermined members' ability to meet their families' basic needs (author interviews with union leaders, January–July 2009, Mexico City).[38] Both the collaboration between unions and *campesino* organizations and the language used to describe that collaboration suggest that tortillas served as a powerful unifier.

As with the water wars, a discourse of ease and inevitability dominated most organizers' descriptions of the mobilization process. Francisco Hernández, leader of the UNT, recalls thinking, "We had to organize. If we weren't going to fight for tortillas, what were we going to fight for?" Hernández treats mobilization as a political imperative, something around which there was no choice. "We could all work together on this," he went on to say. "It was easy" (author interview, July 2009, Mexico City). *Campesino* leader and president of the CCC Max Correa used similar language when describing how the movement came together so quickly. "It was pretty clear to us," he argued. "If we weren't going to fight for tortillas, what would we fight for? We had to mobilize [against the tortilla price increases] and working together seemed like the natural thing to do" (author interview, May 2009, Mexico City). Correa's question suggests not that he was simply looking for a strategic mobilization tool, but rather that there was an "of course" about the protests. He implies that if they are going to fight for anything, it will be for tortillas. Both

---

[37] Commercial corn farmers sell their produce twice per year (or just once if they have only one harvest). The price at the date of sale (fall and spring) is the price these farmers get. As a result, if prices go up between October (a potential date of sale) and December, farmers do not benefit.

[38] See also coverage in *La Jornada* and *Reforma*.

leaders followed these comments with expressions of disappointment. "We
had a moment," Hérnandez recalled, "but it became nothing." Correa called
the period a "lost opportunity." Both men saw a potential for sustained mass
mobilization, but both were forced to reflect on how the movement never
took off. Correa summed it up as "a spark that didn't take" (author interview,
July 2009, Mexico City).

For Hernández, Correa, and others, that Mexicans would mobilize around
tortillas seemed obvious, and, as a result, the ultimate outcome of a short-lived
episode of contention a disappointment. As their statements make clear, the way
in which corn itself served as a uniting force made the necessity for mobilization
seem obvious, and working together "easy" and "natural." Already highly organized, unions and *campesino* organizations had thousands of members in the
state of Mexico alone, and each organization had well-established and tested
mechanisms for mobilization. Once their leadership decided to cooperate, that
these groups were able to rally their constituencies is not particularly surprising.

The mobilizing power of coalitions of citizen and environmental organizations is more puzzling. A number of Mexico City–based organizations were
well versed in small protest and staged action but had little previous experience
getting large numbers of Mexicans to the streets. Others had never organized
outside of their *colonia*. Yet these groups quickly added their voices to the
opposition, and many set to work mobilizing at the neighborhood level. The
alliance of *campesinos*, unions, and other civil society organizations was well
in place by the end of the first week in January.

This coalition joined with political leaders from the FAP on January 10 to
call for a march "in defense of national *soberanía alimentaria* [food/nutriment
sovereignty]" later in the month (Balboa 2007). The press conference included
the electricity, telephone, and social security workers' unions, in addition to six
campesino organizations. PRD leader Porfirio Muñoz Ledo likened the *tortillazo* to the economic crises of the early 1970s and called for a general strike
because there was a "coming together of independent unions" that hadn't been
seen for forty years (Aguirre and Salazar 2007). One *campesino* activist who
appeared to be in his early fifties recalled, "there was a real sense of a coming
together – we were given a moment, a thing on which we could agree" (author
interview, February 2009, Mexico City). He went on to joke that he was even
willing to sit next to the leader of another *campesino* organization with whom
he had had a public and infamous split in the aftermath of ECNAM. "History
was made," he laughed, "when [the other activist] and I took the stage together
at that press conference on the 10th" (author interview, February 2009, Mexico
City).[39]

[39] The analysis here focuses on collaboration among social movement activists within the state
of Mexico. As indicated earlier, the protests were not limited to the capital state or city. At
the national level, a number of civil society organizations came together to call themselves the
Cruzada Nacional en Defensa de la Tortilla. The coalition included, but was not limited to,
groups in Monterrey, Puebla, Morelos, Michoacán, and Jalisco.

Ultimately, tortillas and corn proved items that a variety of interest groups and citizens' organizations could agree on, at least in the abstract. The issue offered them the opportunity to work together, and many social movement organizers were keenly aware of how the tortilla crisis cut across issues of class or occupation. In discussing the cooperation around the tortilla crisis *campesino* leader Max Correa said, "Listen, we could all agree. We all wanted the same thing. Tortillas are part of what it is to be Mexican. Maybe we were not in agreement about some of the answers, but everyone – rich, poor, worker, *campesino* – we all wanted everyone to be able to buy the tortillas they needed" (author interview, May 2009, Mexico City). Laura Becerra, president of *Equipo Pueblo*, an organization aimed at strengthening civil society, reflected,

There was a *conjunto* [coming together] of the demands with the *tortillazo*. The three sectors [unions, *campesinos*, popular sectors] were finally really able to come together. It was a real *coyuntura* [coming together in time, critical moment]. Citizens could really identify with the fight, even those that weren't members of unions or other organizations; we all felt violated so we all participated. (Author interview, June 2009, Mexico City)

Protecting the poor, preserving the countryside

As some of the previous evidence suggests, perceptions of those who would suffer the most and calls to defend them infused the discourse surrounding the *tortillazo*. An oft-repeated phrase of people who participated in events such as the *cacerloazos* on the 17th and those interviewed by local TV news programs (TV Azteca, Televisa) and in Mexico City dailies (*La Jornada, Reforma, El Universal*) was that tortillas were important because a price increase affected "*los que menos tienen* [those who have the least]." Claims of concern for the poor bridged political and class divides. The idea that the poor should be able to afford tortillas (or, at the very least, the expression of the idea) was not limited to the poor themselves but rather emerged as almost a seemingly national consensus. To this author's knowledge, not one newspaper article or editorial called for the poor to simply eat something else. Although there was no consensus on how to make tortillas affordable, to ask Mexicans to replace this most Mexican of foods with something else represented one big step toward losing *lo mexicano*.

Whereas many stated that they themselves were having trouble making ends meet with tortilla prices so high, a number wanted to speak not for themselves, but for "Mexico's poor." The comments of one middle-class participant in the January mobilizations were illustrative of those of many others. "Poor people eat more tortillas than the rest of us," she remarked, "so this was really affecting them. We have to protect them" (author interview, *tortillazo* protest participant, June 2009, Mexico City). In the calls for the first coordinated protests, union leaders used language that would reappear throughout the rest of the crisis, arguing that they were fighting for Mexico's poorest: "This hits those who have the least," so government must act, they claimed (Pensamiento 2007).[40]

Importantly, the right of Mexico's poorest to continue to eat tortillas seemed worth defending. Although middle- and upper-class Mexicans no longer turned to tortillas as a nutritional centerpiece themselves, it seemed critical to some to preserve the tortilla as a staple for the country's poorest. Mexico's wealthiest consume less than 15 percent of their daily calories in tortillas (although, interestingly, these numbers imply that tortilla consumption is, indeed, still a daily matter, even for Mexico's wealthy), whereas its poorest often get more than 70 percent of their daily calories from tortillas. When prices reached their highest point in mid-January, some Mexicans paid more than 150 percent more for tortillas than they had the previous August. A government study estimated that at the peak, spending on tortillas within Mexico's poorest 10 percent reached more than 17 percent of average monthly income – up from 6.8 percent the previous August (Tépach 2007). In contrast, Mexico's wealthiest 10 percent increased their spending on tortillas from 0.3 to 0.4 percent of their average monthly income (ibid.).[41] Tortillas were more expensive, but the increase was hardly going to have a noticeable material impact on the daily lives of Mexico's wealthiest.

Yet even for many who could still easily afford their daily tortilla quotient and for whom the price increase had little impact on monthly spending, the tortilla crisis offended their sensibilities as Mexicans. "It is a shame," one relatively affluent adult male participant in the protests reflected. "The *tortillazo* undermined the way we are supposed to live as Mexicans. We lose a piece of ourselves when we can't all eat tortillas" (author interview with *tortillazo* protest participant, April 2009, Mexico City). Other interviews suggested a sentiment of, "while we can look elsewhere, or even endure the price increases, it is critical that they maintain the foundation of Mexican culture that is the tortilla" (author interviews with *tortillazo* protests participants, April–July 2009, Mexico City). It was almost as if the idea of the accessibility and affordability of tortillas was more important than the actual prices.

With the elimination of Mexican corn subsidies as a part of the agricultural chapter of NAFTA and the slow increase of corn import quotas, *campesino* compensation for their yields slowly declined; a *campesino* way of life was

[40] This discussion suggests that perhaps many Mexicans simply seemed to care about the welfare of the poor regardless of whether the threat manifested itself in high tortilla prices or some other material hardship. There are two reasons to doubt the potential power of this alternative. First, if claims were based purely on material welfare, there would be little reason to protest, as wheat remained a potentially cheaper substitute. Second, there is little historical precedent to suggest that large numbers of Mexicans mobilize when they perceive that the material well-being of the poor is at risk.

[41] The study cited here reports that, in 2006, Mexico's poorest families – those in the bottom 10 percent of income – reported an average monthly income of 906 pesos. Those in the top 10 percent reported 31,498 pesos of average monthly income (Tépach 2007, 5).

becoming increasingly unsustainable. For small-scale producers, the increase foreshadowed what would happen with the full opening of NAFTA – even the largest Mexican producers could not compete with U.S. yields.[42] The *tortillazo* protests were not just about protecting urban consumers. They also put the countryside, and its place as a foundational element of Mexican national culture, on center stage.[43]

Calls to support the countryside were ubiquitous during the protests themselves and appeared in the pages of major newspapers. Demands to use government support to help make the agricultural sector more efficient and able to compete internationally abounded (e.g., see *Reforma* 2007). Letters to the editors of national newspapers blamed low productivity for the vulnerability to international markets that many perceived to have caused the crisis, but the solution was rarely to simply give the corn market over to the more efficient American producers. Instead, the pleas were for "supporting" the Mexican countryside, either to improve efficiency or to encourage investment. Indeed, some understood the problem itself to have come from a failure to support the countryside in the first place. One urban merchant claimed that Mexico needed to value the countryside anew. "I think the polemic is a product of a long time ago when they didn't pay attention to the countryside," he argued. "They didn't invest resources and today we suffer/undergo [*padece*] the crisis with the increase" (quoted in Zepeda 2007). The crisis was, in his estimation, the result of a failure to take proper care of the countryside.

A prominent slogan during the protests throughout the month offers additional support for the notion that conceptions of countryside and nation were intertwined. Protesters shouted, "Defending the countryside, we defend Mexico," and "Without corn there is no country," and carried signs with the same words (or some variation thereof) as they stopped traffic during *cacerolazos* or marched to the Zócalo on January 31 (see Figure 5.2). The countryside becomes synonymous with, or a synecdoche for the nation – something that must be preserved if national community is to be preserved as well. "The countryside is the heart of Mexico," a housewife from Tlalpan commented during an interview two years after the *tortillazo*: "We all have a grandmother

[42] Mexico produces approximately 2 tons/hectare where production is seasonal and 6.5 where production occurs with irrigation. In the United States, average yields are around 8.2 tons/hectare. Mexican producers simply can't compete.

[43] During the *megamarcha* on January 31, images of *campesino* revolutionary hero Emiliano Zapata abounded, and the familiar refrain "¡*Zapata Vive, Vive, la Lucha Sigue, Sigue!* [Zapata lives, the fight continues!]" resounded. Zapata's image at once symbolized hope and disappointment. His leadership helped make land reform a centerpiece of the Mexican Revolution. Yet his plan, embodied in the *Plan Nacional de Ayala*, was never fully implemented. Land reform as Zapata had imagined never occurred, and the adoption of Article 27 of the constitution in 1991 dramatically altered the redistribution and reform that did take place; the article legalized the sale of communally held *ejido* lands. Zapata is on one hand an inspiration and on the other a reminder of how the countryside has, for decades, played second fiddle to Mexico's rapidly urbanizing centers.

FIGURE 5.2. Protesters with a "Sin Maíz No Hay País" banner in Mexico City on January 17 (photo reproduced from lizdenovella).

who made us fresh tortillas in the countryside. Our secrets, our soul is still with those grandmothers" (author interview with *tortillazo* protest participant, May 2009, Mexico City). An increase in tortilla prices became a threat to the countryside, which was, in turn, a threat to the core of this mother's sense of what it means to be Mexican. Of course, every Mexican does not, literally, have a grandmother who made fresh tortillas, although many do. The interviewee's comments, however, suggest the ease with which many Mexicans appropriate the image of a grandmother making fresh tortillas. It was almost as if, without these grandmothers in the countryside growing their own corn and making their own tortillas, a crucial piece of Mexico's heritage – a connection to a valued past – would be lost.

(IN) SECURITY

Anxieties rooted in a discourse of insecurity extended well beyond fears for the countryside or the nation's poor. The *tortillazo* created perceptions of multiple, often overlapping, vulnerabilities. The link between free markets and high corn prices suffused discussions of market-induced vulnerabilities – and *soberanía alimentaria* –in particular. The ability to live generally, to live a Mexican life in particular, and the stability of "the" Mexican nation all seemed to be unsettled through insecurities evoked by the tortilla crisis. The longing for food/nutriment independence was fused with fears of social/state instability.

Corn and markets

By the end of the first week of January, journalists, activists, government officials, and many other Mexicans had clearly articulated whom they perceived the villains in the *tortillazo* to be. Markets, and free trade in particular, bore the brunt of the public critiques. Columnists in national papers, movement organizers, and people on the streets interviewed for television programs revealed that they perceived NAFTA to be responsible for an influx of cheap, American corn, for the elimination of consumer corn subsidies, and for the decline of the Mexican countryside. Markets had rendered access to affordable corn unreliable, infusing the corn market with perceptions of insecurity.

A discussion of the ways in which markets served as the central target highlights corn's status as something particularly special in the Mexican context. In both interviews after the fact and newspaper coverage during the *tortillazo*, many Mexicans underscored corn and tortillas as goods that should not be subject to the vicissitudes of markets because of their place in Mexican culture. The concern appeared to be about knowing how much tortillas or corn will cost and being able to plan or respond accordingly. Markets are often perceived as working to undermine this predictability, even if these perceptions only manifest themselves in social mobilization when the vulnerability is clear – when prices rise or access is otherwise limited.[44] Furthermore, insecurities are heightened during times when a government's willingness to provide for a good in moments when markets threaten access is in doubt. At moments when the state has been pulling away from the predictability that might come with price supports or subsidies (as had been happening in Mexico since the early 1980s), citizens may doubt whether governments will be willing to intervene to ensure broad access. The unpredictability of markets works together with vanishing expectations of the state to produce particularly intense experiences of insecurity.

The link between free trade and the tortilla crisis is particularly surprising in light of research that suggests that many Mexicans, and Latin Americans more generally, are largely supportive of free-trade policies (see Baker 2003, 2009). Indeed, one might conclude that the PAN's election in 2006 was an affirmation of broad public support for market-oriented policies more generally. Yet the blame hurled at markets for the tortilla crisis and the pervasive argument that unfettered markets were simply not appropriate where corn and tortillas are

---

[44] This is not to suggest that mobilization won't occur if a threat to corn comes from, for example, a natural disaster. But the theoretical mechanisms at work may very well look different.

concerned suggests that it is not just markets, but rather the item that is getting marketized, that matters. Markets may, on the whole, be largely popular in Mexico. Yet the evidence presented here suggests that because tortillas and corn mean far more than simply food items that are paid for and consumed, support for market-based prices of these particular goods is another matter entirely.

It is not surprising that, broad-based support for free trade notwithstanding, many Mexicans were quick to make the link between open markets and rising tortilla prices and understand corn as a good for which free trade should not apply. For a smaller crowd, the tortilla crisis revealed deeper problems with markets more generally, and free trade in particular. Alfonso Ramírez Cuellar, president of the debtors' organization El Barzón (which had helped to organize protests throughout January), put it this way: "the *tortillazo* opened the eyes of ordinary Mexicans – it showed them clearly what NAFTA is and why it is bad for Mexico" (author interview, July 2009, Mexico City). Even though Ramírez may have been articulating his own beliefs rather than accurately portraying the reaction of other Mexicans, his comments do reflect discussions of the events among protesters, within the national media, and between legislators. In an interview two years later, Francisco Hernández, president of the UNT, recalled that the *tortillazo* showed that "the magic of neoliberal promises can never come to be" (author interview, July 2009, Mexico City). For him, the *tortillazo* was the unmasking of the Salinas economic reforms, and of NAFTA in particular. Another leader of the movement affiliated with the CNC argued that the tortilla crisis showed that "it is urgent that we stop seeing the free market as the optimal regimen to satisfy basic needs" (author interview, May 2009, Mexico City).

But the predictably anti-NAFTA crowd was not alone in placing markets squarely at the center of the crisis. In particular, officials from every major political party also made the link, suggesting that corn and tortillas are, indeed, understood differently than other commodities included in NAFTA; people with divergent political views could nonetheless come together when tortillas were at stake. In an official statement, the Permanent Congress of the Union argued that the problems began when tortilla prices were left to free markets as a result of NAFTA and called on Calderón to stabilize tortilla prices (Díaz Garza 2007). Markets were to blame, and the answer was government intervention. Even the free-market PAN joined the tortillas-should-not-be-subject-to-markets chorus. Héctor Larios Córdova, the PAN coordinator in the legislative chamber, claimed in an article in *El Universal* that the tortilla should be an "exception" to free market principles. Tortillas, he argued, are a product around which the government should intervene in spite of the fact that he saw few distortions in the market.[45] He called for permanent subsidies for tortillas, saying that the small corn discs had special "characteristics" that warranted special protection (Larios 2007). Again, markets were to blame, and, in

---

[45] Others claimed that there were, indeed, extensive distortions and the government should intervene precisely because of them.

spite of a general commitment to free market principles, tortillas should not be subject to the insecurity that markets can create.

Staunch supporters of free market principles continued to come out in favor of regulation during the tortilla crisis. On January 12, the editorial page of *El Universal* – a paper with editors known for their support for both the PAN and free markets – called on the government to use regulatory mechanisms to "save capitalism from the capitalists." To keep tortillas off the plates of Mexico's poorest families "is equivalent to condemning them to hunger, malnutrition, and sickness. A half a kilo less of tortilla … means some will be left with an empty stomach." The quote not only recalls the general discussion of Mexico's poor in the preceding section on class and nation, but also the particular reference to tortillas as the only thing that can "fill you up." There seems to be a perceived responsibility not only to feed the poor the calories they need, but also to feed them tortillas specifically. Tortillas will both keep Mexicans healthy and help them to be "healthy" Mexicans.

The editorial goes on to say that it is not the market per se that is at fault, but rather "those who have deformed the market for corn and tortillas." Markets remain the answer – capitalism must be saved. But markets can also be corrupted by capitalists and deformed by interests able to run amok in the capitalist system. The answer is in government regulation. The editors ask the government to insert order into the corn/tortilla market. They call on the government to restore security to Mexicans' access to this most critical of foodstuffs through subsidies and interventions. In the same paragraph, the paper calls on Diconsa – the distributional arm of SEDESOL – to complete its job of making sure the poor have access to tortillas. There is, of course, a tension in these comments. The authors profess a commitment to capitalism but argue that some things are too important to be left to markets. The ideal of markets must not be abandoned, yet government intervention remains necessary if markets prove unable to ensure that all Mexicans can access tortillas. The editorial concludes by saying, "the community can't play with hunger." Because an absence of tortillas condemns the country's poorest to hunger, malnutrition, and sickness, their provision is too important to be left to the capitalists. Tortillas should not be subject to the vagaries and vicissitudes of markets – they are not something with which the government can take risks, or "play."

Although the abstract concept of "markets" was often singled out for blame, there were disagreements about the specific ways in which markets were failing Mexicans and who should be responsible. Newspapers, legislators, and activists repeatedly implicated specific corn flour companies such as Minsa and Gruma, monopolies, and speculators more broadly; free trade in general; and the Calderón administration. The state and so-called middle men have long been the traditional boogeymen of Mexican food politics (see Ochoa 2000). With the tortilla crisis, discomfort over the level at which Mexicans were now removed from the production process of staple ingredients in their lives – corn, corn flour, and tortillas – became strikingly apparent. During the crisis, a columnist in *El Universal* wrote, "If the benefit were for the people that produce, that grow corn, it would be perfect. But that's not the way it is. It all stays with the *acaparadores* [hoarders]" (*El Universal* 2007).

But the hoarders not only benefited from the crisis, they were also understood as at least partially responsible. With tortilla prices determined in open markets, many Mexicans imagined hoarders or speculators to be free to stockpile as much corn or corn flour as they could, cutting supply and sending prices soaring. They, too, were undermining the security of the corn market. This is exactly what many perceived to be taking place in late December and early January 2007. Increasing demand for ethanol had, the story went, caused large corn and corn flour companies to release less of the grain (both whole and processed), rapidly driving up prices of both products. Whether these dynamics actually caused the price spike in early January (let alone whether hoarding took place at all) is not relevant to the argument made here.[46] Instead, it is the perceptions that matter. Markets allow hoarders to take advantage of increased demand, rendering perceptions of access to corn insecure.

Maseca, Minsa, Gruma, and others were all singled out – by legislators, newspaper reporters and columnists, and protesters – as helping cause the price increase through hoarding and speculation. Legislators called on leading corn producers and corn flour companies to testify before Congress, signs denouncing Minsa appeared in the protests, newspaper story after newspaper story (opinion, news, and letters to the editor) blamed either specific companies or hoarders generally for taking advantage of the Mexican people, and interviews with protest participants and nonparticipants alike revealed similar perceptions. A *campesino* leader reflected that "these companies have destroyed our countryside. We rely on them now for tortilla. So we are vulnerable. They can do whatever they want" (author interview, May 2009, Mexico City).

The price increase also highlighted a specific set of insecurities as they related to the marketization of corn. A demand that had been present in the *El Campo No Aguanta Más* movement – *soberanía alimentaria* (often translated as "food sovereignty," the phrase more directly means "nourishment" or "nutriment" sovereignty) – took center stage. With rising reliance on corn imports to meet domestic needs, Mexico had become increasingly vulnerable to international prices. The *tortillazo* suggested that the promise of consumer benefits from free trade through lower prices, at least where corn was concerned, was an unstable reality at best. But it wasn't simply high consumer prices that became an issue during the *tortillazo*. There were also perceptions that the nation would no longer be able to feed itself. An environmental activist said that "with a product as important as corn, we can't depend on other nations. We have to be self-sufficient" (author interview with a Greenpeace Mexico employee, March 2009, Mexico City).[47]

---

[46] Although as already indicated, subsequent research suggests that this was at least partially the case (see García Rañó and Keleman 2007).

[47] The Calderón administration's decision to react first by increasing corn imports elicited a strong negative reaction from social movement and political leaders. Community activists responded by

State security

Perceptions of food insecurity translated quickly and seamlessly into perceptions of both state and national vulnerability. From the first shouts of "¡*soberanía, ya!* [sovereignty now!]" during the protests on January 12, many perceived Mexico's sovereignty to be at stake. Indeed, when the January 18 price pact undercut tortilla prices as a single, galvanizing issue, the organizers of the march on the 31st honed in on sovereignty as a concern rooted in the *tortillazo* but with broader political resonance. Former mayor of Mexico City and FAP member Manuel Solís wrote an editorial for *El Universal* blaming the problem on vulnerability to external shocks and called for Mexico to defend itself. Social scientist Alberto Aziz Nassif (2007) called the price increases an issue of national security. With the elimination of corn subsidies to farmers, he argued, Mexico produces less and less of its own corn and is unable to feed its own people. As NAFTA was responsible for the subsidy elimination, it was also responsible for the increase in tortilla prices. In another column, political scientist Pablo Marentes (2007) argued similarly that in the years since NAFTA, Mexico "lost its *soberanía alimentaria* and 2 million *campesinos* were left without work." Marentes goes on to argue that the *tortillazo* is also about migration. NAFTA drove the *campesinos* north and away from the cornfields. As a result, the price increases show how a part of Mexico has been lost – they reveal the country's failure to support its own people in the cultivation of a staple crop.

In the *El Universal* editorial by Alejandro Villagómez cited earlier, the economist also calls the *tortillazo* a national security issue: "Corn is the input in a critical food [*alimento*] in our country. It doesn't only represent a relevant portion of the daily expenses of those who have little, but it is also a food/nutriment [*alimento*] that is hard to substitute in the diet of the majority of Mexicans, simply for historical-cultural reasons." He goes on to say that "the potential for nonconformity and social mobilization that an explosive increase in the price of this product would provoke could surpass any foreseeable and rational limit." Social mobilization was, for many, a predictable outcome, and they often used language suggesting that the mobilizations or unrest could have serious consequences.[48]

arguing that increasing imports would only exacerbate the underlying problems. After a meeting with the directors of the National Confederation of Corn Producers of Mexico, the director of the CNC, Cruz Águilar López, argued (not surprisingly) that the increased imports would only encourage speculation, and that purchasing this fundamental element of the Mexican diet abroad was a grave error (Cárdenas Cruz 2007). With sovereignty over corn, Mexicans could reaffirm sovereignty over their own culture, defending it from the corrupting influences of the north. Corn sovereignty would guarantee that, no matter what happened in international markets – including U.S. decisions to subsidize corn or create incentives for ethanol, Mexicans would always have enough domestic corn available to ensure that corn could remain "in their blood."

48 Villagómez's comment that the mobilizations could surpass "rational" limits is also worthy of note. The reflection suggests that Villagómez understands any mobilization to be motivated not (or not entirely) by a "rational" response to the material burdens of a tortilla price increase, but

Comments from a very different source, the Chiapan bishop from San Cristóbal de las Casas, Felipe Arizmendi Esquivel, suggested fears of social instability and tied those fears to threats to country in ways that echo Villagómez's comments. The bishop argued that a movement "as dramatic as 1994 [the EZLN uprising]" was possible (quoted in Muñoz and Henriquez 2007). He added, "if the poor can't eat even tortillas, the fundamental and basic element of their diet, and almost the only [element], it puts in danger the whole country." Bishop Arizmendi's comments are ambiguous. It is unclear what kind of danger the country faces and what the effects of this danger could be. Yet he clearly perceives the threat to come from restricted access to tortillas and that its implications are national in scale.

For some, issues of national or state vulnerability were rooted directly in the ways in which free trade had altered dynamics in the Mexican countryside. On January 11 the general secretary of the National Autonomous University in Mexico, Enrique de Val Blanco, wrote:

The government should be careful with the theme of the tortilla and, from what we can see now, it would be convenient for someone to illustrate it for them, as until now it looks as though they don't understand what this basic product means for the Mexican community [*pueblo*] and the consequences could be much worse than a simple price increase of a product; it is more, much more than this. (2007)

He goes on in the article to directly attack NAFTA, but not only for the price increases for which he held the treaty responsible. In addition, he argued that the "red light" of social instability was lit because of the millions of people in the countryside who dedicate themselves to cultivation and were left without protection in the face of free trade. He called for the government to enact immediate price controls. "The price of tortillas," he wrote, "is an almost sacred thing for Mexicans, and government should understand it as such." The crisis was so deep that after less than two weeks of dramatic price increases, de Val Blanco expressed an expectation that the government should already have taken action. He also blamed free markets not simply for Mexico's vulnerability to international price increases, but also for the creation of a Mexican countryside in which small-scale agricultural production was no longer financially viable. If only the Mexican countryside were continuing to produce large amounts of corn – then the cities would not be vulnerable to international corn prices. Both tortillas and the Mexican countryside are held up as sacred in his account. And he called for government intervention to save both.

The Calderón administration's initial efforts to lower corn and tortilla prices through increasing imports not only elicited fears of food/nutriment vulnerability, but also state and national insecurity. The turn toward imported corn evoked feelings of pride in and belonging to the Mexican nation across sectoral lines. A union leader argued that by allowing Mexico to rely on other

rather by motivations that could be considered irrational – perhaps, for example, feelings of national belonging.

nations for its corn, Calderón was "putting at risk the stability of the country" (author interview, June 2009, Mexico City). A columnist for *Reforma* accused speculators of harming the "viability of the nation" (Enríquez 2007). Later in the column he goes on to argue, "If the state doesn't intervene, with all of its force, like it is doing against the bands of drug traffickers, goodbye to the state, and goodbye to the country." The author implies that if markets threaten access to tortillas, the crisis will undermine both the state and the country. I do not mean to suggest that the author imagines that the tortilla crisis could, indeed, bring an end to the state of Mexico, understood as a political entity existing within a particular set of geographically defined borders. But the statements do suggest that some understanding of what the state and country are, or perhaps what they should be, would disappear if the government did not bring serious force to bear on solving the tortilla crisis. The security-related anxieties that surfaced during those weeks suggested that conceptions of state, nation, family, and crime were intimately intertwined. The crisis was not just about a conception of cultural independence, but also about understandings of basic issues of national security (del Campo 2007).[49] Markets had left the nation exposed.

Issues of national sovereignty are apparent not only through the discourse used, but also in contentious performances in the streets. Following the national protests on January 12, activists worked to organize an additional march on the 16th – "in defense of the Tortilla and for the resignation of [Minister of the Economy] Sojo" (Galán et al. 2007). The march was to take place at the Monument to the Child Heroes – a symbol of resistance to U.S. intervention in Mexico. The location was particularly fitting – many understood U.S. intervention in the Mexican economy through high ethanol demand and low corn prices (some even suggested that the United States was engaging in illegal "dumping") to be responsible for the high tortilla prices. The *tortillazo* protests were, as a result, a declaration of national sovereignty and a protest of U.S. intervention. The two often go hand in hand, as challenges to Mexican sovereignty are routinely perceived to come from the north, whether through military armies, imported corn, or satellite television. Union leaders and farmers' organizations joined the call, with the CCC, the CROC, and the miners' union all announcing their support and calling for unity among *campesino* organizations and unions.[50]

---

[49] Questions of respect in the international arena also appear to have been at stake. To rely on the United States or South Africa for corn was not just a matter of national embarrassment or perceptions of independence. Some took the argument to the extreme, positing that if Mexico depends on other nations for corn, it will lose its clout in the international arena. The comments of Juan Arturo León López, a researcher at UAM Xochimilco, are illustrative on this point. "If Mexico wants sovereignty on every level," he argued, "it should guarantee nutritional independence. History teaches us that if a country depends on the production of another, it doesn't have the ability to negotiate an important role in the international realm" (quoted in Alatorre 2007a).

[50] I have not yet gotten a clear answer as to why this march didn't take place in the form imagined. No one seems to remember what happened; yet there is no newspaper coverage of any march at

THE PRICE PACT AND THE *MEGAMARCHA*

On January 18 Calderón announced the implementation of the price pact. The dynamics of the movement shifted fundamentally in its wake. The pact hit at the core of anxieties that dominated the tortilla crisis; the government had intervened and generated an expectation of stabilized tortilla prices.[51] Tortillas would not be left to the vicissitudes of markets, and corn would not be subject to monopoly pricing or the evils of speculation. They would, instead, be protected through an intervention of the federal government. Social movement organizers continued to prepare for a large-scale protest at the end of the month. With the price pact in place, however, enthusiasm for the march dwindled, and the movement appeared to lose momentum.

The implementation of the price pact mattered for the trajectory of this episode of contention. There are undoubtedly many reasons why the *tortillazo* protests would not become the Cochabamban water wars. Everything from the challenges in mounting a campaign in a city ten times the size of Cochabamba, to attempts at national-level mobilizing, to the organizational dynamics of the networks involved mattered. Yet government response also had a role to play.[52] While their Bolivian counterparts fanned the flames of unrest by first dismissing initial mobilizations as trivial and later sending in police from La Paz to control the protesters, Mexican authorities created a political spectacle that served to validate protesters' claims, communicate that those claims had been heard, and suggest that the state was on their side. The president declared that he considered the local repercussions of the international increase in the price of corn "unacceptable" and that he would "firmly" punish anyone who "took advantage of the needs of the people" (*Cinco Días*, January 18, 2007). Calderón's words stand in stark contrast to those of Bolivian President Hugo Banzer, who called the initial blockades in Vinto "background music" with which he could easily contend (*Los Tiempos*, September 3, 1999).

The pact itself may have been all show – it was, after all, voluntary, and many *tortillerías* did not sign on. Indeed, by January 20, representatives of millers' associations were already saying that it would be impossible to reduce the price of tortillas to 8.5 pesos/kilo (Gómez 2007). In the state of Quintana Roo in the Yucatán Peninsula local leaders of *masa* and tortilla workers declared that they would continue to sell tortillas at 12 pesos/kilo (Parra 2007).

Nevertheless, the president's show had a political effect. It suggested that Calderón and his team were listening and sent a message that they would

all on the 16th. More important for the points made here, whether the march occurred is largely irrelevant. That the organizers were planning a march to take place at this symbol of independence from the United States is enough to help reveal the connections between the tortilla crisis and conceptions of national independence.

[51] Whether that stabilization was actually accomplished is not what matters. It is the perception here that is important.

[52] See Simmons (2011) for an in-depth discussion of state responses to the two movements.

not, in spite of their commitments to free markets, let the price of tortillas be set by the whims of the market. The price pact said: we understand this is important to you and we think it is important, too. What ultimately happened to prices is almost irrelevant. The pact removed the anxiety that came from insecurity by creating – even if it was only an illusion – the perception that the state would not let the situation get out of control. Reflecting on the events, Víctor Suárez, president of ANEC, recalls that Calderón's price pact served as an *"engaño* [trick]." The pact "tricked the public into thinking the problem was taken care of. We lost the regular, middle-class people we needed with the price pact. They [members of the administration] knew how to co-opt the people" (author interview, February 2009, Mexico City). Suárez interprets the pact as a disingenuous signal that worked to produce quiescence. Disingenuous or not, the pact did send the message that the administration was listening.

The legacies of state intervention – often through clientelistic practices – in the Mexican corn and tortilla market may help to provide some of the answer to the puzzle of rapid demobilization. From the early 1960s the Mexican government has been heavily involved in regulating and subsidizing producers and consumers at almost every stage in the corn-tortilla chain. Much of that support was phased out prior to NAFTA. When the state systematically pulls away from the predictability that can come with price supports or subsidies, citizens may doubt whether governments are willing to intervene during price crises. Insecurities are heightened during times when populations are unsure of how a state will respond in the face of rapid, seemingly never-ending price increases of staple goods. The unpredictability of markets works together with vanishing expectations of the state to produce particularly intense experiences of insecurity. While concerns around small-scale corn farming practices and food systems, as well as food sovereignty more generally, might have remained, the state was able to address the central anxieties around access. The state had sent a strong message that tortillas could remain a staple of the Mexican diet. It seemed to matter less whether they came from Walmart than that they were on the table at all.

Preparations for the march

Yet even as the movement appeared to stall, intersectoral cooperation continued to dominate. The march was a moment of exemplary coordination and unity among and within groups from a variety of backgrounds with a variety of agendas. With the price pact in place, the cost of tortillas no longer appeared as a central rallying cry. Instead, movement organizers turned toward an emphasis on *soberanía alimentaria*, a frame that continued to highlight connections between tortillas and nation. The tortilla crisis helped bring identifications as Mexicans to the fore, encouraging broad-based, if brief, collaboration among unexpected interlocutors.

Even in the wake of the price pact, union, *campesino*, and other civil society leaders continued to organize the drive toward January 31. Leaders from the UNT – representing more than 100 independent unions – and the *Sindicato Mexicano de Electristas* [Electrical Workers' Union] (SME) pledged the support and participation of their members. The union at the *Universidad Nacional Autónoma de México* [National Autonomous University of Mexico] (UNAM), the telephone workers' union, the social security workers' union, and the miners' union also began to rally their memberships for the event. Factions of the farmers' movement, including the CNC, UNORCA, *Consejo Nacional de Organizaciones Campesinas* [National Council of Peasant Organizations] (CONOC), *Consejo Nacional de Organizaciones Rurales y Pesqueras* [National Council of Rural and Fishing Organizations] (CONORP), and the CCC, continued their commitment to both work together and bring in members from all over the country for the march. The debtors' organization El Barzón also joined in the planning and reached out to its national membership to rally participants. The National Citizens' Coalition (a collective of women's groups, environmental groups, consumer organizations, and other civil society organizations) organized participation at the local, neighborhood level. The Democratic Alliance of Civil Organizations [*Alianza Democrática de Organizaciones Civiles*] (ADOC), an umbrella organization that coordinated civil society activities throughout the country, also joined as a driving force in efforts to mobilize previously unorganized citizens. Small-scale protests continued, but all of the organizational effort was now behind putting together a large-scale march on January 31.

As planning for the march progressed, leaders from each organization may very well have had their own interests or goals in mind. A number of Mexican officials called the protests "opportunistic," claiming that the organizations driving the movement cared little about corn prices and had merely been taking advantage of an issue they knew would galvanize a broad base of participants (author interviews with Mexican governmental officials, May–July 2009, Mexico City). Indeed, some leaders claimed unabashedly to have taken advantage of the crisis to push a prior anti-neoliberal or anti-PAN agenda. In the *tortillazo*, they saw an opportunity to mobilize Mexicans to join long-standing fights against free trade, in favor of subsidies for the countryside, or against the PAN (author interviews with Mexican political opposition leaders, January–July 2009). Prominent public intellectual Sergio Sarmiento explicitly called the march a purely political move staged by Calderón's opponents in the PRD and the PRI (Sarmiento 2007). Opposition parties did not want to let a moment of weakness pass without taking full advantage of the potential for organized protest. Yet perhaps counterintuitively, Sarmiento's cry of opportunism offers further support for the argument made here. In the language of social movement theory, the tortilla crisis offered an extraordinary political opportunity – the crisis gave the opposition an issue around which it could come together. But that the opportunity was possible at all is a product of the meanings with which corn was imbued. Social movement leaders may very well have been taking advantage of the tortilla crisis, but that they could do so at all speaks to the universality of the tortilla as an important symbol of life and livelihood across classes and sectors. Regardless of activists' own perceptions of the role of corn in constructing communities, they capitalized on the broad-based appeal of the issue. The political opportunity existed only because of the ways in which tortillas symbolized community in Mexico.

Sarmiento also fails to point out that the call to protest attracted not only members of the declared opposition, but also members of the PAN itself – people who had voted a little more than six months earlier to put Calderón in office. Although PAN leaders were not behind the organization of any of the events in the streets during January, they did not fail to speak out on the floor of the Congress, directly critiquing the president and his appointees. Furthermore, whereas PAN leaders stayed at home on the 31st, many of their constituents took to the streets (author interviews with *tortillazo* protest participants, January–June 2009, Mexico City). Regardless of their own political convictions, PAN leaders had arguably good political reasons to position themselves as fighting against rising tortilla prices. Irrespective of their party affiliation or declared ideological commitments, politicians appeared reluctant to support free market principles when corn and tortillas were at stake.

January 31, Mexico City

Mexican activists began the January 31, 2007, protest from different spots throughout the city, aiming to converge on the central plaza. The protesters easily accomplished their goal – in contrast to events in Cochabamba, neither the central government nor the local police got in their way, and no confrontations between city, state, or federal authorities and the protest participants were reported.[53] The Mexican Union Front [*Frente Sindical Mexicano*] (FSM), led by the SME, started at the Monument to the Revolution. The UNT, including social security, telephone, and transportation workers and pilots, started at the Zócalo itself. *Campesino* organizations began at the Angel of Independence; the Citizens' Alliance for Democracy and other citizens' groups began at the monument to Columbus (Muñoz et al. 2007). The leaders of the protest called it a "march for food independence and in defense of salaries and employment."

With the price pact in place, organizers shifted their focus to broader demands; immediate access to tortillas was no longer a powerful rallying cry. Movement leaders reflecting on the march largely recall that the price pact required that they expand their message and explicitly use the crisis to highlight Mexico's vulnerability to international markets (author interviews with *tortillazo* protest leaders, January–July 2009, Mexico City). *Soberanía alimentaria* became a driving theme, as did concerns around genetically modified corn. For union participants, the recently renegotiated minimum wage also became a focal point as wages were set while tortilla prices were at 70 percent

---

[53] See Simmons (2011) for a discussion of this variation.

FIGURE 5.3. The Zócalo in Mexico City, January 31, 2007 (photo courtesy of *La Jornada*).

of the January 18 price pact level; union leaders argued the wages were now unacceptable given the new cost of tortillas. These new foci were both vague and too targeted. Appeals to a higher minimum wage spoke to urban union constituents but did not have universal appeal. Calls for *soberanía alimentaria* may have had broad appeal but lost their resonance when they could no longer be tied to a direct, immediate threat.

Once assembled, the "plurality" that filled the plaza issued the "Declaration of the Zócalo," calling for a "new social economy" that included revised economic programs, *soberanía alimentaria*, and "sovereignty" over "national goods" (See Figure 5.3; Muñoz et al. 2007). Television journalist Verónica Velasco read the declaration, which argued that the "economic model that was forced on the country is not viable any longer and today is in a crisis" and stated that "a new stage of fighting" had begun (ibid.). The declaration focused on the economic model broadly, arguing that the recent price increases were tied to neoliberal policies, and that the threat to *soberanía alimentaria* was the result of a failure to support the countryside.

While the protest suggested widespread collaboration, there was significant internal disagreement over one issue in particular – the formal participation of the PRD. Union, *campesino,* and other civil society leaders had fought vigorously to keep Andrés Manuel López Obrador, the former presidential candidate for the PRD, from speaking at the march. They wanted to send a clear message that their movement was distinct from the one that López Obrador represented. The corn movement was not only cross-class and cross-region, but also cross–political party, including members of the PRD and the PRI as well as Calderón's own PAN, and its organizers did not want to undermine their message with partisan controversy (author interviews with *tortillazo* protest leaders, January–July 2009, Mexico City). But López Obrador could not be dissuaded and a second march took place that evening at 7PM. By that time numbers had diminished and the rhetoric changed to the familiar slogans of the López Obrador campaign.

National mobilizations

Whereas the mobilization in Mexico City was the most visible, other marches took place throughout the country (Martínez et al. 2007). In the capitals of ten states, union members, farmers, and citizens demanded relief from the tortilla price increase and policies to protect *soberanía alimentaria*. The national nature of the mobilizations stands in contrast to the events in Cochabamba, where protests remained localized until their final days. In each Mexican state, the marches were attended by equally diverse sectors of the local community. Unions joined peasant organizations, consumer advocacy groups, housewives, students, and indigenous organizations, among others.

The largest protest outside the capital appears to have taken place in Morelia, Michoacán, where members of forty-eight organizations, as well as citizens unaffiliated with any particular political or social organization, joined the protest. Union organizations – including large umbrella unions such as the *Asociación de Trabajadores de Estado de Michoacán* [Association of State Workers of Michoacan] (ATEM) and sector-specific unions such as the *Coordinadora Nacional de Trabajadores del la Educación* [National Coordinator of Education Workers] (CNTE) – joined *campesino* organizations and El Barzón in rallying members. But neighborhood associations, housewives, and local business owners also joined the crowds with signs declaring, "*Somos Gente de Maíz* [We are People of Corn]," "*Defendemos el Campo* [We Defend the Countryside]," and "*Defender a Nuestro Maíz, Defendemos a México* [Defending Our Corn, We Defend Mexico]," among others. Members of the State Front of Farmers' Organizations blocked highways and toll booths throughout the state, encouraging drivers to join the movement. Local *campesino* leader Carlos Ramos argued that the protests were taking up the mantel of the ECNAM movement, only this time "it is not only the countryside that can bear no more, but also the pocketbooks of the workers that can't bear anymore either" (*La Jornada de Michoacán*, February 1, 2007).

The mobilization in Mexico City and the marches that accompanied it throughout the country demonstrate the broad-based mobilizing power of a market-driven threat to tortillas. But even though the cross-class, cross-sector, and cross-urban–rural composition of the movements' participants reflected an exceptional coming together of Mexican sectoral and other civil society interests, the protests that day did not draw large numbers of independent citizens. Consumers who were unaffiliated with a union or sectoral organization largely stayed at home. These independent consumers were exactly the people that movement organizers contend they could have mobilized had Calderón failed to act so quickly and so publicly to reassure Mexicans that tortillas were exempt from the regular ups and downs of the market. Nevertheless, tortillas had brought unions, *campesinos*, and citizen organizations together. They had even, for a time, mobilized housewives, middle-class businessmen and businesswomen, and Mexicans who, ordinarily, closed their doors and stayed home when Mexico's sectoral organizations sought to mobilize the masses.

Movement dissolution

The government responded to the January 31 march by proposing a dialogue with the organizing groups; government representatives moved quickly and adeptly to bring movement leaders to the negotiating table (see Simmons 2011). The secretaries of the economy, agriculture, and labor sat down with representatives from CONORP, CONOC, CAP, UNORCA, El Barzón, and the CNC (farmers), as well as the UNT and FSM (workers), CROC (workers and farmers), and the Citizen's Coalition. Although the PAN had notably less experience than its predecessor (the PRI) at effectively managing civil unrest, much institutional memory remained. Standard postprotest policies were quickly put into place. By bringing the opposition to the table quickly, the government effectively undermined any momentum that might have been produced by the January 31 march. Furthermore, government policy makers effectively capitalized on divisions within such a plural group, offering enough favors to some to take them out of the movement, and highlighting differences among those that remained. In spite of a shared declaration, there was little agreement among the groups once they sat down to negotiate. Historical divisions among the organizations that split after ECNAM, as well as new splits resulting from the 2006 election outcome, plagued the negotiations.[54] One participant remarked that the plurality of the groups represented made it easy for government to take advantage of disagreements (author interview, May 2009, Mexico City). The groups met a few times between February and the end of April, and the government offered concessions to various participants. Gradually, participants dropped out, but the conversations continued and the meetings functioned as a link, albeit thin and tenuous, between the administration and organized civil society.

---

[54] Some groups continued to actively support López Obrador; others, still PRD sympathizers, chose to respect Calderón's right to be in office.

The crisis had passed. The government had intervened quickly and decisively. Movements had started to form all over the country, but they quickly subsided. Government concern about the issue, however, remained. The Minister of the Economy now got weekly reports including the price of tortillas (a figure the government had not previously tracked) and efforts continued to keep prices stable. At the end of April, government representatives met again with the signatories of the price pact to renegotiate before the deal expired. The parties signed an extension of the agreement, committing to keep the price of tortillas at 8.5 pesos/kilo until August 15. The administration appeared determined not to have to contend with a spike in tortilla prices again.

CONCLUSION

Corn and community are intimately intertwined in the Mexican context. The preceding analysis of the tortilla crisis shows how a social movement can emerge when markets threaten to weaken or reconfigure these ties. Through both reminding Mexicans of corn's place in their lives and livelihoods and creating a perception of corn's potential vulnerability, the *tortillazo* tapped into deeply rooted connections to family, evoked perceptions of class and countryside, and heightened feelings of national belonging. As a result, politicians crossed party lines to voice common goals, sectoral organizations with histories plagued by disagreement mounted a joint campaign, and "ordinary" citizens banged pots and pans in the streets in protest.

Frames were key in this process, but how and why they worked in the ways they did requires attention to the signifying work that corn does in the Mexican context. Frames related to family, security, sovereignty, and nation can be potent mobilization tools. But to be effective, they must resonate. The meanings with which corn was already imbued could not have been the product of clever framing by social movement activists already opposed to NAFTA, fighting on behalf of *soberanía alimentaria*, or working to secure better union wages. Although a number of organizations were ready to be mobilized in protest, the frames were powerful political tools only because they tapped into what corn and tortillas already meant to many Mexicans.

A counterfactual underscores this point. For example, it is hard to imagine that a frame painting rising sugar prices as a threat to the Mexican "*pueblo*" would gain significant traction within the country. That tortillas can be framed as goods that are synecdochic for or emblematic of the Mexican "*pueblo*" in ways that resonate powerfully throughout the country is the critical point. Tortillas and corn were *already* understood by many Mexicans to symbolize the Mexican nation, and to wed nationalism to domesticity.

Demands for "sovereignty now!" or declarations that tortillas are "*patria*" hardly make sense when high tortilla prices are understood in purely material terms. However, when we see the threat as more than simply a price increase, we can understand how and why the *tortillazo* worked as a reminder of shared heritage, potential national or state vulnerabilities, domestic routines, or commitments to the poor or *lo campesino*. Each helped bring national belonging to the fore and, in doing so, helped produce a broad-based, widespread resistance movement.

6

Conclusions

At its most general, this book argues that the meanings with which grievances are imbued can play an indispensable explanatory role in our understandings of social movement origins and composition. The argument takes the content of social movements seriously, making the case that scholars should not ignore social movements' claims when they seek to explain social movement processes and outcomes. These theoretical arguments help to address many of the critiques that have pushed grievances to the sidelines in the social movement literature. Perhaps the most widely accepted and deployed critique of using grievances as an explanatory variable is rooted in the idea that grievances exist everywhere and always. Since grievances are everywhere, they cannot vary with outcomes of interest. By understanding grievances as meaning-laden, we can helpfully complicate their status as seemingly omnipresent variables.

THE BENEFITS OF STUDYING GRIEVANCES AS MEANING-LADEN

I do not claim to challenge the ubiquity of grievances. Nor do I seek to downplay the importance of material conditions; cultural meanings alone are unlikely to work in the ways outlined here in the absence of a material threat. I do, however, contend that grievances take on different meanings in different times and places and that an understanding of these meanings will give us the tools to productively incorporate grievances into our analyses. For example, as this book has shown, in Mexico, corn can mean family, neighborhood, or nation. Corn can be tied to conceptions of domesticity, sovereignty, and security. High corn prices are not, therefore, simply understood as occasions for material trade-offs. Instead, in addition to material threats, they can also be perceived as threats to a sense of self, family, and nation. In understanding corn in this way, we can make sense of mobilizations around high corn prices and, similarly, the failure to mobilize around high prices for sugar or milk. We are, indeed, likely to find grievances everywhere we look. But only some grievances will take on the meanings that create the conditions of possibility for political resistance.

A meaning-laden approach also helps us to address the challenges that come with seeing grievances as truncated variables. For many analysts, grievances are present or absent, or severe or not severe. Even those scholars who divide grievances into materially derived categories often remain committed to materially based notions of what a grievance is and ground their analyses in levels of severity.[1] As a result, it is not surprising that we have trouble developing systematic analyses of how grievances co-vary with outcomes of interest.[2] However, when grievances are studied as materially and ideationally constituted, they are no longer dichotomous or ordinal variables. Even categories like "austerity programs" or "food prices" are helpfully complicated in ways that allow scholars to explore whether grievances that appear the same should, in fact, be analyzed as such.

These insights help to make sense of the varying approaches to understanding responses to neoliberal reforms that currently dominate scholarship.[3] When we break from essentialist accounts of responses to neoliberal reforms we can see how market liberalization might simultaneously demobilize and fragment popular sectors (e.g., Kurtz 2004), receive high levels of popular support (e.g., Baker 2009), and stimulate social protest in defense of popular interests (e.g., Silva 2009). The effects of markets are contextual, conditional, and highly contingent. Markets may have demobilized and fragmented labor, but in places where neighborhood ties or other associational structures are strong, communities are available to be mobilized if they perceive that they are being threatened. Free trade may very well be popular when it gives consumers access to high-quality, low-priced items (Baker 2009). But trade agreements often involve the elimination of subsidies on a variety of goods. When these goods are consumer staples that are part of cultural understandings and practices, we might see vigorous opposition. Finally, as Silva (2009) acknowledges, the economic and social exclusion that accompanies the imposition of a market society will not always generate a Polanyian double-movement. But attention to political associational space, economic crises, framing and brokerage mechanisms, and reformist commitments (ibid.) do not shed light on all of the processes at work when market societies produce economic, social, and political exclusion. By integrating the material and cultural dimensions of movement claims we can see how movement cyclicality – early periods of quiescence followed by later periods of mobilization – in response to market reforms is not explained exclusively by shifting political opportunity structures. We can also

---

[1] For an example of the former see Almeida (2003). For the latter see Van Dyke and Soule (2002).
[2] For exceptions see Wimmer et al. (2009); Cederman et al. (2013); and Buhaug et al. (2014).
[3] Thanks to an anonymous reviewer for the comments from which this paragraph is drawn.

better understand variation across and within policy types. Attention to the interplay of the material and the ideational in the content of a movement's claims can help us better understand the cycles of contention.

Perhaps surprisingly for some scholars, in adding nuance to, or challenging common categorizations of the claims social movements make, a meaning-laden approach to grievances actually enhances our ability to make generalizable arguments. Far from forcing scholars to make limited, parochial claims, attention to a grievance's meanings can allow us to move from the particular to the general in ways we might not have anticipated previously.

By allowing us to move from the particular to the general, attention to the meanings grievances take on can help to reconcile important scholarly debates. For example, the approach helps to bridge important divides in scholarship on the role of grievances in civil war and violence. Cederman et al. (2013) and Buhaug et al. (2014) show how shifting our analytic lens to group-level analysis reveals the importance of inequality and ethno-political discrimination as causes of civil conflict. Their conclusions challenge a literature that looks largely to individual indicators and finds that grievances give us little leverage in understanding violent conflict (e.g., Fearon and Laitin 2003; Collier and Hoeffler 2004; Laitin 2007).

An approach that incorporates the meanings of grievances seriously can help us understand why this might be the case. Individuals experience inequality and political discrimination differently in different times and places. Laitin is correct to claim that "grievances are commonly felt and latent" and therefore we must look for causation in the factors that make grievances (like inequality or political discrimination) "vital and manifest" (2007, 25). But it may be precisely the differences in how the grievances are experienced that makes perceptions of inequality resonate powerfully in some places and among some people but not others. Inequality matters but so do the processes that transform inequality from a Gini Coefficient to the kind of lived experience that might help to cause social mobilization. Differences among groups may contribute to how inequality is experienced, but what inequality symbolizes and how those symbols work is a critical piece of the causal chain. This suggests a new line of inquiry for scholars of political violence: How and when do perceived differences among groups work to produce political violence? Can we think systematically about what types of perceived differences matter for mobilization? Are there similarities among meaning-making processes in the times and places where perceived inequality generates political violence? Scholars would do well to start looking for the ways in which meaning-making matters in the process of transforming a "latent" variable into one that helps to produce political conflict. More generally, as this example shows, studying grievances as meaning-laden opens up new research questions and research agendas for scholars of contention.

Furthermore, when we study a grievance's meanings, we expand our ability to make comparisons between cases that might, at first blush, appear very different. This is precisely what I intend for the comparison between Bolivia and Mexico to do. Because of their roles in daily life and livelihood, water in Cochabamba and corn in Mexico came to mean community in similar ways. In treating these meanings as part of what the grievance is, corn and water become comparable in ways that are difficult to understand when we base our analyses on materiality alone. While this approach may allow us to challenge the utility of some comparisons (for example, corn in Mexico and corn in Japan), it enables other comparisons that may have seemed surprising before (for example, corn in Mexico and rice in Japan). By employing interpretive analysis in our approach to grievances we do not, as some skeptics might claim, limit our ability to make general claims about patterns of contention. Instead, by paying attention to dynamic semiotic practices, we expand the possibilities not only for nuanced causal arguments about particular cases, but also for surprising comparisons that can shed light on processes of social mobilization.

Finally, by analyzing grievances as meaning-laden we may gain leverage not only on questions of movement (non)emergence, but also on movement composition. A meaning-laden approach can help us to explain why a particular grievance in a particular moment might have helped to spark a sustained, broad-based movement while another grievance sparked a movement limited to particular sectors or classes, or perhaps did not spark a movement at all. Attention to a grievance's meanings can systematically help to shed light on the textures and repertoires of political mobilization.

I do not claim that grievances can work alone to explain political mobilization. Any analysis of contention must pay attention to political context and structures and without resources of some kind a movement is unlikely to emerge. These variables offer important leverage for our analyses. Yet the meanings grievances take on help to inform how political opportunities are perceived, which resources are available for movement mobilization, and how frames resonate and with whom. Although attention to either water or corn alone is insufficient to explain political mobilization in either case (political opportunities, resources, and frames each played critical roles), the dynamics of neither case can be fully explained without it. Attention to grievances can enhance our analyses of which political structures are conducive to social mobilization and why resources are available to particular movements at particular moments.

SUBSISTENCE, MARKETS, AND PROTEST

But convincing scholars that the meanings of grievances matter is not my only theoretical aim. In addition, I seek to make more specific claims about the relationship between subsistence resources, marketization, and political protest. When people perceive subsistence resources to be threatened by markets, conditions of possibility for widespread, broad-based resistance can emerge. The water wars in Cochabamba, Bolivia in 2000, and the *tortillazo* protests in Mexico in 2007 serve as a foundation for a theorization of the connections between market-driven threats to subsistence resources and social mobilization.

The arguments elaborated here rest on the premise that the material and the symbolic are intimately intertwined. Our notions of what the material is and, specifically, what we "need" for survival cannot be pried apart from the meanings that "material" goods take on. This relationship is particularly evident in goods understood as subsistence resources. Goods that have formed a critical part of the "material" life and livelihood for particular populations over long periods of time are likely to have also become central to semiotic practices. Because of the meanings with which subsistence resources are likely to be imbued, market-generated threats to them can be perceived not only as material threats, but also as threats to community – both imagined and quotidian. Claimants understand not only their material relationships with the good, but also broader understandings of nation, region, ethnicity, and local community or family to be at risk. These perceptions then serve as grievances that cross salient local divisions, creating conditions of possibility for widespread, broad-based opposition coalitions.

This book's contribution comes through looking at the cultural understandings of subsistence and the moments when these understandings and markets intersect. Arguments that point to the symbolic role of subsistence goods are not new (see Chapter 1). That corn might be synechdochic for "Mexico," or that water might index region or local community in a place with a history of both agriculture and drought may not be particularly surprising. And, of course, what may be seen as a subsistence good culturally may no longer be physically necessary for survival. My argument rests on a chronological understanding of how subsistence resources are imbued with cultural meanings. At some point in time the goods were not substitutable – a failed corn crop would mean unavoidable famine; a deadly virus that wiped out a community's cows would surely mean extreme material hardship. When goods play an indispensible material role in survival they are likely to take on cultural meanings. These meanings are then likely to be produced and reproduced well beyond the times during which the good plays a critical role in survival; the goods continue to be understood as "subsistence" even if they are no longer necessary for a community to physically subsist.

The combination of marketization and protest may help to both remind people of the role these goods play in communal understandings and identifications and reinforce those same understandings. Meanings are always subject to change but the ways in which subsistence and community are ideationally tied may be subject to less risk in the wake of the kinds of spectacles that took place in Cochabamba and Mexico City. Protest events might bring some of the socially constructed schemas that operate without conscious awareness to the fore. By seeing the semiological system at work citizens might recognize its importance more consciously, rendering that system potentially less mutable. Whereas, prior to the water wars, one can potentially imagine ways in which increasingly mechanized systems of water delivery might have caused water-related *usos y costumbres* to gradually fade from regular practice in Cochabamba, in a post–water war world this seems virtually impossible. The importance of *usos y costumbres* was highlighted during the water wars in ways that will not easily be forgotten. While recognizing that meanings are never fixed, this research suggests that subsistence-related protests might serve to make more visible the connections between subsistence and culture, thus amplifying the potential ideational role of subsistence threats in the future.

The cases also show how relationships with subsistence goods will be textured and nuanced in ways that produce different kinds of communities across time and place. While water in Cochabamba and corn in Mexico both worked to symbolize imagined and quotidian communities, the ways in which they produced those communities were different. A similar logic was at work in both cases – both goods were at the center of life and livelihood and that role helped to produce communities – but the specifics were different. In Cochabamba, relationships with water often involved high levels of social coordination. Whether through irrigators' local governance organizations in peri-urban and rural Cochabamba or through water councils in urban areas, people came together to act collectively and to manage water production and consumption. In many places, accessing water required working together at the neighborhood level. While small-scale production of corn has some similar features – for example, communities coming together during harvest or planting time to make sure the work gets done – and those features are often idealized in conceptions of *campesino* life, they do not play as central a role in relationships with corn in urban Mexico. Even if acts of consumption are shared around a family dining table or at a community celebration, the communities created through these events do not require the kinds of shared work that is so present in Cochabamba. Even as water and corn worked similarly to symbolize community and those meanings helped to produce social mobilization, the differences in how those communities were constructed likely mattered for each episode of contention.

MOVEMENT TRAJECTORIES

In fact, attention to these differences might help us begin to shed light on the different trajectories of the two movements. Protest in Mexico was largely a response to the price shock itself. While some discourse focused on the importance of consuming Mexican corn, much of it was simply about the importance of access to corn and tortillas generally. In Bolivia, the Aguas del Tunari contract not only threatened to increase prices, but also to fundamentally alter local irrigation governance and urban water council practices. Even if prices could be brought under control there were other issues at stake with respect to water governance and management. This may help to explain why, even after significant government concessions on the price issue,

Cochabambans continued to take to the streets in large numbers. Water privatization was materially tied to communal practices irrespective of prices in ways that were more immediately perceptible than corn and free trade. As a result, when people perceived that prices would be kept under control in Mexico, it worked to demobilize the movement while the same move in Cochabamba had little effect. Although these divergent movement outcomes may come as no surprise to social movement scholars or experts in Latin American politics, attention to them can refine our understandings of the relationships between subsistence, markets, and mobilization.

But while policy makers in both Bolivia and Mexico worked to contain the respective price increases, their responses to the movements were remarkably different. This, too, could have played a role in the escalation and de-escalation of the two movements (see Simmons 2011). In Bolivia, government officials were slow to take the movement seriously, dismissing it as "background music" (*Los Tiempos*, September 3, 1999) and something with which they could easily deal. They were quick to send in troops from La Paz to contain the mobilizations. Many Cochabambans perceived the government attitude to have been that if Cochabambans knew what was good for them they would stay home. It was not until massive demonstrations shut down the city in January that the movement seemed to garner much attention and not until a second round of protests in February that government policy makers agreed to reductions in rate hikes.

Here attention to the meanings with which grievances are imbued might once again provide explanatory leverage. Differences in how public authorities understood the threatened good might help to explain why Bolivian and Mexican public officials responded to the protests in the ways they did. In Cochabamba, authorities charged with addressing the mobilizations – many of whom came from La Paz or Santa Cruz – failed to perceive the meanings with which water was imbued in the Cochabamba Valley and, as a result, failed to perceive the potential for widespread mobilization. In Mexico, high-level government actors quickly appreciated the potential for mass mobilization around a threat to tortillas. Some members of the Calderón administration understood that their constituents perceived corn to have meanings deeply rooted in a sense of self and community. Others not only understood the meanings with which corn was imbued for constituents but also understood corn to be highly symbolic themselves. Whether or not corn was symbolic to the officials themselves, the perception that it played an important symbolic role for constituents was enough to orchestrate an immediate government response to rising tortilla prices; public officials anticipated the potential for widespread mobilization and acted to avert major social unrest.

Where government officials appreciated the symbolic value of the goods at stake, they acted quickly to curtail resistance. Where officials failed to grasp the meanings with which the good was imbued, they dismissed the potential for widespread mobilization, not only allowing the movement to grow but also intervening in ways that directly encouraged movement acceleration. Thus, the analysis suggests that we should pay attention not only to what grievances mean to potential social movement participants but also to policy makers. Meaning-making drives patterns of contention because of the ways it informs the perceptions, actions, and interactions of those seeking to anticipate and contain mobilization as well as the people who might mobilize.

BROADER IMPLICATIONS

By theorizing the dynamics at work when the perceived marketization of a subsistence good triggers political mobilization, this book offers insights into both the particular contentious episodes that form the core of the preceding analysis and the broader collective action puzzle that has long motivated social science scholarship. One of the general conclusions that emerges from the book's argument and analysis is both intuitively unsurprising and, at the same time, perhaps unsettling for academicians, and political scientists and sociologists in particular. The evidence presented here suggests that we can understand neither moments nor patterns of contentious politics without grounding our analysis in the particulars of time and place and how we interpret the world around us. This book has focused on the meanings that grievances take on, and the ways in which some grievances that appear the same cannot always be coded as such, while other grievances that appear different may, in fact, work similarly to help produce contentious episodes. But the conclusion from the research can be interpreted more generally. Meanings matter and our analyses of contentious politics should not overlook their constitutive and causal role.

In placing meaning at the center of our analyses of contentious politics, we necessarily limit the kinds of claims that particular methodological and theoretical approaches can make when studying contention. While scholarship that conceives of individuals as purely rational and strategic may help us to better understand some political phenomena, it cannot offer a complete picture when patterns of contentious politics are the subject of inquiry.[4] To understand why people mobilize we must understand what their interests are. Local, intersubjective processes are key to helping us figure out what people care about and why.[5] While there is a significant literature within contentious politics that acknowledges the limits of rational choice approaches (e.g., Aminzade 2001; Goodwin et al. 2001; Goodwin and Jasper 2004; Gould 2009), the evidence offered here explicitly points to the importance of including an understanding of semiotic practices as they relate to the claims at a social movement's core. To explain contentious politics, we must understand actors' perceptions

---

[4] See Wedeen (2002) for a discussion of the ways in which rational choice analyses and interpretive approaches may be incommensurable.

[5] See Herrera (2005) on this point.

of grievances not only as rational and strategic, but also as nonstrategic and embedded in groups.

In addition to offering general theoretical implications, this book also helps scholars to understand oft-studied events in new ways. Chapter 1 suggested that the subsistence theory developed here has implications for bread riots in England and for peasant rebellions in Southeast Asia. Preliminary research also suggests that attention to the meanings with which subsistence claims are imbued sheds light on the dynamics at work in Revolutionary France, the 1930 Indian Salt March, and the 1977 Egyptian "bread riots" (Simmons 2012). Every time subsistence goods and markets intersect we should look to the ways in which perceptions of community shape individual, local, national, and state responses. All of the mechanisms at work in the preceding pages may not appear, but some of them may, and certainly attention to them will shed light on the dynamics at work in whatever political processes we observe.

But the research also has implications for our analysis of state and society beyond the episodes of contention that are at the core of the analysis. Although the mechanisms described in the preceding pages focus on the connections among markets, subsistence, and contention, they might also inform our analysis of policy-making processes and public opinion, perceptions, and actions that don't necessarily lead to mobilization. For example, incorporating the ways in which the family farm has been idealized and revered as something quintessentially American might help us better understand some aspects of the power of the agricultural lobby in U.S. politics. A similar line of analysis might also be helpful in thinking about French policies related to cheese imports. High gas prices are particularly meaningful in the U.S. context and politicians are routinely caught up in efforts to ensure that Americans can continue to drive cars for long distances at relatively low cost. An analysis of how and why cars have come to mean what they do in conceptions of American-ness might shed some light on why gas prices shape U.S. politics and policy in the ways they do.

The research is also an invitation to think more broadly about subsistence practices that may not be related to any particular subsistence good. Whereas land falls outside the definition of a subsistence good offered in the first chapter, threats to it may work in similar ways, depending on the threat itself. Based on his work in Zimbabwe, Donald Moore argues that "historically sedimented livelihood strategies" (2000, 667) are situated practices key to understanding localized cultural politics. For Moore, landscape is both soil and semiotics. The specific, place-based character of relationships to land might foreclose the kind of broad-based resistance discussed in the preceding chapters. But similar processes surrounding perceived threats to community might still be at work. For example, although a particular forest may help constitute self and community for the people who live near it, it may be less likely to take on these meanings for political actors hundreds of miles away. If that particular forest is threatened by marketization (e.g., the commodification of the trees), the theorizing done here suggests that resistance is likely but also that it will be highly localized. If, however, a number of forests across a larger region are threatened and those forests either play or have played a critical role in livelihood strategies in the region, one might see the same kind of cross-cleavage mobilization. The forests might be symbols of regional pride or work to index national or ethnic attachments. They may also help produce quotidian communities throughout the region, as daily practices are likely to relate directly to them.[6]

Further work exploring the intersection of markets, subsistence, and contentious politics will continue to advance our theoretical claims about patterns and processes of contention while shedding light on specific events that have helped to shape political realities. This book invites additional research into the intersection of subsistence and contention, the anxieties produced by markets, how those anxieties might surface when symbols of community are threatened, and how people might experience regional or national vulnerabilities when they understand daily rituals and routines to be at risk. More generally I want to encourage other scholars, through careful attention to how the material and the symbolic are intimately intertwined, to rethink how grievances are coded and categorized.

Insofar as threats to subsistence are understood as threats to imagined and quotidian communities – to nations, regions, ethnic groups, or families – they are likely to generate an emotional reaction. As Deborah Gould (2009) has argued, what people feel can have a tremendous impact on shaping contention. A perceived threat to something that is highly valued (say, an ideal of "the" Mexican family, or "the" Andean cosmovision), and, in particular, when the value of that "thing" is axiomatic and nonconscious, political protest seems almost self-evident. Threats to the everyday take on powerful meanings capable of bridging cleavages and, in the process, shaping patterns of contentious politics.

This line of analysis suggests that the kinds of mechanisms at work in subsistence protests may also be at work when other categories of grievances are at stake. Subsistence threats are only one subset of a larger category of threats to everyday life and livelihood. We might expect that these kinds of threats – whether related to a subsistence good or not – might generate mobilization through some similar mechanisms. Poor municipal service delivery, such as garbage collection or electricity provision, might not tap into the kinds of imagined communities related to subsistence but they could very well activate quotidian communities. Attention to the ways in which threats to everyday life and quotidian communities intersect to help generate episodes of contention could, for example, help us to better understand the dynamics at work in the service delivery protests that have occurred throughout South Africa since 2004. The idea that threats to everyday practices might serve as an increasingly

---

[6] See Kosek (2006) for an excellent account of how conceptions of community and land are intimately intertwined in New Mexico. See also Sawyer (2004) for a discussion of land, national imaginings, and territory in Ecuador.

powerful locus for contention suggests that many movements could remain highly place-based. It might be difficult to aggregate mobilization in one province over garbage collection with mobilization in another focusing on electricity shortages. Because these kinds of claims might not tap into the imagined communities available during subsistence threats, movements could remain limited in their abilities to organize across class and geography. Research on mobilizations organized around threats to everyday practices could produce additional insights into important trends in contemporary contentious politics.

To explain variation in social mobilization we must better understand how people understand and order their worlds, and how ideas are produced through practices. On an important level this book is about the ways in which the politics of the everyday intersect with and shape the politics of the extraordinary. When these axiomatic conceptions of life and livelihood are challenged, the meanings with which they are imbued are abruptly called to the fore and become apparent in discourse and spectacle. Contention will not always be the outcome – social mobilization is capricious and there is undoubtedly an element of contingency in every movement. But to understand contention we must examine the ideas at stake in everyday practices and the meanings at work as they are challenged.

References

Abarca, Meredith E. 2006. *Voices in the kitchen: views of food and the world from working-class Mexican and Mexican American women*. 1st edn. College Station: Texas A&M University Press.

Abercrombie, Thomas. 1991. "To be Indian, to be Bolivian: ambivalence and ambiguity in the construction of ethnic and national identities in Bolivia." In *Indian and nation state in Latin America*, ed. G. Urban and J. Scherzer. Austin: University of Texas Press, pp. 95–130.

1998. *Pathways of memory and power: ethnography and history among an Andean people*. Madison: University of Wisconsin Press.

Agamben, Giorgio. 1995. *Homo sacer*. Torino: G. Einaudi.

Aguayo, Sergio. 2007. "Tacos de lengua." *Reforma*, January 17.

Agüero, Felipe and Jeffrey Stark. 1998. *Fault lines of democracy in post-transition Latin America*. Coral Gables, FL; Boulder, CO: North-South Center Press/University of Miami: Distributed by Lynne Rienner Publishers.

Aguirre, Alberto and Emmanuel Salazar. 2007. "Anuncia el FAP movilizaciones." *Reforma*, January 12.

Alatorre, Adriana. 2007a. "Critican aumento de maíz importado." *Reforma*, January 21.
2007b. "Niegan pérdida de clientela." *Reforma*, January 19.

Albro, Robert. 2005. "The water is ours carajo! Deep citizenship in Bolivia's water war." In *Social movements: an anthropological reader*, ed. J. Nash. Malden, MA: Blackwell Publishing.

Almeida, Paul D. 2003. "Opportunity organizations and threat-induced contention: protest waves in authoritarian settings." *American Journal of Sociology* 109:345–400.
2007. "Defensive mobilization: popular movements against economic adjustment policies in Latin America." *Latin American Perspectives* 34 (3):123–39.

Alvarez, Raúl. 1982. "Semilla del Cuarto Sol." Mexico: Institution Nacional Indigenista.

Alvarez, Sonia E., Evelina Dagnino, and Arturo Escobar. 1998. *Cultures of politics/politics of cultures: re-visioning Latin American social movements*. Boulder, CO: Westview Press.

Aminzade, Ronald, Jack A. Goldstone, Doug McAdam, Elizabeth J. Perry, William H. Sewell, Jr., Sidney Tarrow, and Charles Tilly. 2001. *Silence and voice in the study of contentious politics*. Cambridge; New York: Cambridge University Press.

Anderson, Benedict. 1991. *Imagined communities: reflections on the origin and spread of nationalism.* Rev. and extended ed. London; New York: Verso.

Anonymous. 2000, 1831. *El concinero Mexicano: Tomo I.* Mexico City: CONACULTA.

Appadurai, Arjun. 1988. "How to make a national cuisine: cookbooks in contemporary India." *Comparative Studies in Society and History* 30 (1):3–24.

Appendini, Kirsten. 2001. *De la milpa a los tortibonos: la restructuración de la política alimentaria en México.* 2nd edn. México, DF: Colegio de México Instituto de Investigaciones de las Naciones Unidas para el Desarrollo Social.

2008. "Tracing the maiz-tortilla chain." *UN Chronicle* 45 (2/3).

Arce, Moises. 2010. "Parties and social protest in Latin America's neoliberal era." *Party Politics* 16 (5):669–86.

Arnold, Thomas Clay. 2001. "Rethinking moral economy." *American Political Science Review* 95 (1):11.

Arze, Carlos and Tom Kruze. 2004. "The consequences of neoliberal reform." *NACLA Report on the Americas* 38 (3):23–8.

Aserca. 2010. "Teocintle: el ancestro del maíz." ed. Agriculture. Mexico City. www .aserca.gob.mx/sicsa/claridades/revistas/201/ca201-32.pdf

Assies, Willem. 2003. "David versus Goliath in Cochabamba: water rights, neoliberalism and the revival of social protest in Bolivia." *Latin American Perspectives* 30 (3):22.

Auyero, Javier. 2001. "Glocal riots." *International Sociology* 16 (1):21.

2003. *Contentious lives: two Argentine women, two protests, and the quest for recognition.* Durham, NC: Duke University Press.

2007. *Routine politics and violence in Argentina: the gray zone of state power.* Cambridge; New York: Cambridge University Press.

Aziz Nassif, Alberto. 2007. "¿Fin de la estabilidad económica?" *El Universal,* January 16.

Baker, Andy. 2003. "Why is trade reform so popular in Latin America? A consumption-based theory of trade policy preferences." *World Politics* 55 (April):423–55.

2009. *The market and the masses in Latin America: policy reform and consumption in liberalizing economies.* Cambridge; New York: Cambridge University Press.

Bakker, Karen J. 2002. "From state to market? Water *mercantilización* in Spain." *Environment and Planning A* 34:767–90.

2003. *An uncooperative commodity: privatizing water in England and Wales.* Oxford; New York: Oxford University Press.

Balboa, Juan. 2007. "Llama el FAP a defender la soberanía alimentaria." *La Jornada,* January 12.

Barthes, Roland. 2012. *Mythologies.* New York: Hill and Wang.

Beas, Juan Carlos. 1982. *Como lo usamos.* Mexico City: Árbol Editorial.

Benford, Robert, and David Snow. 2000. "Framing processes and social movements: an overview and assessment." *Annual Review of Sociology* 26: 611–39.

Bentley, Arthur Fisher. 1994. *The process of government: a study of social pressures.* New Brunswick, NJ: Transaction.

Bertran Vilá, Miriam. 2005. *Cambio alimentario e identidad de los indígenas mexicanos.* Mexico City: Universidad Nacional Autónoma de México.

Bizberg, Ilán. 2003. "El sindicalismo en fin de regimen," *Foro Internacional* 43(1), 215–48.

Bob, Clifford. 2005. *The marketing of rebellion: insurgents, media, and international activism*. Cambridge; New York: Cambridge University Press.

Boelens, Rutgerd, David H. Getches, and Jorge Armando Guevara Gil. 2010a. *Out of the mainstream: water rights, politics and identity*. London; Sterling: Earthscan.

2010b. "Water struggles and the politics of identity." In *Out of the mainstream: water rights, politics, and identity*, ed. R. Boelens, D. H. Getches and J. A. Guevara Gil. Washington, DC: Earthscan.

Bonfil Batalla, Guillermo. 1982. "El maíz." *El Día*, October 17.

Bonnell, Victoria E., Lynn Avery Hunt, and Richard Biernacki. 1999. *Beyond the cultural turn: new directions in the study of society and culture*. Berkeley: University of California Press.

Bourdieu, Pierre. 1977. *Outline of a theory of practice*. Cambridge; New York: Cambridge University Press.

1990. *The logic of practice*. Stanford, CA: Stanford University Press.

Bourdieu, Pierre, and John B. Thompson. 1991. *Language and symbolic power*. Cambridge, MA: Harvard University Press.

Bouton, Cynthia A. 1993. *The flour war: gender, class, and community in late Ancien Régime French society*. University Park: Pennsylvania State University Press.

Brubaker, Rogers. 2004. *Ethnicity without groups*. Cambridge, MA: Harvard University Press.

Brubaker, Rogers, and Frederick Cooper. 2000. "Beyond identity." *Theory and Society* 29:1–47.

Buhaug, Halvard, Lars-Erik Cederman, and Kristian Skrede Gleditsch. 2014. "Square pegs in round holes: inequality, grievances, and civil war." *International Studies Quarterly* 58:418–31.

Bustamante, Rocío. 2002. "Legislación del agua en Bolivia." Cochabamba: UMSS, Centro Andino para la Gestón y Uso del Agua.

Bustamante, Rocío, Elizabeth Peredo, and María Esther Udaeta. 2005. "Women in the 'Water Wars' in the Cochabamba Valleys." In *Opposing currents: the politics of water and gender in Latin America*, ed. V. Bennett, S. Dávila-Poblete, and N. Rico. Pittsburgh: University of Pittsburgh Press.

Butler, Judith. 1997. *Excitable speech: a politics of the performative*. New York: Routledge.

Camacho Solís, Manuel. 2007. "Tortillas y petróleo." *El Universal*, January 15.

Cárdenas Cruz, Francisco. 2007. "Pulso político." *El Universal*, January 16.

Castillo, Hernández and Rosalva Aída. 2010. "Towards a culturally situated women's rights agenda: reflections from Mexico." In *Women's movements in the global era: the power of local feminisms*, ed. A. Basu. Boulder, CO: Westview Press.

Cederman, Lars-Erik, Kristian Skrede Gleditsch, and Halvard Buhaug. 2013. *Inequality, grievances, and civil war*. New York: Cambridge University Press.

Chávez M., Ma. C., G. Nava B., and C. Arriaga J. 1999. "Diversidad en el maíz y agricultura campesina mazahua del municipio de san felipe del progreso, estado de méxico." In *El maíz: sustento del pasado y presente en la cultural popular nacional*, ed. R. Marcial Jiménez. Toluca: Universidad Autónoma del Estado de México.

Chong, Alberto, and Florencio López de Silanes. 2004. "Privatization in Mexico." In *Working Paper #513*. Washington, DC: Inter-American Development Bank.

Clendinnen, Inga. 1991. *Aztecs: an interpretation*. Cambridge; New York: Cambridge University Press.

"Cochabamba en emergencia exige rebaja de tarifas de agua." 1999. *Opinión*, December 21.

"Cochabamba unida, rechaza reajuste de tarifas de agua." 1999. *Opinión*, December 23.

"Cochabambinos protagonizaron un paro cívico contudente." 2000. *Presencia*, January 12, 2000.

"Cochabambinos protestarán hoy contra subida de precios." 1999. *Presencia*, December 22.

Collier, George Allen, and Elizabeth Lowery Quaratiello. 2005. *Basta! land and the Zapatista rebellion in Chiapas.* 3rd edn. Oakland, CA: Food First Books.

Collier, Paul, and Anke Hoeffler. 2004. "Greed and grievance in civil war." *Oxford Economic Papers* 56:33.

Comaroff, Jean, and John L. Comaroff. 1990. "Goodly beasts, beastly goods: cattle and commodities in a South African context." *American Ethnologist* 17 (2):195–216.

2009. *Ethnicity, Inc.* Chicago: University of Chicago Press.

"Comenzará hoy resistencia civil por el 'tarifazo' de agua potable." 2000. *Presencia* January 3.

"Comité Cívico no busca anual el contrato, sino modificarlo." 2000. *Opinión*, January 8.

"Comité Cívico rechaza intento de imponer proyecto Corani." 1997. *Opinión*, March 16.

"Coordinadora definó acciones contra el 'tarifazo' del agua." 2000. *Presencia* January 5.

Crabtree, John. 2005. *Perfiles de la protesta: política y movimientos sociales en Bolivia.* 2nd edn. La Paz: PIEB Fundación UNIR Bolivia.

Crespo Flores, Carlos. 1999. "Gestión ambiental: el conflicto por la perforación de pozos profundos en Vinto-Sipe Sipe." In *Conflictos ambientales (dos casos: agua y territorio)*, ed. C. Crespo Flores and R. Orellana. Cochabamba: CERES.

2000. "Continuidad y ruptura: la guerra del agua y los nuevos movimientos sociales en Bolivia." *Revista del Observatorio Socia de América Latinal* 2:21–7. Argentina: CLACSO.

2003. *Water privatisation policies and conflicts in Bolivia: The water war in Cochabamba (1999–2000)*, Oxford: School of Planning, Oxford Brooks University.

Crespo Flores, Carlos, and Omar Fernández. 2001. "Los campesinos regantes de Cochabamba en la guerra del agua: una experiencia de presión social y negociación." Cochabamba: UMSS-CESU.

Cusicanqui, Silvia Rivera. 1990. "Liberal democracy and Ayllu democracy: The case of the Northern Potosí Bolivia." *Journal of Development Studies* 26 (4):97–121.

Davies, James. 1962. "Toward a theory of revolution." *American Sociological Review* 27 (1):5–19.

1969. "The J-curve of rising and declining satisfactions as a cause of some great revolutions and a contained rebellion." In *Violence in America*, ed. T. R. Gurr and H. D. Graham. New York: Praeger.

de Orellana, Margarita. 2006. "Maíz místico." *Artes de México* 78:7–8.

Dehesa, Germán. 2007. "Cosas II." *Reforma*, January 26.

del Campo, David Martín. 2007. "Entre paréntesis/Un taco para Proust." *Reforma*, January 23.

del Val Blanco, Enrique. 2007. "Jugando con fuego." *El Universal*, January 11.

Díaz Garza, Felipe. 2007. "Entre Managua y Davos." *Reforma*, January 13.

Díaz León, Marco Antonio 2003. "Rituales para el Maíz." Mexico: Museo Nacional de Culturas Populares. Film.

Dirección General de Materiales Educativos. 2010. *Historia: 4to grado*. ed. D. G. d. M. Educativos. Mexico City: Secretaría de Educación Pública.

Domínguez, Carlos. 2007. *Public policy and social movements: the cases of Bolivia and Mexico*. Oxford: Development Studies, Oxford University Oxford.

Dunkerley, James. 1984. *Rebellion in the veins: political struggle in Bolivia, 1952–82*. London: Verso.

Eckstein, Susan, and Timothy P. Wickham-Crowley. 2003. *Struggles for social rights in Latin America*. New York: Routledge.

Edelman, Murray J. 1971. *Politics as symbolic action: mass arousal and quiescence*. Chicago: Markham Pub. Co.

Einwohner, Rachel L., and Thomas Maher. 2009. "Assessments of threat and collective action: Jewish resistance in ghettos and death camps during the Holocaust." Paper presented at the American Sociological Association Annual Meeting. San Francisco, CA.

Emirbayer, Mustafa. 1997. "Manifesto for a relational sociology." *American Journal of Sociology* 103 (2):281–317.

"Empezó la obra del túnel: la mejor prueba de que Misicuni es una realidad." 1998. *Opinión*, August 29.

"*En México, 'Sin maíz no hay país'.*" 2001. Univisión [cited March 14, 2012 2011]. Available at http://noticias.univision.com/mexico/actualidad/slideshow/2011-09-30/mexico-sin-maiz-no-hay-pais.

Enciso L., Angélica, 2011. "Preocupa a mil científicos y a la ONU el uso de maíz transgénico." *La Jornada*, October 25.

Enríquez, José Ramón. 2007. "Pánico Escénico." *Reforma*, January 19.

Fearon, James, and David Laitin. 2003. "Ethnicity, insurgency, and civil war." *American Political Science Review* 97 (1):16.

"Fejuve-Pueblo: Resistencia civil contra del tarifazo." 1999. *Opinión*, December 12.

Ferguson, James. 1985. "The bovine mystique: power, property, and livestock in rural Lesotho." *Man* 20 (4):647–74.

"The fight for water and democracy: an interview with Oscar Olivera." 2000. *Multinational Monitor* 21 (6).

Finnegan, William. 2002. "Leasing the Rain." In *NOW with Bill Moyers*, ed. B. Moyers. PBS.

"Firmado el acuerdo que permitirá estabilizar el precio del maíz." 2007. *Cinco Días*, January 18.

Fitting, Elizabeth M. 2011. *The struggle for maize: campesinos, workers, and transgenic corn in the Mexican countryside*. Durham, NC: Duke University Press.

Florescano, Enrique. 1969. *Precios del maíz y crisis agrícolas en México (1708–1810); ensayo sobre el movimiento de los precios y sus consecuencias económicas y sociales*. 1st edn. México: El Colegio de México.

Foweraker, Joe, and Ann L. Craig. 1990. *Popular movements and political change in Mexico*. Boulder, CO: Lynne Rienner Publishers.

Fox, Jonathan. 1993. *The politics of food in Mexico: state power and social mobilization*. Ithaca, NY: Cornell University Press.

Fraser, Nancy, and Axel Honneth. 2003. *Redistribution or recognition?: a political-philosophical exchange.* London; New York: Verso.

Fuentes Aguirre, Armando. 2007. "De Política y Cosas Peores/Al pan, pan." *Reforma,* January 15.

Galán, José, Laura Poy, Gabriel León, and Mariana Norandi. 2007. "'Torpe e irresponsable,' el plan contra alza de la tortilla." *La Jornada,* January 13.

Gallegos Devése, Marisela. 2009. "La fiesta a San Isidro Labrador y los ritos de fertilidad del maíz entre los matlatzincas de San Francisco Oxtotilpan." *Diario del Campo* 52:122–37.

Gamson, William. 1992. *Talking politics.* New York: Cambridge University Press.

García, Alberto, Fernando García, and Luz Quintón. 2003. *La "Guerra del Agua": Abril de 2000, la crisis de la política en Bolivia.* La Paz, Bolivia: Fundación PEIB.

García Linera, Alvaro, Marxa Chávez León, and Patricia Costas Monje. 2004. *Sociología de los movimientos sociales en Bolivia: estructuras de movilización, repertorios culturales y acción política.* 1st edn. La Paz, Bolivia: DIAKONIA OXFAM.

García Rañó, Hugo, and Alder Keleman. 2007. "*La crisis del maíz y la tortilla en México: ¿Modelo o coyuntura?*" Mexico City: Oxfam International.

Garduño, Roberto, and Ciro Pérez. 2007. "Exige la Permanente resolver la crisis alcista." *La Jornada,* January 18.

Gelles, Paul. 2010. "Cultural identity and indigenous water rights in the Andean highlands." In *Out of the mainstream: water rights, politics, and identity,* ed. R. Boelens, D. H. Getches and J. A. Guevara Gil. Washington, DC: Earthscan.

Gerring, John. 2007. *Case study research: principles and practices.* New York: Cambridge University Press.

Geschwender, James. 1968. "Explorations in the theory of social movements and revolutions." *Social Forces* 47 (2):127–35.

Gibson, Charles. 1964. *The Aztecs under Spanish rule: a history of the Indians of the Valley of Mexico, 1519–1810.* Stanford, CA: Stanford University Press.

Gill, Lesley. 2000. *Teetering on the rim: global restructuring, daily life, and the armed retreat of the Bolivian state.* New York: Columbia University Press.

Goffman, Erving. 1959. *The presentation of self in everyday life.* Garden City, NY: Doubleday.

1974. *Frame analysis: an essay on the organization of experience.* Cambridge, MA: Harvard University Press.

Goldstone, Jack, and Charles Tilly. 2001. "Threat (and opportunity): popular action and state response in the dynamics of contentious action." In *Silence and voice in the study of contentious politics,* ed. R. R. Aminzade, J. A. Goldstone, D. McAdam, E. J. Perry, W. H. Sewell, S. Tarrow, and C. Tilly. Cambridge: Cambridge University Press.

Gomez Flores, Laura. 2007. "Llamado a asistir a cacerolazo contra escalada de precios." *La Jornada,* January 17.

Gómez, Leslie, Ana Bertha Ramírez, and Fernando Paniagua. 2007. "Un vistazo." *Reforma,* January 15.

Gómez, Noel. 2007. "Anuncian marcha por el incremento a las tortillas." *Sipse,* January 20.

Gómez, Ricardo. 2006. "Diputados 'toman' la tribuna por alza a leche." *El Universal,* November 17.

González Aktories, Susana, and Gonzalo Camacho Díaz. 2006. "Los rituales de tlamanes." *Artes de México* 78:15–21.

González Martínez, Velia. 1999. "Repercusiones de la implementación de un programa agrícola en el cultivo del maíz en el llano de solidaridad, municipio de tanatico, estado de méxico." In *El maíz: sustento del pasado y presente en la cultural popular nacional*, ed. R. Marcial Jiménez. Toluca: Universidad Autónoma del Estado de México.

Goodwin, Jeff. 2001. *No other way out: states and revolutionary movements, 1945–1991*. Cambridge; New York: Cambridge University Press.

Goodwin, Jeff, and James M. Jasper. 2004. *Rethinking social movements: structure, meaning, and emotion*. Lanham, MD: Rowman & Littlefield Publishers.

Goodwin, Jeff, James M. Jasper, and Francesca Polletta. 2001. *Passionate politics: emotions and social movements*. Chicago: University of Chicago Press.

———. 2004. "Emotional dimensions of social movements." In *The Blackwell companion to social movements*, ed. D. Snow, S. A. Soule and H. Kriesi. Malden: Blackwell.

Gotkowitz, Laura. 2007. *A revolution for our rights: indigenous struggles for land and justice in Bolivia, 1880–1952*. Durham, NC: Duke University Press.

Gould, Deborah B. 2009. *Moving politics: emotion and Act Up's fight against AIDS*. Chicago: University of Chicago Press.

Gould, Roger V. 1995. *Insurgent identities: class, community, and protest in Paris from 1848 to the Commune*. Chicago: University of Chicago Press.

Grillo Fernández, Eduardo. 1994. *El agua en las culturas Andina y occidental moderna*. Lima: Proyecto Andino de Tecnologías Campesinas.

Grindle, Merilee Serrill. 2003. "Shadowing the past? Policy reform in Bolivia 1985–2002." In *Proclaiming revolution: Bolivia in comparative perspective*, ed. M. S. Grindle and P. Domingo. Cambridge, MA: ILAS and David Rockefeller Center for Latin American Studies.

Guardia, Víctor. 1994. *Misicuni, realidad técnico-económica o simulación política?* Cochabamba: Universidad Mayor de San Simon.

Gudeman, Stephen. 2001. *The anthropology of economy: community, market, and culture*. Malden, MA: Blackwell.

Guerrero, Claudia, Armando Estrop, Claudia Salazar, Mayolo López, and Daniel Pensamiento. 2007a. "Piden legisladores subsidio para el producto. Advierten perredistas con movilizaciones de no ser modificados los nuevos precios." *Reforma*, January 10.

———. 2007b. "Urgen a Gobierno regular la tortilla." *Reforma*, January 10.

Gurr, Ted Robert. 1970. *Why men rebel*. Princeton, NJ: Published for the Center of International Studies, Princeton University [by] Princeton University Press.

Harvey, Neil. 1998. *The Chiapas rebellion: the struggle for land and democracy*. Durham, NC: Duke University Press.

Heidegger, Martin. 1977. *The question concerning technology, and other essays*. New York: Garland Publishers.

Hendrix, Cullen, and Stephan Haggard. 2015. "Where and why food prices lead to social upheaval." In *Monkey Cage*, ed. M. J. Graff, *Washington Post*.

Hendrix, Cullen, Stephan Haggard, and Beatriz Magaloni. 2009. "Grievance and opportunity: food prices, political regime, and protest." Paper prepared for presentation at the International Studies Association Annual Meeting. New York, NY.

Herbas Camacho, Gabriel. 2004. "Foro Cochabambino del Medio Ambiente." In *La guerra por el agua y por la vida*, ed. A. E. Ceceña. Cochabamba: Fabrilco.

Hernández, Érika, and Armando Estrop. 2007. "Reclaman acciones legales." *Reforma*, January 18.

Hernández García, Gabriel. 2009. "Kali akgwahu kin tiyatkan, kali akgwahu kin kuxi kan: La defensa colectiva del maíz nativo en la Sierra Norte de Puebla." *Diario del Campo* 52:122–37.

Hernández Navarro, Luis. 2007. "La nueva guerra de la tortilla." *La Jornada*, January 12.

Herrera, Yoshiko M. 2005. *Imagined economies: the sources of Russian regionalism.* New York: Cambridge.

Hewitt de Alcántara, Cynthia. 1994. *Economic restructuring and rural subsistence in Mexico: corn and the crisis of the 1980s.* San Diego: Center for U.S.-Mexican Studies, University of California San Diego.

Higgins, Nicholas P. 2004. *Understanding the Chiapas rebellion: modernist visions and the invisible Indian.* Austin: University of Texas Press.

Hobsbawm, E. J. 1992. *Nations and nationalism since 1780: programme, myth, reality.* 2nd edn. Cambridge; New York: Cambridge University Press.

Hobsbawm, E. J., and T. O. Ranger. 1983. *The invention of tradition.* Cambridge [Cambridgeshire]; New York: Cambridge University Press.

Hochstetler, Kathryn. 2006. "Rethinking presidentialism: challenges and presidential falls in South America." *Comparative Politics* 22(1):401–18.

Holben, Symantha. 2007. *Expanding the focus of water management: an investigation of cooperative irrigation in Sacaba (Cochabamba) Bolivia* (Doctoral dissertation), Anthropology, The Catholic University of America, Washington, DC.

Huasteca, Programa de Desarrollo Cultural de la. 2000. *Cuerpos de maíz: danzas agrícolas de la huasteca.* Mexico City: Ediciones del Programa de Desarrollo Cultural de la Huasteca.

Imaz, Rubén, and Michel Lipkes. 2003. "Somos Gente de Maíz." Mexico: Museo Nacional de Culturas Populares. Film.

"Inicia marcha de las cacerolas a Secretaría de Economía." 2007. *El Universal*, January 17.

Instituto Nacional de Estadísticas. 2006. Cochabamba: Estadísticas e Indicadores de Pobreza Según Sección Municipal, 2001. Available at www.ine.gov.bo, accessed February 20, 2007.

Instituto Nacional de Estadísticas. 2007. Instituto Nacional de Estadísticas 2006. Available at www.ine.gov.bo/default.aspx, accessed February 2007.

Instituto Nacional de Salud Pública. 2006. "Encuesta Nacional de Salud y Nutrición," ed. Secretaría de Salud. Mexico City.

Inter-American Development Bank. 2006. *Country indicators* 2006 [cited December 2006]. Available at www.iadb.org/countries/indicators.cfm language= English&id_country=BO&pLanguage=ENGLISH&pCountry=BO&parid=8.

Jackson, Robert H. 1994. *Regional markets and agrarian transformation in Bolivia: Cochabamba, 1539–1960.* 1st edn. Albuquerque: University of New Mexico Press.

Jasper, James M. 1997. *The art of moral protest: culture, biography, and creativity in social movements.* Chicago: University of Chicago Press.

Jiménez, Verónica, Lev García, and María Teresa del Riego. 2007. "Un vistazo." *Reforma*, January 13.

Jung, Courtney. 2003. "The politics of indigenous identity: neoliberalism, cultural rights, and the Mexican zapatistas." *Social Research* 70(2):433–61.

2008. *The moral force of indigenous politics: critical liberalism and the Zapatistas.* Cambridge; New York: Cambridge University Press.

Kahneman, Daniel, and Amos Tversky. 1979. "Prospect theory: an analysis of decision under risk." *Econometrica* 47:263–91.

Kaplan, Steven L. 1996. *The bakers of Paris and the bread question, 1700–1775.* Durham, NC: Duke University Press.

Katznelson, Ira. 2003. "Periodization and preferences: reflections on purposive action in comparative historical social science." In *Comparative historical analysis in the social sciences,* ed. J. Mahoney and D. Rueschemeyer. Cambridge: Cambridge University Press.

Klein, Herbert S. 1992. *Bolivia: the evolution of a multi-ethnic society.* 2nd edn. New York: Oxford University Press.

2003. *A concise history of Bolivia.* Cambridge; New York: Cambridge University Press.

Knight, Alan. 1991. "The rise and fall of Cardenismo." In *Mexico since independence,* ed. L. Bethell. New York: Cambridge University Press.

Kohl, Benjamin. 2003. "Democratizing decentralization in Bolivia: the Law of Popular Participation." *Journal of Planning and Education Research* 23 (2):12.

Kosek, Jake. 2006. *Understories: the political life of forests in northern New Mexico.* Durham, NC: Duke University Press.

Kurtz, Marcus. 2004. "The dilemmas of democracy in the open economy: lessons from Latin America." *World Politics* 54 (January):262–302.

Kurzman, Charles. 2004a. "Poststructuralist consensus in social movement theory." In *Rethinking social movements: structure, meaning, and emotion,* ed. J. Goodwin and J. M. Jasper. New York: Rowman and Littlefield.

2004b. *The unthinkable revolution in Iran.* Cambridge, MA: Harvard University Press.

"La Suprema falló a favor de la Alcaldía." 1997. *La Razón,* July 3.

Laitin, David D. 2007. *Nations, states, and violence.* Oxford; New York: Oxford University Press.

Larios, Héctor. 2007. "El mercado: cuándo intervenir." *El Universal,* January 25.

Larson, Brooke. 1998. *Cochabamba, 1550–1900: colonialism and agrarian transformation in Bolivia.* Expanded ed. Durham, NC: Duke University Press.

"Las tortillas y el capitalismo salvaje." 2007. *El Universal,* January 12.

Laurie, N., and S. Marvin. 1999. "Globalisation, neoliberalism, and negotiated development in the Andes: water projects and regional identity in Cochabamba, Bolivia." *Environment and Planning A* 31:1401–15.

Leblang, David, and William Bernard. 2011. "Blame it on the Benjamin: U.S. monetary policy, global food prices, and the onset of civil conflict." Paper presented at the American Political Science Association Annual Meeting. Seattle, WA.

Ledezma, Mariana. 2007. "Protestan por aumentos a básicos." *El Universal,* January 13.

Locke, Richard, and Kathleen Thelen. 1995. "Apples and oranges revisited: contextualized comparisons and the study of comparative labor politics." *Politics & Society* 23 (3):337–67.

López-Austin, Alfredo. 1996. *The rabbit on the face of the moon: mythology in the mesoamerican tradition.* Salt Lake City: University of Utah Press.

Lustig, Nora. 1998. *Mexico: the remaking of an economy.* 2nd edn. Washington, DC: Brookings Institution Press.

Maher, Thomas. 2010. "Threat, resistance, and collective action: the cases of Sobibór, Treblinka, and Auschwitz." *American Sociological Review* 75(2):252–72.

Maldonado Rojas, Gonzalo. 2004. *H2O: La Guerra del Agua.* La Paz: Fondo Editorial de los Diputados.

Mallo, Sandra. 1997. "Misicuni: ¿un mito o una realidad?" *La Razón*, August 24.

Malloy, James M. 1970. *Bolivia: the uncompleted revolution.* Pittsburgh, PA: University of Pittsburgh Press.

Marentes, Pablo. 2007. "Maíz amargo." *El Universal*, January 16.

Martin, Isaac William. 2008. *The permanent tax revolt: how the property tax transformed American politics.* Stanford, CA: Stanford University Press.

Martínez, E., S. Ocampo, D. Carrizales, J. Narváez, M. Chávez, J. Lastra, J. Valdez, I. Sánchez, C. Camacho, G. Flores, and H. Martoccia. 2007. "Protestan miles en ciudades de 10 estados contra la carestía." *La Jornada*, February 1.

Martínez, Alejandra. 2007. "Jefe de Gobierno pide ayuda federal para ayuda en tortilla." *El Universal*, January 16.

McAdam, Doug. 1982. *Political process and the development of black insurgency, 1930–1970.* Chicago: University of Chicago Press.

   1999. *Political process and the development of black insurgency, 1930–1970.* 2nd edn. Chicago: University of Chicago Press.

McAdam, Doug, John D. McCarthy, and Mayer N. Zald. 1996. *Comparative perspectives on social movements: political opportunities, mobilizing structures, and cultural framings.* Cambridge, England; New York: Cambridge University Press.

McAdam, Doug, Sidney G. Tarrow, and Charles Tilly. 2001. *Dynamics of contention.* Cambridge; New York: Cambridge University Press.

McClintock, Cynthia. 1984. "Why peasants rebel: the case of Peru's Sendero Luminoso." *World Politics* 37 (1):48–84.

   1998. *Revolutionary movements in Latin America: El Salvador's FMLN & Peru's Shining Path.* Washington, DC: U.S. Institute of Peace Press.

McVeigh, Rory. 2009. *The rise of the Ku Klux Klan: right-wing movements and national politics.* Minneapolis, MN: University of Minnesota Press.

Monsiváis, Carlos. 2008. "De las ciudadanías culturales en el siglo XXI." In *Cultura mexicana: revisión y prospectiva*, ed. F. Toledo, E. Florescano and J. Woldenberg. México, DF: Taurus.

Moore, Donald. 2000. "The crucible of cultural politics: reworking 'development' in Zimbabwe's eastern highlands." *American Ethnologist* 26 (3):654–89.

Morales Valderama, Carmen. 2009. "De un diario de campo: 'El San Isidro de Oxtotilpan' y el registro del patrimonio cultural inmaterial." *Diario del Campo* 52:122–37.

Morales Valderama, Carmen, and Catalina Rodríguez Lazcano. 2009. "Desangrando una mazorca: orígenes y etnografía de los maíces nativos." *Diario del Campo* 52.

Munn, Nancy. 1977. "The spatiotemporal transformation of Gawa Canoes." *Journal de la Société des Océanistes* 33:39–53.

Muñoz, Alma E., and Elio Henriquez. 2007. "Minimiza Rivera efectos del tortillazo: 'no es una tragedia ni el acabose.'" *La Jornada*, January 15.

Muñoz, Patricia, Matilde Pérez, and Fabiola Martínez. 2007. "'Nuevo pacto social', piden miles en el Zócalo." *La Jornada*, February 1.

Nadal, Alejandro. 2000. "The Environmental and Social Impacts of Economic Liberalization of Corn Production in Mexico." Gland: Oxfam GB and the World Wildlife Fund International.

Nash, June C. 2005. *Social movements: an anthropological reader*. Malden, MA: Blackwell Pub.

Neurath, Johannes. 2006. "La boda del maíz." *Artes de México* 78:41–51.

Nickson, Andrew, and Claudia Vargas. 2002. "The limitations of water regulation: the failure of the Cochabamba concession in Bolivia." *Bulletin of Latin American Research* 21 (1):22.

Noakes, John A., and Hank Johnston. 2005. "Frames of protest: a road map to a perspective." In *Frames of protest: social movements and the framing perspective*, ed. John A. Noakes and Hank Johnston. Lanham, MD: Rowman & Littlefield.

"Nueva tarifa pone en apuros a Aguas del Tunari y gobierno." 2000. *Los Tiempos*.

Núñez, Ernesto, and Margarita Vega. 2007. "Reclaman a FCH aumento a tortilla." *Reforma*, January 12.

Ochoa, Enrique. 2000. *Feeding Mexico: the political uses of food since 1910*. Wilmington, DE: Scholarly Resources.

Ohnuki-Tierney, Emiko. 1993. *Rice as self: Japanese identities through time*. Princeton, NJ: Princeton University Press.

Olivera, Oscar. 2004. *Cochabamba! Water war in Bolivia*. Cambridge, MA: South End Press.

Olivera, Oscar, and Raquel Gutiérrez. 2008. *Nosotros somos la Coordinadora*. Cochabamba: Fundación Abril.

Ostrom, Elinor. 1990. *Governing the commons: the evolution of institutions for collective action*. Cambridge; New York: Cambridge University Press.

Ostrom, Elinor, Roy Gardner, and James Walker. 1994. *Rules, games, and common-pool resources*. Ann Arbor: University of Michigan Press.

Otero, Gerardo. 2008a. "Contesting neoliberal globalism and NAFTA in rural Mexico." In *Contentious politics in North America: national protest and transnational collaboration under continental integration*, ed. J. Ayers and L. McDonald. Basingstoke: Palgrave.

2008b. *Food for the few: neoliberal globalism and biotechnology in Latin America*. Austin: University of Texas.

Otero, Gerardo, and Armando Bartra. 2005. "Indian peasant movements in Mexico: the struggle for land, autonomy, and democracy." In *Reclaiming the land: the resurgence of rural movements in Africa, Asia, and Latin America*, ed. S. Moyo and P. Yeros. New York: Zed.

Oxhorn, Philip, and Graciela Ducatenzeiler. 1998. *What kind of democracy? What kind of market?: Latin America in the age of neoliberalism*. University Park: Pennsylvania State University Press.

Pacheco, Cristina. 1983. *Para vivir aquí*. 1st edn. México, DF: Editorial Grijalbo.

Parra, Lanry. 2007. "Mantienen molineros en $12 el kilo de tortilla." *Sipse*, January 20.

Paz, Octavio. 1985. *The labyrinth of solitude: life and thought in Mexico*. Harmondsworth; New York: Viking Penguin.

Pearlman, Wendy. 2013. "Emotions and the microfoundations of the Arab uprisings." *Perspectives on Politics* 11 (2):387–409.

Pensamiento, Daniel. 2007. "Rechazan alza a tortilla." *Reforma*, January 9.

Peredo, Carmen, Carlos Crespo Flores, and Omar Fernández. 2004. *Los regantes de Cochabamba en la guerra del agua: presión social y negociación*. Cochabamba: CESU-UMSS.

Perreault, Thomas. 2001. "Developing identities: indigenous mobilization, rural livelihoods, and resources access in Ecuadorian Amazonia." *Ecumene* 8 (4):381–413.

2005. "Why *chacras* (swidden gardens) persist: agrobiodiversity, food security, and cultural identity in the Ecuadorian Amazon." *Human Organization* 64 (4):327–39.

2006. "From the *guerra del agua* to the *guerra del gas*: resource governance, neoliberalism and popular protest in Bolivia." *Antipode* 38(1):150–72.

2008. "Custom and contradiction: rural water governance and the politics of *usos y costumbres* in Bolivia's irrigators' movement." *Annals of the Association of American Geographers* 98 (4):834–54.

Petras, James F., and Henry Veltmeyer. 2005. *Social movements and state power: Argentina, Brazil, Bolivia, Ecuador*. London; Ann Arbor, MI: Pluto Press.

Pierson, Paul. 2004. *Politics in time*. Princeton, NJ: Princeton University Press.

Pilcher, Jeffrey M. 1998. *Que vivan los tamales!: food and the making of Mexican identity*. Albuquerque: University of New Mexico Press.

Piven, Frances Fox, and Richard A. Cloward. 1977. *Poor people's movements: why they succeed, how they fail*. 1st edn. New York: Pantheon Books.

Polanyi, Karl. 2001. *The great transformation: the political and economic origins of our time*. 2nd Beacon Paperback edn. Boston, MA: Beacon Press.

Polletta, Francesca, and Edwin Amenta. 2001a. "Conclusions." In *Passionate politics: emotions and social movements*, ed. J. Goodwin, J. M. Jasper, and F. Polletta. Chicago: University of Chicago Press.

2001b. "Second that emotion? Lessons from once novel concepts in social movement research." In *Passionate politics: emotions in social movements*, ed. Jeff Goodwin, James M. Jasper, and Francesca Polletta. Chicago: University of Chicago Press.

Posada, Miriam, and Matilde Pérez. 2007. "No habrá control de precios para frenar el aumento a las tortillas: Sojo." *La Jornada*, January 9.

Programa Nacional de Riego (PRONAR). 2000. "Inventario Nacional de Sistemas de Reigo." Cochabamba: PRONAR.

Profeco. 2007. "Informe Annual Procuraduría Federal del Consumidor 2007." Secretaría de Economía. Mexico City, Mexico.

Przeworski, Adam, and Henry Teune. 1970. *The logic of comparative social inquiry*. New York: Wiley.

"Queman centenares de facturas del tarifazo de Aguas del Tunari." 2000. *Opinión*, January 19.

Ragin, Charles C. 2000. *Fuzzy-set social science*. Chicago: University of Chicago Press.

Ramos, Jorge. 2007. "Presenta PRD iniciativa para subsidiar gasto en tortillas." *El Universal*, January 15.

Ray, R., and A. C. Korteweg. 1999. "Women's movements in the third world: identity, mobilization, and autonomy." *Annual Review of Sociology* 25:47–71.

"Realizan coronación de Reina del Maíz 2012." 2012. *El Guardián*, January 26.

Rice, Roberta. 2012. *The new politics of protest: indigenous mobilization in Latin America's neoliberal era*. Tucson: University of Arizona Press.

Rioja Vasquez, Oswaldo. 2002. "La Guerra del Agua." Bolivia. Film.

Riva Palacio, Raymundo. 2007. "Maldita tortilla." *El Universal*, January 24.

Rubio, Blanca. 2007. "El Campo no Aguanta Más: claroscuros de un movimiento campesino." In *El Campo no Aguanta Más*, ed. A. Sánchez Albarrán. Mexico: Universidad Autónoma Metropolitana Miguel Angel Porrúa.

Rulfo, Juan. 1955. *Pedro Páramo*. 1st edn. México: Fondo de Cultura Económica.

1986. *El llano en llamas*. México: Fondo de Cultura Económica.

SAGARPA. 2011. "Será MASAGRO punta de lanza en esfuerzo global para incrementar producción de alimentos." ed. SAGARPA. Mexico City.

Sahlins, Marshall David. 1976. *Culture and practical reason*. Chicago: University of Chicago Press.

Salazar, Horacio. 2009. "Genoma del maíz permitirá indagar en sus orígenes." *Milenio*, November 22, 2009.

Salazar, Luis. 1997. "Agua y cultura: comunidad de aguas." Cochabamba: CESU-UMSS.

Sánchez Albarrán, Armando. 2007. *El Campo no Aguanta Más*. 1st edn. Mexico: Universidad Autónoma Metropolitana Miguel Ángel Porrúa.

Sarmiento, Sergio. 2007. "Jaque Mate/Contradicciones." *Reforma*, February 1.

Sawyer, Suzana. 2004. *Crude chronicles: indigenous politics, multinational oil, and neoliberalism in Ecuador*. Durham, NC: Duke University Press.

Schelling, Thomas C. 1960. *The strategy of conflict*. Cambridge: Harvard University Press.

Scott, James C. 1976. *The moral economy of the peasant: rebellion and subsistence in Southeast Asia*. New Haven, CT: Yale University Press.

Sewell, William H. 1999. "The concept(s) of culture." In *Beyond the cultural turn*, ed. V. E. Bonnell and L. A. Hunt. Berkeley: University of California Press.

1980. *Work and revolution in France: the language of labor from the Old Regime to 1848*. Cambridge; New York: Cambridge University Press.

Shultz, Jim. 2003. "Bolivia: the water war widens." *NACLA Report on the Americas* 36 (3):34.

2013. *Bechtel vs. Bolivia: Cochabamba's water bills from Bechtel*. n.d. [cited August 23 2013]. Available at: http://www.democracyctr.org.

Silva, Eduardo. 2009. *Challenging neoliberalism in Latin America*. Cambridge; New York: Cambridge University Press.

Simmons, Erica. 2011. "The next French Revolution? Explaining government response to subsistence protests." Paper presented at the American Political Science Association Annual Meeting. Seattle, WA.

2012. *Markets, movements, and meanings: subsistence resources and political protest in Latin America* (Doctoral dissertation), Political Science, University of Chicago, Chicago.

Simmons, Erica, and Nicholas Rush Smith. 2015. "Comparative ethnography: possibilities for political science." Paper presented at the American Political Science Association Annual Meeting. San Francisco, CA.

Simón, Angélica. 2007. "GDF: este lunes, plan contra alza a tortillas." *El Universal*, January 13.

Skocpol, Theda. 1979. *States and social revolutions: a comparative analysis of France, Russia, and China*. Cambridge; New York: Cambridge University Press.

Slater, Dan, and Erica Simmons. 2013. "Coping by colluding: political uncertainty and promiscuous powersharing in Indonesia and Bolivia." *Comparative Political Studies*, 46(11): 1366–93.

Slater, Dan, and Daniel Ziblatt. 2013. "The enduring indispensability of the controlled comparison." *Comparative Political Studies*, 46(10): 1301–27.

Smelser, Neil J. 1963. *Theory of collective behavior*. New York: Free Press of Glencoe.

Snow, David, and Robert Benford. 1992. "Master frames and cycles of protest." In *Frontiers in social movement theory*, ed. A. Morris and C. Mueller. New Haven, CT: Yale University Press.

   1988. "Ideology, frame resonance, and participant mobilization." *International Social Movement Research* 1:197–217.

Snow, David A., Daniel M. Cress, Liam Downey, and Andrew W. Jones. 1998. "Disrupting 'the quotidian': reconceptualizing the relationship between breakdown and the emergence of collective action." *Mobilization* 3(1): 1–22.

Snow, David, E. Burke Rochford, Steven Worden, and Robert Benford. 1986. "Frame alignment processes, micromobilization, and movement participation." *American Sociological Review* 51(4): 464–81.

Snow, David A., and Sarah Anne Soule. 2010. *A primer on social movements*. New York: W. W. Norton.

Spronk, Susan J. 2007a. *The politics of third world water privatization: neoliberal reform and popular resistance in Cochabamba and El Alto, Bolivia* (Doctoral dissertation), Political Science, York University, Toronto.

   2007b. "Roots of resistance to urban water privatization in Bolivia: the 'new working class,' the crisis of neoliberalism, and public services." *International Labor and Working-Class History* 71:8–28.

Stallings, Anne Marie. 2006. *Culture, history, and property rights in the emergence of groundwater irrigation: Cochabamba, Bolivia* (Doctoral dissertation), Anthropology, The Catholic University of America, Washington, DC.

Starn, Orin. 1994. "Rethinking the politics of anthropology: the case of the Andes." *Current Anthropology* 35 (1):13–38.

Stepan, Alfred C. 1978. *The state and society: Peru in comparative perspective*. Princeton, NJ: Princeton University Press.

Stolle-McAllister, John. 2005. *Mexican social movements and the transition to democracy*. Jefferson, NC: McFarland & Co.

Tabone, Francesco Taboada. 2002. "Los últimos zapatistas, héroes olvidados." Mexico. Film.

"Tarifazo: una semana de conflicto en Cochabamba." 2000. *Los Tiempos*, January 16.

Tarrow, Sidney G. 1998. *Power in movement: social movements and contentious politics*. Cambridge; New York: Cambridge University Press.

   2010. "The strategy of paired comparison: toward a theory of practice." *Comparative Political Studies* 43 (2):230–59.

Tedlock, Dennis. 1996. *Popol vuh: the Mayan book of the dawn of life*. Rev. ed. New York: Simon & Schuster.

Tépach M., M. en E. Reyes. 2007. "El impacto en los hogare del país del incremento en el precio de la TORTILLA." ed. S. d. E. Cámara de Diputados. Mexico City: Centro de Documentación, Información y Análisis.

Thompson, E. P. 1971. "The moral economy of the English crowd in the eighteenth century." *Past and Present*, 50: 76–136.

Thompson, Eric S. 1964. *Grandeza y decadencia de los mayas*. Mexico City: Fondo de Cultural Económica.

Tilly, Charles. 1978. *From mobilization to revolution*. Reading, MA: Addison-Wesley Publishing Company.

2002. *Stories, identities, and political change*. Lanham, MD: Rowman & Littlefield.

Tönnies, Ferdinand. 1988. *Community & society*. New Brunswick, NJ: Transaction Books.

Truman, David Bicknell. 1981. *The governmental process: political interests and public opinion*. Westport, CT: Greenwood Press.

Tutino, John. 1986. *From insurrection to revolution in Mexico: social bases of agrarian violence, 1750–1940*. Princeton, NJ: Princeton University Press.

Valdez Ruiz, Roberto. 1999. "La importancia del maíz en las culturas de México." In *El maíz: sustento del pasado y presente en la cultural popular nacional*, ed. R. Marcial Jiménez. Toluca: Universidad Autónoma del Estado de México.

Van Dyke, Nella, and Sarah A. Soule. 2002. "Structural social change and the mobilizing effect of threat: explaining levels of patriot and militia organizing in the United States." *Social Problems* 49 (4):497–520.

Vargas Quevedo, Francisco. 2006. "El Violín." Mexico: Camara Camal Films. Film.

Villagómez, Alejandro. 2007. "El complejo problema de las tortillas." *El Universal*, January 16.

Walsh, Katherine Cramer. 2009. "Scholars as citizens: studying public opinion through ethnography." In *Political ethnography: what immersion contributes to the study of power*, ed. E. Schatz. Chicago: University of Chicago Press.

Walton, John, and David Seddon. 1994. *Free markets and food riots*. Cambridge: Blackwell.

Walton, John, and Charles Ragin. 1990. "Global and national sources of political protest: third world responses to debt crisis." *American Sociological Review* 55 (6):876–90.

Warman, Arturo. 2003. *Corn & capitalism: how a botanical bastard grew to global dominance*. Chapel Hill: University of North Carolina Press.

Wedeen, Lisa. 2002. "Conceptualizing culture: possibilities for political science." *American Political Science Review* 96 (4):713–28.

2008. *Peripheral visions: publics, power, and performance in Yemen*. Chicago: University of Chicago Press.

2009. "Ethnography as interpretive enterprise." In *Political ethnography: what immersion contributes to the study of power*, ed. E. Schatz. Chicago: University of Chicago Press.

2010. "Reflections on ethnographic work in political science." *Annual Review of Political Science* 13:255–72.

Williams, Heather L. 2001. *Social movements and economic transition: markets and distributive conflict in Mexico*. Cambridge; New York: Cambridge University Press.

Williams, Rhys H. 2007. "The cultural contexts of collective action: constraints, opportunities, and the symbolic life of social movements." In *The Blackwell companion to social movements*, ed. D. A. Snow, S. A. Soule, and H. Kriesi. Malden: Blackwell.

Wimmer, Andreas. 2013. *Waves of war: nationalism, state formation, and ethnic exclusion in the modern world*. Cambridge; New York: Cambridge University Press.

Wimmer, Andreas, Lars-Erik Cederman, and Brian Min. 2009. "Ethnic politics and armed conflict: a configurational analysis of a new global dataset." *American Sociological Review* 74 (April):316–37.

Wittgenstein, Ludwig. 1958. *Preliminary studies for the "Philosophical investigations," generally known as the Blue and Brown books.* Oxford: B. Blackwell.

1973. *Philosophical investigations: the English text of the third edition.* New York: Macmillan.

Wolford, Wendy. 2003. "Families, fields, and fighting for land: the spatial dynamics of contention in rural Brazil." *Mobilization* 8 (2):157–72.

Womack, John. 1999. *Rebellion in Chiapas: an historical reader.* New York: New Press, distributed by W. W. Norton.

Wood, Elisabeth Jean. 2001. "The emotional benefits of insurgency in El Salvador." In *Passionate politics: emotions and social movements*, ed. J. Goodwin, J. M. Jasper, and F. Polletta. Chicago: University of Chicago Press.

2003. *Insurgent collective action and civil war in El Salvador.* New York: Cambridge University Press.

World Bank. 2006. *2006 World development indicators* [cited December 2006]. Available at http://siteresources.worldbank.org.proxy.uchicago.edu/DATASTATISTICS/Resources/table2-7.pdf.

Wutich, Amber. 2007. "Vulnerability, resilience, and robustness to urban water scarcity: a case from Cochabamba, Bolivia." In *SOURCE*, ed. K. Warner. Bonn: United Nations University Institute for Environment and Human Security.

Xochimilco, Delegación. 2012. "Feria del Maíz y la Tortilla" 2012 [cited March 14 2012]. Available at www.xochimilco.df.gob.mx/tradiciones/ferias/maizytortilla.

Yashar, Deborah J. 2005. *Contesting citizenship in Latin America: the rise of indigenous movements and the postliberal challenge.* Cambridge; New York: Cambridge University Press.

Zepeda, Germán. 2007. "Libran alza en tortilla." *Reforma*, January 15.

Zolov, Eric. 1999. *Refried Elvis: the rise of the Mexican counterculture.* Berkeley: University of California Press.

Zorrilla, Leopoldo. 1982. *El maíz.* Mexico City: Museo Nacional de Culturas Populares.

Index

Books in the Series (*continued from p.iii*)

Printed in Great Britain
by Amazon